Feeling Cinema

Feeling Cinema
Emotional Dynamics in Film Studies

Tarja Laine

B L O O M S B U R Y

NEW YORK · LONDON · NEW DELHI · SYDNEY

Bloomsbury Academic
An imprint of Bloomsbury Publishing Plc

175 Fifth Avenue	50 Bedford Square
New York	London
NY 10010	WC1B 3DP
USA	UK

www.bloomsbury.com

First published 2011
Paperback edition published 2013

Library of Congress Cataloging-in-Publication Data
A catalogue record for this book is available from the Library of Congress

ISBN: HB: 978-1-4411-6815-3
PB: 978-1-6235-6150-5

Printed and bound in the United States of America

Contents

Acknowledgments

Jacques Derrida once wrote that the heart is the organ of thoughts, and not only the organ of feelings, love, and desire. My heart has been thinking about this book for a very long time. My fascination with cinematic emotions began when I was a student in the mid-nineties, and it has formed the undercurrent of my academic thinking ever since, both as a teacher and as a scholar. Many people—colleagues, friends, students—have contributed to this book in countless stimulating conversations. Thank you—you are too numerous for me to mention you all, but you know who you are. In addition I would like to express my particular gratitude to Sudeep Dasgupta, Thomas Elsaesser, Charles Forceville, Dan Hassler-Forest, Tina Kendall, Jaap Kooijman, Susanna Paasonen, Mari Pajala, Patricia Pisters, Gerwin van der Pol, Wim Staat, Wanda Strauven, and Maryn Wilkinson. Many thanks also to David Barker and Katie Gallof at Continuum for their editorial guidance and support. Furthermore, I must thank my soul sister Saskia Lourens for her warmth, kindness, and generosity. And last, but certainly not least, I am enormously grateful to Charles France, not only for his insightful remarks on the first draft of my manuscript, but also for his intellectual encouragement, as well as his invaluable friendship and love. The origins of this book lie in the postgraduate seminar "Fictional Events and Actual Emotions"[1] that I taught at the University of Amsterdam from 2005 to 2009. I feel greatly indebted to all the students who participated in that course, and it is therefore to them that this book is dedicated.

Introduction

Poetry [. . .] takes it origin from emotion recollected in tranquility.
(William Wordsworth)

People are always quoting that and all of them seem to agree
And it's probably most unwise to admit that it's different for me.
I have emotion—no one who knows me could fail to detect it—
But there's a serious shortage of tranquility in which to recollect it.
So this is my contribution to the theoretical debate:
Sometimes poetry is emotion recollected in a highly emotional state.
(Wendy Cope)

The poem above, entitled "An Argument with Wordsworth," is written by Wendy Cope as a response to the famous Wordsworth quotation from his *Lyrical Ballads.*[1] Similar, I feel, is the task of the scholar studying cinematic emotions: to "recollect" emotions in such a way that the act of recollecting (close analysis) does not obscure the emotional experience itself. The reason why this should be so, is that we are neither outside observers of cinema, nor located in particular, fixed viewing positions within cinema as if cinema were some kind of container. By contrast, we are *part* of cinema in its emotional eventfulness. This experience is a cyclical, rather than linear, process in which our affective ("bodily") and cognitive ("cerebral") states are inextricably intertwined. Consequently, cinematic emotions should not be recollected as components, as indicators of their objects' properties for instance, but as processes that are intentional in a phenomenological sense, supporting the continuous, and dynamic exchange between the film's world and the spectator's world. The recollection of cinematic emotions should therefore entail participatory understanding of both the film and the spectator in their mutual constitution, as a process in which both are indispensable to each other.

Just like our real-life emotions, our cinematic emotions are composed of affective appraisals and emotional evaluations. An affective appraisal is the pre-reflective bodily mechanism that underlies all emotion and that gives pre-semantic meaning to information that originates from our bodily system, and more in particular from our senses. An emotional evaluation is the semantic account of the affective appraisal that can be narrated and remembered. Through this, we experience our being-in-the-world as subjectively, historically, and culturally particular individuals. Affective appraisal, such as the flash of anger or the sudden weigh of despair, strikes the body, immediately in and through the flesh. But emotional evaluation collects and gives significance to the "surplus" of affective appraisal by transforming it into a memory, a mental reserve, or a data bank, to emulate Michel Serres.[2] In film theory the emphasis often seems to be either on the affect (the Deleuzian tradition) or on the emotion (the cognitivist tradition) as separate, rather than unified states. By contrast, I attempt to approach cinematic emotions as unified states or processes that involve both affective appraisals and emotional evaluations, affect being an implicit quality of the stream of emotion. Therefore I employ the concept "cinematic emotion" as an umbrella term that covers both affective appraisals and emotional evaluations.

A further distinction between affective appraisals and emotional evaluations is that the former consist of incidents that matter to the individual as an "organism" and that occur very fast: instinctively and pre-reflectively, below the threshold of reflective consciousness. These incidents are succeeded by emotional evaluations that concern the individual as an autobiographical person, as they function as reflective monitoring of the situation that can be given semantic meaning. An affective appraisal is situational, the "with-ness" in the midst of the world, while an emotional evaluation is contextual, an awareness of the affective appraisal.[3] However, as Sianne Ngai points out, this does not mean that affective appraisals lack contextual structure altogether, or that they are devoid of hermeneutic interpretation. For Ngai the difference is "taken as a modal difference of intensity or degree, rather than a formal difference of quality or kind."[4] In this same vein it must strictly be kept in mind that the "components" of my umbrella concept cinematic emotion are not mutually exclusive, but rather two sides of one phenomenological experience. Emotions are not singular responses to events, but processes in which affective appraisals and emotional evaluations constantly and reciprocally modify each other by folding over each other in negotiation. Furthermore, these components can be seen to correspond with two kinds of self. According to neurologist Antonio Damasio the sense of self which emerges in affective appraisals is the core self, a transient entity that is constantly re-created for each and every experiential event in the individual's life. The other sense of self which emerges in emotional evaluations is the autobiographical self, which corresponds with the more traditional notion of "self" that has memories of previous, similar experiential events.[5]

To approach cinematic emotions as unified states that involve both affective appraisals and emotional evaluations would seem to require a special methodology from a scholar. This methodology entails a form of openness to experience that enables the film to "speak back" as an "object" of study.[6] The hermeneutical tradition in film studies often consists of positioning oneself as a "reader" with a proper experiential distance to the film as an objectively readable text. By contrast, the hermeneutical stance that is endorsed in this book requires a methodology in which scholars position themselves as critical and attentive participants *within* the cinematic event. As cinema addresses our imagination directly through the senses in ways that are immediately felt in the body, it calls forth emotion from the *inside*.[7] Yet cinema is not so much an emotion *machine*, in Ed Tan's suggestion, as an emotional *agent*. In his recent book *Filmosophy*, Daniel Frampton argues that films "have agency" in that they "think" about their subject matter by making their "thoughts" visible and audible.[8] Yet not only is the film a self-thinking "filmind," but it is also a "film-heart" that possesses emotional intentionality—the "aboutness" and "towardness" of emotion. Films both feel about their subject matter and possess an emotional attitude toward the spectators, moving them with a greater or lesser degree of success within an emotional gamut that runs from horror through amusement to consolation.[9]

I propose to approach films as intentional agents with emotional states that are analogous, but not identical, to human emotional states, because all films have an operational, intentional structure of their own that I call the *emotional core* of the film. At least for the time being, and for the sake of the argument, it might be agreed upon that this emotional core is boredom in Andy Warhol's *Empire* (1964), guilt both in Michael Haneke's *Hidden* (*Caché*, 2005) and in Gus Van Sant's *Paranoid Park* (2007), joy in Jean-Luc Godard's *A Woman Is a Woman* (*Une femme est une femme*, 1961), and nostalgia in Andrey Tarkovsky's *Nostalghia* (1983). Essentially, in my view not only do films express emotions, but they also embody emotions. Thus an emotional core is not a quality "attached" to the film externally. Rather, it is an "affective quality" (to use Mikel Dufrenne's term) that is immanent to the film and inseparable from the spectator's aesthetic experience. We could not apprehend the affective quality of a film, if we were not already in possession of the affective categories that enable us to feel this quality as a certain *kind* of quality—boring, guilt-ridden, joyful, nostalgic, etc.[10] In fact, feeling this affective quality even seems to be a precondition for the spectator's engagement with the emotional event that is the cinematic experience. As Francesco Casetti writes, referring to Léon Pierre-Quint:

> If a film expresses something, it does so departing not from an idea, but from an immediate emotion. For such an expressive capacity to be affirmed, it is necessary that these impressions be multiplied, organized, and take on a rhythmic progression that they wind up evoking great human feeling.[11]

Therefore, cinematic emotions as such are not purely to be defined only in terms of human feelings. They are strategic and operational processes *within* the film, which can inform us about the "salient techniques" (to use David Bordwell and Kristin Thompson's term) that evoke bodily affectivity and give semantic meaning to the cinematic experience. Methodologically this means that an inquiry into cinematic emotions should be performed as part of an inquiry into film aesthetics, since the operational structure of a cinematic emotion is inextricably interwoven with the operational structure of film as an aesthetic system—the filmic poetics, if you will.

I propose that to think about emotions in relation to the cinematic event, is to shift from questions of representation (what the film is) or signification (what the film means) to matters of agential practices, actions, and intensities (what the film *does*).[12] In my consideration, a film is not an immutable system of representation that is meant for one-way communication, but an agential participant in the cinematic experience as an emotional event. This means that cinematic emotions should not be considered in terms of what we see on screen, but in terms of how the film directs our attention toward what cannot be seen, that which can only be detected by means of intersubjective sharing of experience. As one dialogically engages with the film as a co-participant in an analytical discussion, the film becomes a "partner" that contributes in scholarly production.[13] As the cinematic experience is a process of interaction in which the emotional system of the film engages with the emotional system of the spectator immediately and reciprocally, it is best approached as an event that is "a continuing interchange, neither beginning nor ending at any specific point."[14] Notably, the emotion that the film embodies is not necessarily the same emotion that the spectator feels in this dialogical process. Even though spectators of horror regularly experience fear toward the film, more or less simultaneously with the characters *in* the film feeling fearful toward its fierce creatures, fear is not what the film *itself* embodies. Instead the emotional core of a horror film is often malevolence. Furthermore, the horror movie spectator's emotion is not a matter of simply sharing the film character's fear, but a result of immediate and autonomous engagement in the process of emotional exchange between the film and the spectator. In this exchange, the spectator's emotion may either correspond with or differ from the emotional core of the film. Hence, the spectators may respond to a "sad" film with sadness, but also with anger directed at the unjustified suffering or cruelty it embodies—or perhaps at the cheap sentimentality they consider the film to be expressive of.

It has often been suggested that cinematic emotions regularly emerge as a result of character identification or sympathetic engagement, emotionally experienced as concern for the characters, and affectively felt as changes in action tendency.[15] I am by no means denying this. Yet I propose that, just as often, cinematic emotions are essentially different from those reactions that arise, say, as a result of the structures of sympathy (to use Murray Smith's terminology). A mimetic response for instance, such as a visceral reaction or an impulse for action, is often a *cause for* rather than a consequence of the spectator's sympathy for the character. Yet so far the study of cinematic emotions seems to be all too narrowly focused on the aspects of empathy and sympathy in film experience. Alternatively, the argumentative emphasis in *Feeling Cinema* is on the way in which film aesthetics directly engage the spectators emotionally—albeit in a historically and culturally habituated fashion. In this process not only is the film present for me, but I am also present for the film in both my objectivity and subjectivity. Admittedly it may seem like an impossible task to discuss, say, the narrative distribution of knowledge without taking character engagement into consideration as a mode of emotional mediation. Yet the films discussed in this book rely more on what Gérard Genette calls focalization and Murray Smith coins alignment: an aesthetic engagement with the character, be it perceptual or mental, that always precedes but never guarantees identification, allegiance, sympathy, or empathy with them. By shifting the focus from character-affinity to aesthetic elements that are less character-bound, *Feeling Cinema* hopes to complement rather than to challenge the earlier views on cinematic emotions.

Hence, for an inquiry into cinema as an emotional event, the scholar needs to be aware both of the film's emotional core and its emotional attitude toward the spectator. The emotional core of Michael Haneke's

Funny Games (1997), for instance, is fury and menace, and the film literally assaults its spectators with the aggression that is epitomized in John Zorn's dissonant score in its opening scene. This is a case of affective nonsynchronicity between the emotion embodied in the film (fury) and the emotion with which the spectator responds (anxiety). By contrast, a melancholic film such as Ingmar Bergman's *Wild Strawberries* (*Smultronstället*, 1957) establishes an emotional congruence between the spectator and the film due to its harmonic affective qualities. This is a case of affective synchronicity between the spectator's emotion and the emotion embodied in the film, similar to the connection between sad music and the listener who responds with sadness even when not "truly" sad.[16] Furthermore, the way in which the spectator engages with cinema emotionally can take at least two different forms apart from sympathetic or empathetic responses to the characters. First, spectators can respond to the emotional attitude of films with a different emotion of their own, in a manner of "emotional dialogue." Secondly, spectators can respond by reproducing the emotion embodied in the cinematic event in a manner of "emotional resonance." This is the starting point of the analysis conducted in this book. An obvious objection to my approach is the apparent fact that cinema is a technology that is unable to "emote" in an analogous fashion to sentient creatures such as humans. Yet both films and spectators attribute degrees of salience to the world through similar modes of affective intentionality. These shared affective modes enable us to "tune in" to the fluctuating frequency of the film's emotional energy in the first place. Thus within my argument emotional core stands for the way in which the aesthetic system of film serves as "affective glue" that sensitizes us to a dual capability of picking up the emotions that film embodies and reacting to them.

My "emoting with cinema" has brought me to the conclusion that our affective responses to cinema often emerge from an immediate engagement with the cinematic event itself. In this process, we "take in" and respond to the emotions embodied in the film, but in such a way that the emotional sensations that we undergo remain our own, stimulated and influenced by our personal motivations, goals, preferences, memories, and life histories. Cinema as an emotional event is conditioned not only by its aesthetic system, but also by the spectators' view of the world, their sense of self, their valuation of phenomena such as love that are important for their own well-being, and their willingness to "accept" the film in general. Within these bounds the spectator may also choose to reject the film for instance for its lack of artistry, or for its "artsy-fartsiness."[17] After all, same films move different spectators in emotionally distinctive ways.

But how then should we organize the field of study into cinema as an emotional event, which in the same way as "ordinary" life is anything but constant, when no spectator position "inscribed" in the film is prearranged?[18] In film theory, every so often emphasis is given to a conceptual framework that does not necessarily do justice to the film as an aesthetic whole, including the spectator's experience. Instead the cinematic event is reduced to an illustration of the theoretical hypothesis that a scholar wishes to prove. In return this approach can damage the scholar's "authentic encounter" with the film. As David MacDougall points out, "meaning, when we force it on things, can also blind us, causing us to see only what we expect to see or distracting us from seeing very much at all."[19] For the purpose of this book, cinema will be defined as an emotional event that offers itself to be engaged with by means of its aesthetic system. This stance has epistemological and methodological consequences. Making sense of cinema as an emotional event requires making sense of *oneself* as a sentient subject, interacting emotionally with the film.[20] As Serres puts it, "knowing things requires one first of all to place oneself between them. Not only in front of them in order to see them, but in the midst of their mixture, on the paths that unite them."[21] At the same time as a participant of such methodological encounter, one should remain strongly aware of the nature of scholarly practice. As Edgar Morin wrote in 1956:

> The cinema unveils and opens up the intellectual structures of participation, the participative structures of intelligence, and thus, as well as the theory of magic and affectivity, it illuminates the theory of the formation of ideas and their development. Its natural and fundamental movement is none other than the natural and fundamental movement of the human mind at its source, that is, in its first totality. *It is because all participation at the time leads to a subjectivity and objectivity, a rationality and an affectivity, that a circular dialectic carries the film along an objective-subjective, rational-affective system.*[22]

Feeling Cinema remains well within the tradition of continental (film) philosophy and its mode of taking on emotions. In addition, it embraces several other approaches, among others analytical philosophy, cognitive psychology, gender studies, neurobiology, sound theory, and trauma theory. Various aspects of these approaches have inspired me and continue to be useful while I formulate my own views on cinematic emotions, since it is my conviction that no one theory or paradigm can adequately explain cinematic emotions, and that no critical position as regards their nature is orthodox. While I believe that diverse insights lead to a more enriched understanding of cinematic emotions, it is not my intention to provide an overview of different approaches to the subject, nor to examine the extent to which these approaches are valid, or to provide an all-embracing account of what cinematic emotions "are." More than anything else, this book is a plea for a method "in action," endorsing a mode of thinking "through" emotions that emerge in the process of participating in the cinematic event. This process is similar to what I understand Jean-Luc Nancy to aim for when he speaks of "sharing of Being." Nancy writes: "To partake of existence [. . .] is not to share any common substance, but to be exposed together to ourselves [. . .] to the happening of ourselves."[23] The cinematic event as "mutual exposure" means, that in order for the film's and the spectator's emotional configurations to be able to "meet," both parties must "exit themselves," so as to come into contact with each other in the manner of "being-with." This, according to Nancy, is "to make sense mutually, and only mutually."[24] *Feeling Cinema* offers itself as an exploration of what happens when one encounters cinema not in terms of well-known categories like auteur or genre, but by means of directing one's "thinking through" cinema co-creatively around different emotional events. Furthermore it hopes to express an attitude of wonder, surprise, attentive awareness, honesty, and astonishment in the sense of Luce Irigaray when inquiring into what puts the motion in the cinematic "e-motion." As Philip Fisher writes:

> Each of the strong emotions or passions designs for us an intelligible world and does it by means of horizon lines that we can come to know only in experiences that begin with impassioned or vehement states within ourselves.[25]

Feeling Cinema is made up of seven chapters, all of which call attention to the impassioned interaction between films and their implied spectators. In this interaction the spectators' emotions function as their "designers" of an intelligible cinematic world. This book aims at gaining insight, not only into how emotions work in the cinematic experience, but also into the ways in which cinematic emotions function as "philosophical agents." Agents that help us to understand in what ways our primal fears and desires are integral to our selfhood and how we deal with our basic relatedness to others, also in moral terms. Chapter 1 on horror argues that many scary films scare one through more immediate means than can be explained by spectators entertaining in thought the disgusting and dangerous properties of the films' monsters, as Noël Carroll has suggested.[26] It will show that in such examples as *The Shining* (Stanley Kubrick, 1980) and *Repulsion* (Roman Polanski, 1965), the films themselves are the monsters that frighten, by "taking over" or possessing the spectator so that their experience of the film is thoroughly "contaminated" by the "spirit" of horror. Chapter 2 on hope explores the evoking of suspense through the operational logic of (hopeless) hope at the core of the film's narrative structure, which functions independently from the spectator's sympathetic regard for the characters. George Sluizer's *The Vanishing* (1988) and Nicolas Roeg's *Don't Look Now* (1973) will be discussed as examples of films that put the spectator into a "clairvoyant," although not omniscient, position, and thus confront them with a dilemma: will they prefer the satisfaction of their aesthetic desire or the satisfaction of their moral desire? Chapter 3 deals with trauma. It will explain the emotional effect of contemporary melodrama through the operational structure of trauma, as based on the aesthetic strategy of matching in a parallel construction the world of possibility and the world of despair. This parallelism creates "twofold attention" to the trauma victim's identity deadlock that cannot be communicated through empathetic sharing. Instead, the other's traumatic experience remains inaccessibly remote in films such as *The Sea Inside* (Alejandro Amenábar, 2004), *Elementary Particles* (Oskar Roehler, 2006), and *Reprise* (Joachim Trier, 2006), even when it inspires compassion, albeit conditioned by experiential distance.

Chapter 4, which is on anguish, discusses the ways in which music both expresses emotion and induces affective experience by means of mutual resonance between music and listener. The same can be claimed about sound in general. Sound in itself can express emotion by conveying an affective atmosphere into which the listener can "tune in" by opening up to this resonance. This is how both musical and non-musical sound functions in the cinematic experience, as will be shown through a "resonance analysis" of *Dancer in the Dark* (Lars von Trier, 2000) and *The Silence* (Ingmar Bergman, 1963). Chapter 5 on shame explores Ruth Leys's notion of the "spectatorial logic of shame." This refers to the feelings of shame which an individual experiences as a result of being conscious of negative exposure. In cinema, the aesthetic axis between seeing and being seen embodies the possibility that shame will be acknowledged as a mode of self-reflection. In turn this becomes a question of moral agency and of multiplicity of coexisting viewing positions. This often makes such "shame films" as *American Beauty* (Sam Mendes, 1999) and *Borat: Cultural Learnings of America for Make Benefit Glorious Nation of Kazakhstan* (Larry

Charles, 2006) dialogic in the spirit of Mikhail Bakhtin, the spectators being forced into a position between two different value systems, rather than finding themselves within only one of them. The concept of moral agency will also be central in Chapter 6, which is on anger. This chapter discusses the various ways in which films can appeal to the spectators' justified feelings of anger, based on their desire for a rightful world. This operates through an "emotional threesome" of contempt, hate, and resentment, as embodied in Gus Van Sant's *Elephant* (2003), Steve McQueen's *Hunger* (2008), and Cristian Mungiu's *4 Months, 3 Weeks & 2 Days* (2007). The chapter argues that in these films anger functions as an essential element in the system of ethical reasoning and political compassion, but beyond spectator identification with the protagonists or acceptance of their actions. The final chapter explores love, not so much as an emotion epitomized in the phrase "being in love with," but as an intersubjective attitude that films can embody. This process can take a cynical, ironic, or authentic "form," which can either seduce spectators into the game of love or nauseate them out of it. In this chapter three films will be discussed: *Dangerous Liaisons* (Stephen Frears, 1988), *Romance* (Catherine Breillat, 1999), and *Eternal Sunshine of the Spotless Mind* (Michel Gondry, 2004). They will be dealt with as examples of films that encourage "evaluative perception" of our own "loving preferences," whether based on sexual desire, romantic fantasies, familial arrangements, narcissistic mirroring, or authentic reciprocity.

In this vein *Feeling Cinema* as a whole aims to explore and to understand the complex unfolding of cinema as an emotional event, by directing attention to affective dynamics and emotional operations both within the film and between the film and its spectator. As already stated, cinematic emotions emerge when the cinematic affective system encounters the human affective system in a manner that transcends generic patterns. The correspondence between these human and cinematic affective systems is the reason why emotions embodied in a film are so easily soaked up as they are. Cinema, therefore, is the art of emotion in the mode of "being-with," which resonates and exchanges its affective energy with us even if we are not always open to this current of emotional reciprocity. In fact, we are always also free to turn away from this affective resonance by focusing our attention on something else for instance.[27] Edgar Morin phrased this beautifully when he wrote:

> Magic is integrated and reabsorbed into the vaster notion of affective participation. The latter determined the fixation of the cinematographic

into spectacle and its metamorphosis into cinema. It still determines the evolution of the "seventh art." It is at the very heart of its techniques. In other words, we must conceive of affective participation *as a genetic stage and structural foundation* of the cinema.[28]

This book, then, hopes to show that cinema does not strike our "emotional chords" in any straightforward or causal manner, but that the process of emotional engagement with the film is a dynamic event of interaction. Contemporary media scholars, not only interested in cinematic emotions, but also in—to mention just a few possibilities—the daily news and political rhetoric, will most certainly have to take into account the complexity of emotional "meaning-making" strategies. As they function as "determinate patterns of salience among objects of attention, lines of inquiry, and inferential strategies,"[29] emotions are central when it comes to meaning-making practices in the media, which in specific ways render some articulations more salient than others. Yet the process of "tracing salience" requires turning one's attention to the dynamic, co-creative, and reciprocal nature of an emotional event, be it fictional or factual, since both the media and its "consumers" are active, agential participants in the "becoming" of that event. In cinema what truly "binds" the spectator to the film, is the very act of participation in the co-creation of the cinematic event as a whole. Therefore the nature of cinema as an emotional event can only be accurately comprehended by making sense *with* instead of making sense *of* cinema. A "distanced" scholar can dissect the film into a series of elements and learn something about the way in which its formal system functions. However, I feel that this far from exhausts the experience of films as emotional events. These can only be apprehended by scholars who open themselves up in affective sensitivity toward the film as a "shared existence," and listen to what the film actually wants to communicate. This is a matter of methodological preference. In "real life" emotion is a phenomenon that is neither spontaneously nor consciously *pro*-active, since we cannot consciously decide what to feel, when to feel, and how to feel. [30] However, as a methodology the affected act of scrutiny involves consciously and voluntarily adopting an attitude that is open, erotic even, in allowing a form of emotional sensitivity to arise between the film and the film scholar.[31] Fortunately the "affective turn" in contemporary film theory seems to have deliberately moved away from the cinema as an objectively readable text, and toward the cinematic as an emotionally experiential event.

Chapter 1

Horror

Noël Carroll has suggested that scary films scare, because our fear is structured by the disgusting, horrible, and dangerous properties of the film monsters in ways that mirror, but do not duplicate, the emotions of their characters.[1] Yet not all horror films feature a monster, and it might even be more correct to say that some films are monsters themselves, with all the appropriate, gruesome properties. Even then, our emotional response is not necessarily structured by these properties, since our fear can also be a reaction to the malevolent, intentional attitude that is embodied in the film itself and as such directed toward the spectator. This chapter argues that scary films scare through more immediate means than can be explained by spectators entertaining in thought, say, the impure properties of Count Dracula, or by their feeling concern for film characters in horrific situations. Philosopher Robert Solomon has written that our worst fears are generated by the threat of possession, the threat of our body and mind being taken over by a malevolent being.[2] Similarly, many horror films scare by taking over the spectators, so that both their reflective and their pre-reflective consciousness is thoroughly "contaminated" by the "spirit" of horror. This state of "being done by horror" is achieved through the cinematic salience itself in both films discussed in this chapter: Stanley Kubrick's *The Shining* (1980) and Roman Polanski's *Repulsion* (1965).

Overwhelming Fear: *The Shining*

The Shining still strikes many filmgoers as the scariest and the most impressive horror film ever made,[3] due to its sheer reliance on a film style that can be rightly characterized as Kafkaesque.[4] The film opens to an ominous soundtrack, an orchestration of the Gregorian chant *Dies Irae*, with a series of eerie aerial shots of a tiny little car dwarfed by a rugged landscape, without a sign of any human settlement whatsoever. The contrast between the car and the landscape, combined with the score, immediately gives the spectator the impression that apparently the people in the car are not only heading toward complete isolation, but also toward uncontrollable, evil powers that in all likelihood will be the cause of impending disaster. The spectator responds to these shots with fear regardless of the fact that nothing has happened so far. We simply know nothing about the characters in the film or the situation they will soon find themselves in. Even after we have learned about the ghastly history of the Overlook Hotel, supposedly built on an Indian burial ground (what else?), the frightening, intense atmosphere that is maintained throughout the film plays a more prominent role in our emotional response, than, say, empathy or concern for the characters.

The Shining tells the story of tormented writer Jack Torrance (Jack Nicholson). He and his wife Wendy (Shelley Duvall) become the winter caretakers of an isolated hotel, the evil powers of which gradually take a total hold of Jack's mind. The narrative focuses on Jack and Wendy's son Danny (Danny Lloyd), who has supernatural "shining" powers, and who is often shown cruising the narrow hallways of the hotel in his pedal car. As argued, the film carries a palpable sense of tension and menace throughout, but this is felt most intensely in these sequences, where the camera follows Danny like a presence that is haunting him. These sequences develop toward their disturbing climaxes, every time Danny stops, be it out of curiosity for what is in a mysterious room 237, or because the axe-murdered daughters of an earlier hotel caretaker appear before him. In fact, the association of an evil presence with the camerawork has been established from the opening sequence, when the camera follows the Torrences' car from an all-seeing bird's eye perspective, the camera movements resembling a playful but mean predator shark swimming around its unsuspecting prey before attacking. Apart from the cinematic intensity that is created through the mobile frame, the frequent use of deep focus in the hotel's long hallways and wide rooms with high ceilings also contributes to the Kafkaesque ambiance in the film. The decor is often highly stylized, extravagant even, and rich with deep colors and geometric shapes that signify the characters' entrapment. The disturbing images, such as Danny's psychic visions of the murdered little girls in the hallway and of the blood gushing from the lift shaft, are accompanied by an intense, shivering score that marks a transformation of the affective significance of such scenes.

As indicated, the fear to be taken over by a malevolent being might just be our primal fear, and in fact the best horror movies often seem to make the most of this. Apart from *The Shining* one only has to think of such films as *Repulsion*, which will be discussed in the second part of this chapter, *The Exorcist* (William Friedkin, 1974), *Invasion of the Body Snatchers* (Philip Kaufman, 1978), and *Alien* (Ridley Scott, 1979), as well as of David Lynch's television serial drama *Twin Peaks* (1990–1). Perhaps it could even be claimed that the best horror films work because we are literally taken over by them. The fear that we feel when watching horror films, dominates our consciousness so completely that it becomes impossible to create an intellectual distance to the emotion. As Martin Buber points out, the most powerful experiences are not the ones that we have, but rather the ones that *have us*, overwhelming us to the point where one can no longer view the experience in its proper perspective.[5] This argument is related to the famous paradox of fiction, as first introduced by Colin Radford, and to the question as to what extent existence beliefs concerning fictional characters and situations are necessary for our emotional engagement with them.[6] One of the most plausible solutions to this paradox is Carroll's suggestion that cinematic emotions are generated by entertaining the thought of something terrifying without believing in its actual existence.[7] For instance, in the case of the gruesome alien in *Alien*, which we know not to exist, we feel fear because we entertain its threatening properties in thought: its unfathomable hostility, its phallic, extendable proboscis, its labia-like jaws that Barbara Creed has described as a "toothed vagina,"[8] and the disgusting slime that covers its perfect amour.

However, this is not how cinematic emotions are generated in *The Shining*, since the fear it evokes is not easy to overcome, work around, or even ignore by *not* entertaining it in thought, by reminding oneself that "the film is just a film." Therefore this kind of paralyzing fear is marked by its obsessive quality. In comparison, "regular" fear is an imperative emotion that in real life directs our attention to relevant details of the dangerous or fearful situation, alerts us to be on the lookout for more relevant details that are imperative to our assessment of the situation, and encourages us to form expectations about how we should respond to the possible evolvement of the situation. Unlike what is often believed, this means that we are not merely in the grip of our emotions as passive "victims of passion," but that we actively employ them in order to gain insight into and knowledge about specific aspects of experiences that are particularly meaningful and important to us.[9] This is valid for cinematic emotions as well. Murray Smith, for one, argues that by assessing our emotional responses to fictional situations, we use emotions to explore unfamiliar situations, after which we can use this newly gained knowledge to act in the world in new ways.[10] By contrast, the overwhelming horror-fear evoked by *The Shining* baffles our (emotional) agency and leaves us powerless, apart from the choice of leaving the very theater building. This kind of film-fear seems to go against the notion of agency advocated by Smith since it lacks a utilitarian function and simply overwhelms the spectator.

Admittedly, this may sound as if the spectators were totally passive after all. But it must be stressed that the horror-fear that I am describing here, only makes them passive inasmuch as it paralyzes their agency. Philip Fisher describes this phenomenon as follows:

> In fear we are overwhelmed by something outside ourselves or by something else we believe may damage or destroy us. [. . .] With fear we are the victim or potential victim of something coming towards us in the world, something that undermines, for at least the moment, our capacity to think ourselves as agents.[11]

This means that such overwhelming horror-fear has to do with the "radius of agency" (to emulate Fisher), the question as to where our emotional agency "begins" and "ends." This is not the same thing as passivity, since our attention always remains active, continuously and consciously in motion toward and away from the object of fear, while at the same time the very same object of fear constitutes a threat to our agency. By contrast, a truly passive response would be an apathetic one, apathy being the opposite of motion as well as emotion. More precisely, we may enter our participation in a horror filmic event with the agential conviction that we can handle the threat it imposes upon us, because of our knowledge of genre conventions for instance. But how powerful the film actually turns out to be, remains outside the scope of our emotional agency and therefore outside our control. According to Fisher: "The passions occur around an *active* [agency], one that expects to fare well in the world and can, for that very reason, be startled, surprised, and even angered by insults and injuries to [the individual] and [his] expectations about the future."[12]

The Shining is overwhelming, as all its elements strike the spectators' "emotional chords," while at the same time the film "blocks" the spectators' agency by preventing them from releasing their emotional stress by identifying with the action on the screen, at least until the very end of the film. Torben Grodal and Ed Tan have written that cinematic emotions function as motivational forces to potential actions, stimulating our action tendencies[13] that are experienced as feelings of urgency for something to be done for or done by the character.[14] Mostly such action tendencies are lacking in *The Shining*. A scene as the one in which Jack grabs his axe and Wendy and Danny finally catch up with what the spectator already knows, does not take place until the 90-minute mark of the film, that is past three quarters of the feature. Instead, the menace becomes enduring, bespeaking the claustrophobic reality of complete isolation, with no means of escape. This is depicted quite literally in the scene in which Wendy and Danny take a walk in the Overlook maze. Again, the camera follows them like a haunting presence. The scene is crosscut to Jack watching Wendy and Danny in the miniature maze at the entrance hall. Needless to say, the maze itself is a powerful symbol for entrapment. Yet in the end the maze saves Danny and destroys Jack, who freezes to death among its branches. The final shot of the film is that of an old photograph hanging in the main hall, showing Jack attending the Fourth of July Ball at the Overlook Hotel in 1929, trapped forever in the eternal return of the past.

I would like to return briefly to the role of existence beliefs in our emotional engagement with fiction. Some theorists, such as Eva Schaper, have rightly pointed out that it is not really necessary to have existence beliefs concerning fictional characters and events.[15] However, what we need are evaluative beliefs about the qualities of such characters and the events that render them scary, disgusting, tragic, or amusing.[16] Starting from such reasoning, I would have to believe that the ghosts of the Overlook Hotel are unfathomable, cruel, and evil in order to be frightened by the thought of them. I can even make true statements about the Overlook Hotel regardless of the fact that it does not really exist, since "truth is not confined to the factual,"[17] as R. T. Allen argues. This means that I can truthfully say that the Overlook Hotel is a scary place to stay at, even though I am perfectly aware that *The Shining* is not a factual presentation of events that took place at the hotel. This seems plausible indeed, but I am inclined to think that even evaluative beliefs are not always necessary in order for us to be emotionally moved by fiction. For instance, I do not have evaluative beliefs that the lovers should unite in Roger Michell's romantic comedy *Notting Hill* (1999). In fact, I could not care less whether or not they will do, but my eyes become teary anyway when Julia Roberts stands in front of Hugh Grant, "as a girl, asking a boy to love her."[18]

For some it may seem like a bold statement to claim that (cinematic) emotions do not necessarily include belief. In his inaugural article,

Radford argues for instance that in order to be emotionally moved by the plight of others, we must believe that these people and their plight really exist or have existed. In all likelihood, Radford would label my tears in the example above as "irrational, incoherent and inconsistent."[19] Yet the element that moves here is not some belief in the actual existence of love trouble between a Hollywood film star and a London travel bookstore owner.[20] Instead, the element is affectivity, the pre-reflective "component" that puts motion in e-motion and that "cannot be explained away, accounted for, or described just in terms of nonaffective words and nonaffective judgments."[21] In other words, the affective qualities of films move us directly within a gamut of emotions, ranging from fear through anxiety and shame to compassion, in ways that "do not discriminate between real and imagined scenarios."[22] Recent findings in neurobiology have shown for instance, that certain areas in our brains that are called "shared circuits" are involved, when we observe other people in emotional situations. These shared circuits are also functioning when we watch a film, causing our hearts to beat faster in suspense when we see a character slipping from the roof of a tall building, causing our faces to get red and hot in anger when we witness social injustice taking place, and our bodies to relax in delight when we finally see the two unfortunate lovers in an affectionate embrace. In these instances, an emotional response is not a reaction to entertaining such situations in thought, but an intuitive sharing of emotions and sensations.[23] Or in Vittorio Gallese's words:

> When we enter in relation with others there is a multiplicity of states that we share with them. We share emotions, our body schema, our being subject to pain as well as to other somatic sensations.[24]

Gallese calls this phenomenon the "shared manifold" of intersubjectivity based on mirror neurons, and what this paradigm is actually capable of showing as well, is the way in which the spectators affectively and kinetically "tune in" to film style as well. Among all the scary scenes in *The Shining* for instance, the long shots of the Overlook Hotel lobby with blood gushing from the lift shaft are the most powerful. The first such shot already occurs in the beginning of the film, establishing the frightful atmosphere from early on, along with the opening sequence I already described. In this particular scene Tony, the little boy that "lives in Danny's mouth," shows Danny a vision in a bathroom mirror, in answer to Danny's question as to why Tony does not want to go and live in the Overlook Hotel for the winter. The shot is filmed with a static camera and a wide-angle lens. The blood gushes down the shaft, splashing all over the walls. This is cut to another vision of the Grady twins, standing in the hallway hand in hand, while a horrified Danny observes both visions. The shot ends with the blood drowning the total frame and the image fading out. Danny's vision comes right after the interview scene, in which Jack is told about Charles Grady having massacred his family, and therefore it can be seen as a symbolic representation of the past events at the hotel. The vision could also be seen as a strong premonition of the terrifying events yet to come. But the reason why the scene is actually so powerful, is its implicit suggestion that in fact the hotel is a living entity, capable of possessing its residents.

This is why Danny's second vision of blood gushing from the lift shaft takes place at the moment when Wendy proposes to leave the hotel together with Danny and Jack furiously objects. It is the hotel itself that does not want its residents to leave, because they are "fuel" for its machinery. After the killing of chef Halloran (Scatman Crothers) blood gushes down for the third time, but this time the hotel really bleeds. The scene is so powerful that Kubrick used it in the original trailer of *The Shining.* This trailer is a replica of Danny's vision, showing a static wide-angle shot of the elevator doors from a low height, the red lift shaft functioning as a blood vessel. At first, nothing happens within the frame, but as soon as the "blurb" has rolled, the blood comes gushing down. The music is different from that used for the scene in the film, consisting of various clinging, booming, and pinging sounds, each of which has its own rhythm. At first, only a metronomic cling can be heard, but as the trailer progresses, other sounds join in one by one, producing a cacophonic and disturbing rhythm that, together with the image, has a blood-curdling effect. This trailer literally forces upon the spectators the effects of blood phobia (hemophobia), the extreme, irrational, and persistent fear of blood that is often experienced with an increase in heart rate.

Another scary element in *The Shining* is the appearance of the Grady twins, always wearing the same light blue dress and white knee socks, always hand in hand, always smiling.[25] The twins appear to Danny even before the Torrance family has settled in, as if they had already been waiting for a new playmate. In the Tuesday sequence, the Grady twins appear for the second time when Danny stops pedaling his little car in front of room 237. In the Saturday sequence, the twins appear to Danny at the very end of a lengthy hallway, done in an extreme long shot with a wide-angle lens. The shot is abruptly cut to a long shot of the twins, then to another (flashback?) shot of the axe-murdered girls in the same hallway, their blood smeared all over the walls. Following the staccato rhythm of the sound track and the meter of the hollow lines that the twins recite ("Hello Danny. Come play with us. Come play with us, Danny. Forever . . . and ever . . . and ever"), the camera leaps disturbingly closer and closer to the twins. Why are the Grady twins so terrifying? This might have something to do with childish innocence turned evil and menacing, with the theme of abjection and the collapse of meaning in a state between life and death, good and evil, in Julia Kristeva's sense.[26] But in fact the twins are scary, because they embody the terrifying possibility that death is not salvation but entrapment: to lose one's life at the Overlook Hotel means to be forever taken over by the hostile presence that it embodies.

Yet another scary element in *The Shining* is the ghastly phenomenon of room 237. As argued above, the Overlook Hotel seems to have a life of its own. It is a living entity and room 237 is its beating heart. The hotel definitively wakes up from its hibernation the moment Jack has entered the room. This scene of Jack's entrance is crosscut to chef Halloran in Florida, who gets a "shining" premonition that things are going terribly wrong at the hotel. This premonition is channeled through insistent heart beating. As he is an essential part of the hotel, the room's bloodstream extends to Halloran even as far away as Florida. The beating of the heart accompanies Jack into the room, where he embraces the beautiful woman that rises from the bathtub, who then turns into a horrifying, decaying corpse. The beating of the heart continues to be heard at regular intervals in the film. Not only does this signify Jack's growing determination to murder his family on the instigation of the ghosts, so as to make sure that the Torrances would never have to leave the hotel, but it is also a confirmation of how the Overlook Hotel bloodstream has now extended into Jack himself. Halloran's death can also be seen as a human sacrifice to the hotel. As soon as his blood is shed, the hotel truly becomes alive, resurrecting all of its fierce ghosts. In this way, Halloran's blood becomes nourishment for the hotel.

Brigitte Peucker has argued that "the corridors of the hotel are corporeal passageways—arteries for the transport of blood—[that turn the Overlook Hotel] itself into a body."[27] Actually, the Overlook Hotel is more than "merely" a body. It really is an embodied mind in the Merleau-Pontyean sense. The Overlook Hotel is both a physical (architectural) structure and a mental (conscious) structure, brought together and intentionally directed toward its residents—in a destructive way. What is intriguing and ultimately frightening in *The Shining*, is the way in which the film itself offers the spectator the experience of being a guest at the Overlook Hotel from the inside out. In other words, the film itself becomes alive with intention, turning into a malevolent agent of possession. *The Shining* does not merely depict possession but it becomes possession, embodying the threat of possession to which we respond with fear. In his theory of "filmind" influenced by Merleau-Ponty, Daniel Frampton argues that in "film-thinking" meaning is united to the cinematic form organically, which allows us to experience meaning in the "cinematic gesture" itself.[28] The haunting presence of the camera in *The Shining* is an excellent case in point about the ways in which films not only wield meaning but also intention by themselves. In *The Shining* the intention is to scare by means of possession. In my opinion, the camera in *The Shining* functions as a pure point of view.[29] Its movement being beyond our control, we are nevertheless forced to become one with it. A pure point of view is different from a perceptually subjective point of view, since the former draws its force from being recognized solely as a presence, not as a person. This is a visual equivalent to Michel Chion's *acousmêtre*, a voice that is neither inside nor outside the diegesis.[30] Whereas many horror films, most notably John Carpenter's *Halloween* (1978), successfully use the killer's perceptual subjectivity in order to enhance the horror effect, the pure point of view is even more effective because it appeals to our archaic fear of being possessed by an entity that is utterly beyond any control.

Much has been written about the emotional effects of perceptual subjectivity in cinema by authors such as Richard Allen, who explains the aesthetic experience of the point of view shot through Richard Wollheim's notion of centered imagining. In this the spectator shares the embodied standpoint of a character internal to the scene, both visual and mental. By contrast, in a-centered imagining the spectator still has a viewpoint as regards the events, but this point of view is not embodied in a character.[31] Sharing Michael Myers's embodied standpoint in *Halloween* enhances our primal fear of being trapped inside another person who is vastly different from us in character and action. In contrast to many horror films that treat spectators as privileged witnesses to the events depicted, allowing them to experience the terrifying events from a safe distance, films such as *Halloween* force the spectator "into a deeper sense of participation in the ensuing action."[32] Through perceptual subjectivity the camera and the spectator both "become" the character, sharing his or her "total subjectivity."[33] However, the characteristic pure point of view in *The Shining* enhances the designated horror effect still further, because here we share the embodied standpoint of an internal presence within the scene, a presence that lacks bodily materiality. The pure point of view exerts its hold on the spectators as an external force or entity more powerful than them. This shows how a powerful cinematic experience can sometimes become an overwhelming event, in which the film takes over the spectator's emotional agency by exercising its affective influence. Therefore, I claim that *The Shining* frightens me not because I entertain the thought of being trapped at the Overlook Hotel, but because actually I *am* trapped at the Overlook Hotel, psychologically if not physically, by means of its cinematic salience. Even though I am placed in the same position of entrapment that Wendy and Danny experience, I am more concerned about my *own* peace of mind than about their safety. As a result, *The Shining* works because it gives the spectators no means to resist its overwhelming power, for instance by allowing them to release their action tendencies. Instead, at any given moment the film threatens to become almost unbearable for the spectators as emotional agents.

Imprisoned in Madness: *Repulsion*

In another masterpiece of psychological horror, Polanski's *Repulsion*, the threat of one's body and mind being taken over comes from inside the self, trapping the spectator in madness in such a way that it "drains the life out of us with a sense of despair," as Daniel Shaw puts it.[34] In *Repulsion*, Catherine Deneuve plays Carol, a young Belgian woman living in London with her sister Helen (Yvonne Furneaux), to whom she is pathologically attached. At the same time, Carol appears overtly disgusted by men, and especially by men touching her, such as her would-be suitor Colin (John Fraser) and Helen's married boyfriend Michael (Ian Hendry). Afraid of being left alone, Carol gradually develops a psychosis when Helen is off to Italy with Michael, locking herself into their apartment that soon becomes a living hell for her—living in the literal sense of the word, as we shall see. First the walls start cracking up with loud noises. A "man"—who earlier on in the film verbally harassed Carol in the street—appears in her dressing mirror for a split second and then disappears. That night in her bed Carol hears footsteps behind the closed door, even though she is alone in the apartment. The next night the man forces his way through a barricaded door into Carol's bedroom and brutally rapes her. Potatoes sprout and the rabbit that was seasoned but never cooked by Helen rots away in the corner of the room as Carol's condition worsens. She kills Colin with a heavy candlestick and puts him in the bathtub, bleeding. Walls become flesh and start bleeding and sweating. Carol forgets to eat and does not bathe, while in the beginning of the film she did nothing but. Her landlord attempts to rape her and she attacks him with a razorblade. In the most memorable scene of the film, hands protrude from the walls of the dark narrow hallway, grabbing at Carol as she forces her way to the other end of it. Upon their return, Helen and Michael finally discover Carol in a catatonic state under the bed. Michael takes her in his arms away from the prying neighbors that by now have invaded the apartment. For Michael it is a "heroic" gesture, but it is performed without any awareness whatsoever of the repulsion that his touch must make her feel.

For many *Repulsion* illustrates the workings of psyche in particularly suggestive ways. One could claim for instance that both Carol's feelings of disgust toward men and her pathological attachment to her sister are symptoms of failing in what Jacques Lacan calls the original organization of the ego in the mirror stage. Evidence for this is found for example in the scene in which Carol sees her reflection in the surface of a teapot. This reflection is distorted and suggests Carol's alienation from the Symbolic/law of the father. In other words, it could be argued that Carol has failed in attaining her heterosexual adulthood. According to Lucy Fischer: "Clearly, Carol's mental illness involves regression—a move from psychological adulthood to a stance associated with youth, and there are many hints of this inversion in the film."[35] Equally common are the interpretations that attribute Carol's psychosis to a childhood of sexual abuse. Indeed, the film begins with a shot in which the camera zooms out from Carol's eye pupil, filmed in extreme close-up, after which the opening credits appear on top of her cornea. And there is the final shot of the film of a family photo in which Carol stares into nothingness without even a trace of a smile, standing apart from the rest of the joyful family. The camera zooms in on Carol's eye until the image goes grainy, closing the circle between the opening and the closing shots of the film. This operational similarity between the two shots suggests that the explanation for Carol's severe mental breakdown as a whole can be found in her childhood, but the film does not explicitly address the issue of sexual abuse. Finally, a feminist reading of the film could argue that Carol's repulsion equals agony over her body that does not fit into the social categories offered to her in the form of marriage and motherhood, and Helena Goscilo even reads the film in terms of male instrumentalization of the female body.[36] Carol's disgust can be seen as a symptom of unsuccessful refusal to commit to what Judith Butler terms a gendered cultural identity. In other words, Carol's reluctance to enter into heterosexual relationships is thoroughly entrenched in her body in the form of disgust.

By contrast, I suggest that *Repulsion* is about being ultra-sensitive to the world and the resulting state of insane fear of intimacy, into which the spectators are directly induced by the film itself. Jennifer Barker makes a similar claim when she describes how the film

> . . . draws us in with a caress, but that caress quickly becomes a repulsive smear. *Repulsion* insidiously invites us to get close [. . .] only to horrify us when those images begin to slither, creep, and erupt with things we'd rather keep at a distance.[37]

For Barker cinema functions as a tactile membrane that touches the spectators and leaves traces on their skins through a visceral connection, a sensuous exchange between the film and the spectator. Like Barker, I too move away from the idea of character engagement to highlight the importance of the cinematic experience as enacted through the encounter between the body of the film and the body of the spectator. But for me the exchange between cinema and the spectator is first and foremost affective, where the aesthetic system of the film serves as an "emotional core" with its own affective intentionality. The exchange enables the spectator to pick up the affects that the film embodies, to resonate with them, and to respond to them.

In my view, in *Repulsion*, as in *The Shining*, the spectator is threatened with getting possessed, this time in a fashion analogous to the way in which Carol's apartment, actually her own mind, keeps her captive in her own disgust. The disgust that Carol feels is not merely disgust toward men, but disgust toward the world in general. This is suggested in the scenes in which Carol walks the streets. Already in the beginning of the film the camera follows her very closely in the outdoor scenes, suggesting the obtrusive nearness of an incorporeal presence, the camera again functioning as a pure point of view. Aurel Kolnai has characterized the experience of disgust precisely as this kind of proximity, when the object of disgust comes obtrusively close and almost penetrates the body.[38] In a later scene, when Carol's mental collapse has already begun, the camera gets even closer to her, and her nervous, aversive gestures imply an attempt to get rid of the disgusting presence (image 1). At that time the music that accompanies the scene has changed from cheerful jazz to

IMAGE 1 Disgusted by the world: *Repulsion*

chaotic drumming and trumpeting that drowns out every other sound. In the beginning of the film Carol resists the outside world by securing her personal boundaries through compulsive cleansing. Later, however, she attempts to shut out the exterior world altogether by barricading her apartment and covering all the windows. But the exterior world refuses to stay outside, and penetrates through the walls, taking the shape of the man that rapes Carol night after night.

Above I have argued that the Overlook Hotel in *The Shining* is an embodied mind that has a physical and a mental structure with an agency and intentionality of its own. Similarly, one could claim that Carol's apartment is a living entity that is capable of possessing its residents. The difference is that, unlike the Overlook Hotel, Carol's apartment is an analogy for her own mental state and in fact we are positioned inside Carol's head. Whereas in *The Shining* the threat of possession comes from the outside, in *Repulsion* the one that is possessed, is the same one that causes the possession. In other words, the threat of possession comes from within the self, which equals the fear of losing one's sanity. What is more, by inviting the spectator to participate in this insanity from the inside, the film again touches on the fear of our mind and body being taken over beyond our control. Whereas *The Shining* possesses the spectators by forcing upon them the effects of claustrophobia and hemophobia, *Repulsion* hits our emotional buttons by addressing our agatheophobia, the fear of insanity.

That is to say, if the apartment can be seen as an analogy for Carol's embodied mind, then it is an embodied mind utterly beyond her control. On the level of film style this is achieved through the organization of sound and mise-en-scene.

The first sign of Carol's pending insanity is the emergence of cracks in the walls and the ceiling of her apartment. Already at an early stage of the film, Carol forgets her date with Colin. This is due to what appears to be an unusual fascination with a rupture in the pavement that she stops to stare at for a long period of time. Later, after Helen has left for Italy, a crack that has the exact same shape as the pavement rupture appears in the kitchen wall. In a previous scene Carol has stumbled on Michael's worn undershirt, which has made her vomit violently. In this scene, Carol is drinking water by the kitchen sink, when suddenly a sharp jolting sound that one might expect to hear during an earthquake, can be heard. The camera moves into a close-up of Carol's eyes, and sharing her perceptual point of view (POV), we witness the newly formed crack in the wall too. She seeks safety outside, only to lock herself up again in order to protect herself from the world. But then this quested protection turns out to be the means of perpetual torment, as the outside forces its way in through the ruptures, thereby shattering the boundaries between the sane and the insane. Simultaneously, the spectators get confused about where and how their state of mind meets Carol's, as the film forces upon them the effects of her loss of sanity from the position of her perceptual and mental subjectivity. The organization of the shots in the scenes where the cracks appear often follows the same pattern: they are always unexpected and they are accompanied by a loud bang. Moreover, they are often arranged around a structure that involves a POV shot and an extreme close-up shot of Carol's wide, frightened eyes. According to Murray Smith, this combined structure of the POV shot and the reaction shot prompts us "to imagine seeing as the character does."[39] Yet, I actually think that this process is more immediate, an embodied vision shared uniquely from within, without the mediating presence of imagination. Or better yet, here the affective appraisal of the situation is a precondition for central imagining, that is the spectator's awareness of the protagonist's perceptions, thoughts, and emotions.[40]

Apart from the cracks, the outside world also forces its way into the "safety" of Carol's apartment in the shape of the imaginary man, first as a reflection in the mirror, then as footsteps behind the barricaded bedroom door, and finally as an intruder of "flesh and blood." This intrusion is likewise filmed in the combined structure of Carol's POV and her horrified face, inducing the effect of the intruder coming right up to us as well. The scene is silent, except for the ticking of a clock that is reminiscent of an earlier scene, in which Carol listens to the sounds of her sister's lovemaking with a similar clock ticking sound in the background. In the second scene the man is already waiting for Carol in bed, suddenly appearing from out of nowhere as Carol removes the duvet. Again the clock is ticking prominently, and the mobile frame highlights Carol's helplessness and her lack of control of the situation—even though the events take place in her mind only. The third time the man appears, Carol actually prepares herself for his nightly visit. Playing what she must imagine to be a good housekeeper, she irons Michael's dirty undershirt, although the iron is not plugged in, and puts lipstick on before going to bed, smiling in "joyful" anticipation. Yet when the man appears she responds in terror once more. This time the intruder's appearance is announced by the booming bells of a neighboring monastery, the same that had been heard earlier in a scene in which Carol's landlord assaulted her. It is especially the way in which the sounds are organized in these scenes that demonstrate the violence by which the external world enters the apartment, leaving Carol shattered on the inside. This is how madness overwhelms. It enters a person without distance, and it is precisely by this frightening, violent attitude that the film "enters" its spectator as well. Consequently, as emotional agents we find ourselves immediately present in the bed with Carol and the rapist.

As argued, the apartment itself is often rightly seen as an analogy for Carol's mental deterioration. It conveys the sense of Carol's lived experience. In the beginning of the film, the place is bright and tidy, but as soon as insanity stealthily moves in, the apartment starts showing signs of neglect and decay. First Carol leaves the uncooked rabbit to rot outside the refrigerator. Then she leaves the bathtub water running and shuts out all daylight, so that the apartment turns into a cavernous, shadowy chamber. She leans against a wall in search of support only to find that it has turned into flesh, on which she can leave imprints with the palms of her hands. Later on in the film the walls literally touch her back, grabbing and clutching at her as she walks by, an event accompanied by cacophonic drumming. All this is filmed with harsh lighting and a wide-angle lens, often from a low height with a straight-on angle that emphasizes the claustrophobic atmosphere of the apartment. Carol endures constant terror and isolation, but cannot escape her situation, since there is no escape from the hell that is one's own insanity. The film suggests that self-isolation as a means of protection against the proximity of the penetrating external world can be a cause for insanity. For Carol the outside world triggers her anhedonia, the inability to gain pleasure from enjoyable experiences. But for the spectator, what is truly frightening in this film, is the feeling of helplessness and lack of control during the course of events. While Carol is under the delusion that she is being controlled and menaced by an external force, the spectators are "swept away" by the force of the film, the events seeming to occur without any narrative motivation. Yet, their being "swept away" by the film is not the same as being passively at its mercy. Rather, they are situated in its "force-field" as weakened, overwhelmed emotional agents, where weakened and passive are not the same. It is the result of the film's powerful affective force drawing the spectators into its life-space. Like Carol, they experience the devastating, schizophrenic terror of being unable to trust one's own senses. But again, it is the film itself that forces the spectators to live through this effect, rather than to merely imagine it.

As I hope to have shown in my close analysis of *The Shining* and *Repulsion*, by embodying a threatening menace to take over the spectators, a possessive horror film often directly addresses their "reasons of the heart" instead of their reasoning minds. When such happens, emotions are not the result of the audience entertaining in thought the film monsters' properties, but rather of the film's operational core being intermingled with the emotional system of its spectators. In films of this kind identification with the protagonists and their actions, or concern for their safety, seems to be of lesser importance for the emotional eventfulness, because the spectators are too preoccupied with the effect that the film itself exercises upon them. Instead, these films organically relate to our innards, our emotional and embodied existence, an effect both *The Shining* and *Repulsion* demonstrate particularly well.

Chapter 2

Hope

Suspense is an affective state that ranges from a sense of mounting terror, at one extreme, to feelings, at the other, that are much more tranquil: inquisitiveness about a problem that has been posed, idle but engaged curiosity about an odd event and its consequences as they unfold in the plot, concern about the welfare of fictional persons whom we find interesting for whatever reason, or just aesthetic involvement in a fascinating story.[1]

As identified by Irving Singer in the above quotation: terror, inquisitiveness, curiosity, concern, and fascination are the affective states evoked in experiencing a suspense film. However, none of these states capture the emotional core as such. For me it is the affective state of hope that seems to lie at the heart of the most suspenseful thrillers. Moreover, the states described by Singer often seem to go hand in hand with affinity for the unswerving hero, while hope depends more on the narrative distribution of knowledge, regardless of how sympathetic or unsympathetic we consider the character to be. In this chapter I will discuss improbable, hopeless hope as an operational structure embodied in *The Vanishing* (*Spoorloos*, George Sluizer, 1988) and *Don't Look Now* (Nicolas Roeg, 1973). Both films enable an approach to the notion of suspense that is less dependent on character-affinity and more reliant on the flow of story information. It is this information that allows the spectators to participate in the protagonist's project that they know to be hopeless from the beginning. This operational structure of hopeless hope allows the spectators to "play God" in a peculiar manner, as "ignorant clairvoyants" as it were.[2] Furthermore, as the above quotation also indicates, curiosity about odd events is often a central element in suspense.[3] In this chapter I also hope to show how narrative moments in which curiosity outweighs hope, can evoke morbidity in the spectator, which in turn leads to ethical consequences. That is because at that point spectators are faced with the dilemma of choosing between the satisfaction of their aesthetic desire and the preference for their moral desire.

Morbid Curiosity: *The Vanishing*

The highly praised, extremely disturbing Dutch film *The Vanishing*, based on Tim Krabbé's novel *Het gouden ei* (1984), can rightly be considered a textbook example of a psychological thriller. The story evolves around the disappearance of a young woman, Saskia Ehlvest (Johanna ter Steege). During a vacation in France with her boyfriend Rex Hofman (Gene Bervoets) she goes to get soft drinks at a gas station and never returns. Three years later a French chemistry teacher called Raymond Lemorne (Bernard-Pierre Donnadieu) approaches Rex, who is still obsessed with Saskia's disappearance. Raymond admits to kidnapping, but not to killing Saskia, and promises to show what happened to her if Rex agrees to come with him to France and experience the exact same events. Rex hesitates, but finally takes the sedative offered by Raymond, and the film ends with the shocking twist of Rex waking up buried alive in a cramped coffin,[4] thus addressing yet another of our archaic fears.

In the beginning of the film, while traveling through the South of France, Saskia tells Rex about her recurring nightmare of being trapped inside a golden egg, which is the literal English translation of the title of Krabbé's original novel. Of course this turns out to be a premonition of the horrific fate that is awaiting both her and Rex later on. Suddenly their car runs out of gas inside a tunnel and the premonition becomes terrifyingly palpable. As Saskia and Rex are now trapped inside a dark tunnel, with approaching trucks flashing their lights and blowing their horns aggressively, Rex heartlessly abandons her to get gas for the car. The next sequence takes place at the gas station, where Rex solemnly promises never to abandon Saskia again. Only minutes later Saskia vanishes. Rex searches for her all over the station, getting more and more desperate, but eventually he fails to alert the police in time. From this point forward, the plot presents us a series of flashbacks that reveal the identity of Saskia's abductor and the course of events leading to her disappearance, but not the abductor's proper motives. When three years later Raymond invites Rex to put himself in his power and then shares his motivation with him, this is illustrated for us in another series of flashbacks.

Noël Carroll has argued that in order for a film to be suspenseful, its course of events must in all likelihood be running toward a very probable outcome that the hero would rather not reach. In other words, the odds must be against an outcome that the hero prefers, or conversely, the odds must be in favor of an outcome that the hero dislikes.[5] Therefore many thrillers contain a built-in emotional core of *hope*, since the hero believes that a particular outcome would be preferable. At the same time the hero is convinced that this preferable outcome is unlikely to occur, but nevertheless does not give up pursuing it. Moreover, if the spectators are able to evaluate the hero as an agreeable character, they tend to accept his goals and to sympathize with him, responding emotionally in an appropriate way to the troublesome situations in which the hero is placed.[6] *The Vanishing* embodies this emotional core of improbable hope too, but the suspense it generates is different from that based on sympathy, since its narrative distribution of knowledge is less dependent on the spectator's positive attitude toward the "hero" than in more "conventional" thrillers. Furthermore, instead of improbability, inevitability functions as the narrative *primus motor* of *The Vanishing*, since the film's course of events seems to be running toward an outcome that actually is both preferable and probable, instead of undesirable and unlikely. Rex is driven by an insatiable desire which can only be satisfied if he finds out what happened to Saskia, no matter at what cost. Meanwhile Raymond appears to be driven by genuine eagerness to satisfy this desire. Still, something is not right. This has to do with free will. There can be no "true" hope for the desired outcome of a course of events without exercising free will to influence it positively. Rex's hope to find Saskia alive is hope against hope, since due to his obsession, he has lost free will. Rex is merely under the illusion that he is still a rational agent, capable of choosing a course of action from among various alternatives. The only character who truly possesses free will is Raymond, and this is why he is in control. The only problem is that he is a sociopath, though. In a crucial moment of recollection Raymond explains to Rex that his sole motivation for randomly kidnapping Saskia was, that he was fascinated by the idea of tempting fate and the possibility of committing an act of pure evil.

In the first flashback 16-year-old Raymond is reading a book on the second-floor balcony of his house, which faces the same square in Nîmes that at an earlier stage in the plot order was an important setting for a "virtual confrontation" between Rex and Raymond. I will return to this shortly. He puts his book away and leans against the railing, only to climb over and reach down. Before he jumps, we get to share his point of view of the square pavement. Raymond explains:

Everyone has those thoughts, but no one ever jumps. I told myself: "Imagine you're jumping." Is it predestined that I won't jump? How can it be predestined that I won't? So, to go against what is predestined, one must jump. I jumped. The fall was a holy event.

In the second flashback Raymond is 42, taking a holiday picture of his family on a bridge, while a little girl is in the water, drowning. Again Raymond climbs over the railing, and before he jumps to the girl's rescue we share his point of view of his own shadow on the surface of the river, which makes him recall the other jump 26 years before. Afterwards Raymond's daughter bursts with pride, calling her father a hero, to which he answers: "Of course I'm a hero. But never trust a hero. A hero is capable of rash gestures." This realization is the *primus motor* for events that lead to Saskia's disappearance. Raymond explains furthermore that in order to be considered a hero he must first envisage the most horrible deed that he could imagine, and finally commit it.

The logic of this rationalization, Raymond's initial conviction, and his subsequent acting upon it could be seen as proof of his free will, unhindered by anything external, such as moral considerations. For freedom of will requires that one even has the capability of choosing to engage in horrific acts of evil. At the same time Raymond's free will incorporates what Immanuel Kant calls a "pure" will, which is indifferent to all personal interests—and in this case, to any acknowledgment of moral responsibility. In other words, Raymond's reasoning is too cold-blooded as to be considered motivated by personal interest. More than anything else, his deed is a thought-experiment in action, performed by what Roland de Sousa would call a Kantian monster: "an emotionless being [. . .] with a computer brain and a pure rational will."[7] By contrast, Rex exercises little control over his actions and decisions, and he acts solely out of a limited form of personal interest. His determination to find Saskia is not proof of free will, because he is driven by obsession. For instance, in the course of events Rex unintentionally alienates his new girlfriend Lieneke (Gwen Eckhaus). Then in the middle of the night he puts up a scene on the square in Nîmes, where Raymond has agreed to meet him earlier that day, using a false name. Finally Rex loses his hold of reality altogether and experiences a series of hallucinations about Saskia. Rex himself is now trapped inside the golden egg from which he can only escape when Raymond approaches him with his offer to put an end to Rex's misery. Even when Rex creates a public challenge in his television appeal to Raymond, this does not qualify as an act of free will, since he has let himself be manipulated into doing it, with Raymond always one step ahead. Or why else would he say: "I'm prepared to do anything"? Therefore, Rex's fate is predestined, unlike Raymond's. What happens to Rex is inevitable and overdetermined, and his frenzy to find Saskia is hopeless hope from the beginning.

In fact, as the narrative develops, Saskia's disappearance almost becomes of secondary importance, as the battle of wills between Raymond and Rex escalates. As already mentioned, Rex challenges Raymond to enter into a confrontation, to which Raymond responds in turn by challenging Rex to take part in an experiment. Rex will only be capable of profiting from this situation, if he puts himself into Raymond's hands, out of his own "free" will. The film builds up this dual tension gradually, for instance by crosscutting between Rex and Raymond on the square in Nîmes. First Raymond observes Rex from his front balcony, opening unto the square, and later on once more in the café where Rex is waiting, unaware that he is being observed. Meanwhile we already know that Raymond has something to do with Saskia's disappearance, and so we monitor the scene as privileged witnesses, to use Ed Tan's terminology. We recognize the disparity between the two characters, when it comes to the amount of control they exercise over their actions, and this disparity contributes to the feeling of suspense throughout the narrative dynamism of the film.

In a crucial scene toward the end of the film, Rex and Raymond have arrived at the same gas station where Saskia vanished. It is night, and it is raining. Raymond offers Rex a sedative, explaining to him that the only way to find out the truth about Saskia's fate is for Rex to undergo the exact same experience. At first Rex refuses. But then under the headlights of Raymond's car, he finds the two coins that Saskia and he had buried under a tree three years before, as a symbol for their newly found loyalty to each other. In a frenzy, Rex starts running circles around the tree, while we watch him from Raymond's point of view, who is sitting in the car. Then in an abrupt gesture Rex swallows the sedative, repeating almost literally Raymond's earlier words as an explanation:

I told myself: "Imagine you're drinking. Where is it predestined I won't drink? So, to go against what is predestined, I must drink."

Needless to say, this is exactly what beforehand Raymond had always known that would happen, and Rex's fate is sealed. The film ends with a close-up of a newspaper article about Rex and Saskia's mysterious double disappearance, in which their photos appear framed in two circles, enclosed together in eternal separation. The film is full of references to circles and circularity: the headlights of the cars, the coins, the key ring, the circular frames. These mise-en-scene elements could all be considered to refer to Saskia's dream about two golden eggs flying through space, one enclosing Saskia, the other enclosing Rex. But circularity in *The Vanishing* can also be seen as a reference to the obsessive spiral Rex has leapt into, which keeps him captive, as in a gravitational field. This has two consequences. First of all it denies Rex any possibility of free will, and secondly all hope for a preferable outcome is rendered hopeless. It is this notion that organizes the whole narrative structure of the film.

Therefore, in my view inevitability is the narrative driving force in *The Vanishing*, and hopeless hope is its emotional core. But how does this operational structure engage the emotional system of the spectator? Among film scholars it is widely acknowledged that cinematic emotions are often firmly related to the concept of character engagement. For instance in *The Vanishing* the spectator is driven by the same curiosity that drives Rex. As a result we concentrate on the events on screen with feelings of suspense, with growing tension combined with curiosity about the mystery that the film narrative challenges us with. We are preoccupied with the shifting possibilities concerning Raymond's current motivation for revealing his secret to Rex, and what will happen to Rex himself. In this way the narrative of *The Vanishing* is *criterially prefocused* for the spectators, eliciting an affectively triggered response (anxiety, concern), and encouraging them to evaluate the events in an emotionally relevant way, that is by means of suspense. This idea is taken from Nöel Carroll's notion of criterially prefocused text, which he describes as:

> . . . a text structured in such a way that the description [. . .] of the object of our attention is such that it will activate our subsumption of the event under the categories that are criterially relevant to certain emotional states. Once we recognize the object under those categories, the relevant emotion is apt [. . .] to be raised in us. We will undergo some physical changes [. . .] with suspense we may feel our muscles tense [. . .] and, in addition, our attention becomes emotionally charged and the object of the emotion rivets our attention.[8]

In contrast to a real-life situation, in which our emotions direct our attention to relevant features in a mass of unstructured details, the criterially prefocused text emphasizes the details that are emotionally salient for the course of events, so that our attention is attracted to such details "auto-matically." Thus, in *The Vanishing* the role of the car key ring is under-lined, which Mladen Dolar speaking of Hitchcock could have labeled a "privileged object."[9] At first the key ring is the object of a playful argu-ment between Rex and Saskia about who gets to drive the car. Secondly, it is a piece of evidence which proves that Raymond was behind Saskia's disappearance. Thirdly, it is an object Rex threatens Raymond with, as it was also the very reason Saskia stepped into Raymond's car in the first place. And finally the key ring is a symbol for the obsessive circle Rex has spiraled into. Yet merely presenting the spectators with a criterially prefocused text does not guarantee the elicitation of an emotionally trig-gered response. The narration must encourage the spectator to experi-ence concern for the fictional characters and events in accordance with the criterial features of those events. In other words, the spectator must be invested with pro and con attitudes about the fictional events. Or again, a narrative film must be criterially prefocused in such a way that the spectators develop expectations about probable and improbable out-comes, as well as a hunch as to which outcomes they desire and which they dislike. It is generally acknowledged that a film needs to introduce an agreeable character in order to enable the spectator to share the con-cern of this character. In this context, Ed Tan writes:

> . . . when we watch a film, our general interest in the fortunes of our loved ones and friends takes the form of sympathy with the fate of a particular character or characters. In the same way, it is our general sense of justice that underlies our hope for the triumph of this hero and the defeat of this villain.[10]

Thus, in a conventional thriller our general sense of justice underlies our hopes for, say, Roger Thornhill (Cary Grant) to be rewarded in *North by Northwest* (Alfred Hitchcock, 1959) and Phillip Vandamm (James Mason) to be punished for his amoral behavior. Yet, *The Vanishing* is more complicated than that. As mentioned before, hope against hope structures the narrative of *The Vanishing* throughout, and this applies to the spectator's concern as well. The outcome of its most central event, Saskia's disappearance, is obvious for the spectator even before the film has started. For a contemporary viewer watching the film on DVD, this information is given away on the back cover, but it is safe to assume that even spectators in a movie theater in 1988 were aware of its outcome, alerted by the title of the film, if not by its prescient opening. In contrast to more conventional thrillers with similarly ominous openings, which nevertheless end with a happy and safe hero(ine), *The Vanishing* breaches our trust in the "task" of cinema to create a happy end for us. Yet due to our superior range of knowledge—or is it in spite of—we cannot help but develop concern for Saskia's safety from the very beginning. For this reason the film can be considered a classic case of Hitchcock's "let the audience play God" anecdote. First, Saskia is stranded inside the tunnel. When Rex drives out of this tunnel—his point of view being shared by us—and he finds Saskia unharmed waiting outside, we respond with relief. Later at the gas station when Saskia goes inside, our concern returns with a vengeance. But again, she returns unharmed. Very often a thriller is suspenseful through delaying the desired but unlikely outcome of a certain situation. *The Vanishing* works in an opposite way. By delaying the undesired but likely outcome of Saskia's disappearance, the spectator's concern is augmented. And when Saskia disappears for a third time, never to return, we do respond with anxiety. However, this is blended with a tiny sense of relief, as the outcome we have anticipated so nervously is finally over and done with.

Another remarkable element in this operational structure is, that every time we think Saskia is endangered, we hope against hope that she will return unharmed, even when we know that sooner or later she will not. I think that the reason for this is, that we naturally feel hope when we are concerned, even in a hopeless situation. This paradox is related to another paradox, the question of why we regularly feel suspense when re-watching a film with an outcome we already know. Carroll rightly points out that suspense is a future-oriented emotion, and that we normally do not feel suspense about what happened in the past, such as the outcome of World War II.[11] In cinema things are more complicated, as every time I watch *The Vanishing*, I experience suspense anew when Rex is about to accept the sedative offered by Raymond, although not necessarily as intensely as the first time. My suspense is evoked regardless of the fact that I have seen the film before, and that I am perfectly aware of Rex's inescapable fate. I think that the answer to this paradox is to be found in a distinction between the affective appraisal and the emotional evaluation of a cinematic event. As I explained in the Introduction, emotional evaluation takes place on the level of what Antonio Damasio calls extended consciousness, which depends on the memory of past events and the anticipated future. By contrast, affective appraisal takes place on the level of core consciousness that is not depending on memory or reflective reasoning.[12] It would seem that suspense in cinema is always "fresh," since at the suspenseful moment core consciousness outweighs extended consciousness, so that we feel the tension intensely even the second time around, and even though we are already aware of the outcome of the event.

As already mentioned, films often play with the spectator's concern for the possible outcome of a course of events, be it a desirable or an undesirable ending. For many scholars, such as Carroll, morality is the card that many films play, since we tend to accept the goals of those characters that strike us as virtuous:

> The virtues in question here—strength, fortitude, ingenuity, bravery, competence, beauty, generosity, and so on—are more often than not Grecian, rather than Christian. But it is because the characters exhibit these virtues—it is because we perceive (and are led to perceive) these characters as virtuous—that we cast our moral allegiance with them.[13]

In his structure of sympathy model, Murray Smith also argues that allegiance, the "highest" level of character engagement, is based on moral evaluation of a character by the spectator. In a thriller, this moral structure frequently functions along the line of characters that are presented as "good" or "bad," although there are often subtleties. The character of Roy Earle, played by Humphrey Bogart in Raoul Walsh's 1941 film *High Sierra*, is an obvious example of this. Broadly speaking, this notion of character engagement engendered by the spectator's moral evaluation is undoubtedly correct, but in my view it is not the whole story. For instance, Rex in *The Vanishing* is a rather dull and uninspiring person who hardly strikes us as virtuous, despite the fact that he is basically a "good" character. It is even questionable whether or not he is likable, because in the scene when Saskia is trapped inside the tunnel, Rex cruelly abandons her, and he even smiles coldheartedly at her pleading cries as he walks away from her. Obsessive behavior as shown by Rex, is not an attractive quality either, as it can block one's free will and, in the end, prevail over any form of common sense altogether. So even though both Rex and the spectator share the desire to know what happened to Saskia, this does not automatically result in an allegiance with him, because Rex is a highly damaged character, morally imperiled and isolated unto himself. I am not even convinced that our shared desire counts as a "pure" form of alignment either. True, we are aligned with Rex informatively, as the spectator has focalized access to his actions, thoughts, and feelings, but we are not aligned with him affectively. There is hardly any reason to perceive him as someone who deserves our sympathy.

Yet the film lures the spectators into feeling concerned about what might happen to Rex by channeling the "narrative desire" through him, by inviting them to ponder with Rex how and why Saskia has disappeared. This has more to do with the way in which narration distributes story information than with sympathy, though. In *The Vanishing* accidents, coincidences, and chance encounters are more significant in the creation of suspense, than moral allegiance is. An appropriate objection to this point of view might be that surely we could never experience suspense if we did not care for the protagonist at all. However, I think that more than for Rex himself, we care for his *mission*. We find an example of such a coincidental narrative element in Rex's quarrel with Saskia, when his car keys play a role in the reconciliation. Rex asks Saskia jokingly if he may still go on vacation, and she gives her "permission" on the condition that she may drive for the rest of the way to their destination. Upon receiving his car keys Saskia asks: "You'd give a key ring this ugly to a lovely lady like me?" Later we find out that the key ring was the reason for Saskia and Raymond's ill-fated encounter in the first place, and to crown it all, this is caused at a moment when Raymond had already abandoned his carefully drawn-up abduction plan. In this way, *The Vanishing* weaves random incidents together in such a way that the spectator submits to its world, anxiously waiting to find out—precisely as Rex does—how everything falls into place, how the whole intrigue was orchestrated, and how the parallel narrative streams come together in a coherent story.

On the other hand, Raymond is contrasted with Rex as imaginative and out of the ordinary.[14] However involuntarily, one can only admire the meticulousness and determination with which he draws up his watertight abduction plan. Hence, the spectator is tossed back and forth between moral alternatives. Even if we care about what happens to Rex, we are even more curious to find out what Raymond's motives are, and it is this complexity that renders the film into a moral exercise. Elias Baumgarten argues that curiosity normally is a moral virtue, since it promotes other virtues such as caring, but this is not always so. Curiosity can be a vice too, and while often we may even have a duty to be curious, there are occasions when we definitely have a duty *not* to be curious, when the object of curiosity is inappropriate, for example. Baumgarten uses the term "morbid curiosity" to describe a form of immoral curiosity that requires "debasing oneself," such as voyeuristic curiosity about the private life of another person. Morbid curiosity is immoral, because it degrades the person who experiences it.[15] Although understandable as such, Rex's obsession with Saskia's disappearance can also be seen as morbid curiosity, because it deprives him of free will—by necessity a precondition for all ethics. But the spectators are placed into a morbid position too, as aesthetically speaking, their curiosity aligns them with an immoral character. This is because at least to a certain extent both Rex and the spectator have to "accept" Raymond's perverse motivation, if they want to find out what happened to Saskia. And just like Rex, the spectators are punished for their curiosity, since the ending sequence from inside the coffin is so unexpected and shocking. The unexpected ending sequence signifies that any attempt to defeat Raymond's master plan was a hopeless project to begin with. For even though Raymond explicitly describes himself as a sociopath, he is also portrayed as an amiable father and husband. Therefore it is hard to imagine the immense contrast between Raymond's inner and outer life, and it could be said that the spectators are fooled by the same "cordial familiarity" of the character that fools Saskia to step into his car.

As just mentioned, the ending sequence really shocks, since it invites the spectator to imagine Rex's terrifying situation "from the inside." In Chapter 1 I introduced the cognitivist notion of centered imagining, which is the spectator sharing an embodied visual or mental standpoint with a character internal to the scene. This centered imagining often functions through a two-part structure, consisting of a point of view shot and a reaction shot. The former renders the perceptual experience of the character visible, and the latter tells us what is emotionally relevant about the situation.[16] The final sequence of *The Vanishing* opens with an establishing shot of Raymond filling Rex's grave, which already gives us an idea of the complete situation. The next shot from inside the coffin only shows us darkness at first, but nevertheless it gives us access to Rex's aural standpoint, a sound perspective of soil falling on top of the coffin and his heavy breathing in a closed space. Then Rex flicking his cigarette lighter forms the reaction shot that brings the horror of his situation even closer. The sequence then switches between the POV shots and the reaction shots, thereby intensifying the horror and the madness of the situation, until the flame of Rex's lighter gradually fades. In contrast to its more congenial variations, the form of "empathy" that is called forth here is felt without requiring any sympathetic concern for the character. It is an instinctive response, involuntary even, in the manner of "emotional telepathy,"[17] "affective mimicry,"[18] or "emotional contagion."[19] The end of the sequence is a final shot from inside the coffin, which dissolves through a graphic match between the flame and the opening of the tunnel into a flashback of Rex driving toward Saskia, shot from his point of view. Now the circle is closed. Raymond has fulfilled Rex's hope to find closure, be it too exhaustively, as if he knew that the only answer that Rex would fully be satisfied with, was indeed experiencing exactly the same fate that Saskia had suffered. Nor could the film have ended in any other way, which perhaps explains why the Hollywood remake that Sluizer also directed, turned out to be a critical catastrophe because of its contrived "happy end."

To turn back to the question of morality and morbid curiosity, Rick Altman has interestingly argued that genre films, such as thrillers, typically offer the spectator the "crossroads" of two narrative paths, each representing a different type of pleasure for this spectator.[20] One might say that in *The Vanishing* the neglected path of narrative development offers morally sanctioned pleasure. This would be Rex overcoming his obsession and saving his life. However, the chosen path departs from moral norms in favor of generic pleasure. It is safe to assume that many spectators would have left the theater with feelings of disappointment, should the film have ended differently. Perhaps one could argue that the crossroads presented to us by *The Vanishing* address the spectator as an ethical agent on the one hand, and as an aesthetic agent on the other. Furthermore, this "double addressing" is analogous with the tension between Raymond and Rex, but in the spectator's experience it becomes an inner conflict.[21] In *The Vanishing* the aesthetic position clearly outweighs the ethical, but this is not followed by a reward in the form of pleasure. It is rather a punishment, as the horror that the film's ending depicts stays with the spectator for a disturbingly long time after the film has actually finished.

Clairvoyant Spectatorship: *Don't Look Now*

As in *The Vanishing*, circularity is a central theme in Nicolas Roeg's *Don't Look Now*. But while *The Vanishing* generates suspense through hope, resulting from tension between the two main characters, *Don't Look Now* addresses the spectator's concern through its strong visual symbolism. After having lost their daughter in a drowning accident, a grieving couple John (Donald Sutherland) and Laura (Julie Christie) reside in Venice, where John has been contracted for the restoration of a Byzantine church.[22] While John attends to the restoration project, Laura befriends two elderly sisters, Heather (Hilary Mason) and Wendy (Clelia Matania). Heather is blind, but has a gift of "second sight." She warns Laura to leave Venice, as an accident is about to happen to John, should they choose to stay. At the same time John starts seeing a small, red-coated figure in the recesses of Venice's maze of alleys. The running figure reminds him of his daughter, but in the end it turns out to be a serial killer on the loose, who then proceeds to kill John gruesomely, wildly stabbing him to death in a shadowy palazzo.

Thomas Elsaesser and Malte Hagener write that openings often cover the whole film in a nutshell, offering "watching instructions" that give the spectator a sense of what the inner dynamics of the film will be.[23] This could also be said about the film's emotional core by the way. *Don't Look Now* is no exception. The seven-minute opening is the whole of the feature length film in a condensed version. The first shot of the film consists of imagery of rain falling on a water surface. The camera zooms in on the raindrops, then the shot is dissolved into a shot of the louvers in a closed shutter, through which sunlight filters in. Church bells can be faintly heard in the background. The first shot anticipates that of the rain that accompanies John and Laura leaving England. The second prefigures the later shot of the window in front of John's drawing table in Italy. Then we witness Christine, John and Laura's daughter, in a red hooded coat playing in a garden, while a neighing white horse gallops by. The reflection of the girl's coat is crosscut to an interior shot of an open fireplace in a room where John and Laura are seated. John is watching a slide of the Venetian church, showing a red-hooded figure sitting in a pew. This shot is cut back to the exterior shot of the reflection of Christine's coat in the water. Next she steps in a puddle, which is juxtaposed with a shot of her brother breaking a piece of glass with the wheel of his bicycle. Then the slide gets damaged and starts to "bleed," with John simultaneously sensing that something is terribly wrong. He rushes outside, but Christine has already sunk to the bottom of the pond. When John rises from the pond with Christine in his arms, the red stain in the slide enlarges, forming a circular shape. The reflections and the streaming water form identical circular shapes around him, while John's movement is repeated seven times. Combining crosscutting with graphic matches, this editing structure suggests that everything is circular as well as interconnected and therefore inevitable.

Throughout the whole film juxtaposed and recurring mise-en-scene components, such as the colors red and white, or the element of water, especially in a religious or spiritual setting, become tremendously powerful, thus generating suspense. This visual symbolism enlarges, enriches, yet even electrifies the emotional core of the film, and conveys its essence to the spectators as emotional agents. Their perception of suspense in

Don't Look Now pertains to something that they "know," namely that something terrible will happen to John, but that John does not know it himself—and will he discover in time? This suspense is conditioned by hope. Their hoping that John will not be harmed, structures the spectators' participation in the flow of story information in *Don't Look Now* throughout. But there are also elements of ignorance and curiosity at stake, which prevent the spectator from being omniscient: how will John meet his supposed fate? Will he find out more about his daughter's death, or more specifically, its meaning?

As mentioned before, the presence of water in the film is striking, and not only because Christine drowns in a pond. The setting of the film is Venice, an archipelago surrounded by water and cleaved by hundreds of canals. In the film water is the element of death from which there is no escape, as indicated by the way in which the beams of sunlight reflected in the canal that John stares at, dissolve into the violent raindrops on the surface of the pond Christine drowned in. But even more important are the red and white mise-en-scene elements in the film that function both as signs of "inevitability" and as warning signs. The white warning signs produce hope, that perhaps John will eventually take such signs seriously and save his life, whereas the red signs of inevitability render this hope hopeless. The combined effect of red and white elements addresses the spectators as "ignorant clairvoyants," thereby enhancing their suspense experience of the film. These elements include the white horse from the opening sequence, the red pencil in John's breast pocket juxtaposed with the white gondola brooch attached to Wendy's overcoat, red scales in a white bathroom, the furniture covered in white sheets in the hotel lobby that is divided by a red carpet, Laura's red boots, Heather's red scarf contrasted with her milky-white blind eyes, and the white rats from which a frightened Laura escapes in a Venetian tunnel. In the scene in which the Venetian police are searching for a murder victim in the canal, the camera sweeps by a bright red cap worn by a casual onlooker, before the pale body is lifted from the water. The red color section in the scarf that John wears around his neck, suddenly stands out more as his pending murder draws nearer. John stops to stand next to a red, oblong graffiti drawn onto a brick wall, while a white cat at the window of the opposite house meows him a "warning." But the most prominent red element is Christine's red raincoat that is repeated in the killer's hooded overcoat. The killer appears to John for the first time when he and Laura are lost in the dark alleys of Venice, right after they have run into the white rats in a dead end tunnel. The second appearance occurs when

John is wandering aimlessly round the streets of Venice. He looks at the water and sees a "reflection" of Christine, which is the exact same shot as seen in the opening sequence. Lifting his eyes he sees a red figure disappearing behind the corner. Somebody throws water into the canal from an open window and the reflection disappears, after which the image dissolves into a shot of John wearing a scarf with the color red in it. It is this graphic match, that is the color red and the identical shape of the two red overcoats combined with the color section of John's scarf, that connects the destinies of these three characters.

The film uses crosscutting as a constant stylistic technique. The most famous example of this technique is the lovemaking scene between John and Laura early on in the film. Here the "crosscut" is not to a different space, as is customary with this technique, but to a different temporal layer, when the couple are dressing right after they have had intercourse.[24] As the film progresses, this parallel editing becomes more frequent. In one crucial scene John is working on the restoration of the church, while Laura wanders off and runs into Heather and Wendy. The conversation between the three of them about John's "psychic gift" is crosscut to John balancing on an unsteady ladder, holding a monstrous statue, as if the statue and John were lovers in embrace. Later during Laura's psychic session, where Heather utters her premonition about John being in danger in Venice, he is confronted in a hallway by an aggressive man wearing a bright red bathrobe. In another scene John climbs up a ladder in the church to examine the small bits of a mosaic icon. The reflection of a spotlight in the background forms a circle in the frame, and the image of a laughing Wendy appears in the middle of it. As John is balancing on some unsteady scaffolding near the church ceiling, a plank comes loose and crashes through a glass window that serves to verify the correct color for the mosaic's replacing parts. The whole construction collapses and grabbing on to a rope, John hangs on for dear life for quite a while before he is rescued.

The crosscutting between the slow movement of the plank and John working with concentrated attention on the icon has a very powerful effect, especially as it is combined with the insert of a laughing Wendy. It suggests that John's predestined death is merely postponed, not annulled, and therefore the scene embodies the hopeless hope at the core of the film. In the scene with the murder victim that follows closely, John gets a vision that might be labeled as an "alternative flashback," in which he actually falls to his death in the church. Soon after this John is on a boat that passes a funeral gondola heading in the opposite direction, carrying

Laura accompanied by Heather and Wendy, all dressed in black. In the end we will find out that this boat is indeed for John's own funeral, after he has been killed by the red-hooded murderer. The circularity implicit in these scenes suggests that John's death has already taken place in the future, and that his fate is now both irreversible and inevitable. Furthermore, the organization of events suggests that the scene in the church was a moment of parallelism with two alternative courses, John falling to his death, or John getting his throat slit. So John can escape death only to die, and there is no different outcome in the direction that the course of events has actually taken.

The extent to which John's fate is inevitable is obvious in the murder scene itself. John follows the red figure that he associates with Christine into a dilapidated palazzo. He climbs a spiral staircase, which is reminiscent of the staircase in Hitchcock's 1958 masterpiece *Vertigo*, up into a shady room where the killer already awaits him. A flashback of the "bleeding" slide from the opening sequence is a hint for John that he is mistaken about the red figure and his facial expression suddenly changes from friendliness to caution. Right then the killer turns around, revealing his grotesque face, walks right up to him and strikes at his throat with a large knife. Next there is a series of flashbacks of previous scenes with premonitive signs, accompanied by a loud clanging of church bells. Among other things there is John's "embrace" with the monstrous statue, John rising from the water holding Christine's lifeless body, and John hanging on to the rope in the church. Toward the end of the sequence, the camera starts gyrating uncontrollably, shooting the ceiling and the walls of the palazzo, thereby signifying the "spinning of the world" at the moment of death. The film then cuts to a close-up of Heather's eyes in which a similar spiraling shape can be detected (image 2). The flashback sequence finishes with a shot of the bleeding slide, in which the leaking color stuff reaches its full circle. Then the film ends with the funeral retinue, which has already been witnessed both by John and the spectator.

The spiral staircase, the circular camera movement in the end, as well as the circular shape in the irises of Heather's eyes, epitomize the way in which the two main narrative strains are circularly intertwined. Two driving narrative forces are at play throughout the film. On the one hand there are the narrative elements that aim at influencing the course of events positively, warning John as it were by means of premonitions. On the other hand there is the inevitable development toward John's impending murder, again done by different premonitions. Therefore the premonition of John's death leads to its own fulfillment

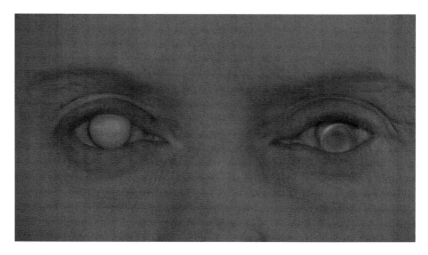

IMAGE 2 Clairvoyant vision in *Don't Look Now*

like a self-fulfilling prophecy. But what does this inevitability have to do with suspense? The suspense in *Don't Look Now* is generated by directing the course of events toward an outcome that is undesirable for the sympathetic couple, but unlike in conventional thrillers, the spectator has no doubt about the inevitability of John getting murdered. First, it is not at all difficult to figure out early on that the subplot of the film, the serial killer on the loose, has something to do with the mysterious red figure. Secondly, the film addresses the spectator as a clairvoyant by means of its precognitive hints, the bleeding slide, a red scarf, a monstrous face, sharp objects, the funeral gondola. These function both as warning signs and signify the inevitability of the approaching tragedy.[25] Again, the suspense generated here is based on hope against hope, because John's fate is inevitable and overdetermined, the events always conceived as already having happened. However much we may *wish* that things will eventually go well for our sympathetic couple, John and Laura, we *know* that they will not, due to the way in which the film gives the spectator supernatural, "psychic" hints about its ending.

Thus, in this film suspense arises from the tension between wishing and knowing, which makes *Don't Look Now* a criterially prefocused text of a special kind. The film encourages us to be on the lookout for the salient details that are relevant to our emotional assessment of the situation the characters find themselves in. But at the same time it also presents these very details as inevitable as regards their fate. The mise-en-scene elements discussed above are narrative agents for both sides of the story: on the one hand there are signs that suggest that the course of events could be subject to alteration, but on the other hand the very same signs actually create the inevitable quandary. In other words, the positive and negative elements not only work against each other, they also confirm each other, and with a thrill of suspense the spectator knows this to be so. An intriguing aspect of films with such built-in logic of inevitability is that they are often more suspenseful than the thrillers with an obviously positive outcome, even when this outcome is presented to us as improbable. What is more, the suspense in such films as discussed in this chapter, has less to do with character engagement than with the spectators being kept in suspense by the cinematic event itself. This occurs by feeding their morbid curiosity in *The Vanishing*, or by signaling the inevitability of the situation that prevents any course of action in *Don't Look Now*. The resulting effect is that what spectators as "invisible witnesses" normally experience as virtual action tendencies, now takes the form of a clogged-up, paralyzing emotional interaction with the film that enhances the intensity of suspense.[26] In conclusion, in films such as *The Vanishing* and *Don't Look Now* suspense is less dependent on the spectator's concern for sympathetic characters, than on the hopeless hope that they embody. It is this embodied hope that the spectator participates in, be it through narrative tension between aesthetic and ethical possibilities as in *The Vanishing* or through premonitive knowledge and impossible desire for a preferable outcome as in *Don't Look Now*.

Chapter 3

Trauma

As already discussed in the previous chapter, it has often been assumed that the emotional logic of suspense is predominantly based on the spectator's sympathy toward the unswerving hero. In a similar fashion, in melodrama it is empathy that is often seen as the main sharing response to the (undeserved) suffering of a cinematic character. This empathy works in a manner of "affective telepathy," by which "the feelings of the persons in the [film] are transmitted to our own soul," as Hugo Münsterberg defined it in 1916.[1] Empathy is often associated and even confused with sympathy, but the nature of empathy is essentially different from that of sympathy, so a brief clarification is called for. When we experience empathy, it is as if we feel the other's emotion as our own. We spontaneously and contagiously focus our emotional attention on the other's situation, and this may occur without any feelings of good will toward the other. A good example of this is the shame and sorrow we share almost involuntarily with the pedophile father (Henning Moritzen) in Thomas Vinterberg's *The Celebration* (*Festen*, 1998) when at the end of the film he asks forgiveness from his family and friends, knowing he will never see any of them anymore. By contrast, sympathy often seems to entail a positive regard or a more than superficial concern for the other person, for it occurs less contagiously. Douglas Chismar summarizes this difference as follows: "In the case of empathy, familiarity with [the recipient's] situation is the chief parameter, whereas for sympathy, agreement with the recipient, liking him and what he stands for [. . .] appear to be the important variables."[2]

Yet, as recent studies in melodrama as a "cultural syndrome" seem to suggest, this genre is more "traumatic" in its emotional core than assumed in generic readings, in which the emphasis is mainly on character engagement and the transmission of emotion on the level of interpersonal relationships.[3] The formal aspects of melodrama have made it possible for film scholars to describe the genre as traumatic in its affective bearing or emotional orientation, both toward its inner world and toward the spectator. More specifically, melodrama is now seen as representing and enacting trauma by means of its peculiar temporal logic, through which the spectators immediately engage with the film as "cinesthetic subjects."[4] This means that the "melodramatic event" can no longer be thought of in terms of empathy. For empathy to take place the film must produce identification through some transitional interplay between the character and the spectator, and by necessity this interplay is missing in the transmission of trauma. Instead, I propose that the emotional engagement with melodrama is characterized by a form of parallelism, enabling the spectator to invent an alternative universe next to the one depicted in the film. At the same time this parallelism allows a mode of affective participation in the cinematic event that imposes the effects of trauma upon the spectator through conditionality, or rather modality. This is an operational structure that in linguistics is called *irrealis*. In Latin *irrealis* is the term for the conditional mode that refers to contrary-to-fact past, present or future events in such sentences as: "If only I had won the lottery, I would have been rich" (contrary-to-fact past conditional), "If only I won the lottery, I would be rich" (contrary-to-fact present conditional), and "If only I am rich, I will buy a car" (contrary-to-fact future conditional, in which the fulfilled condition will make the consequence possible in the future). These modalities can be found in the operational structure of the three films discussed in this chapter: *The Sea Inside* (the contrary-to-fact past conditional), *Elementary Particles* (the contrary-to-fact present conditional) and, *Reprise* (the contrary-to-fact future conditional). In this chapter I will first discuss these films that embody *irrealis* as the operational modality of trauma, before I move on to whatever consequences this concept entails for the spectator.

Even though it is not my intention to lay out a "new" theory of melodrama as a genre in this chapter, a word of justification for the case studies I have chosen might be in order. The three films discussed here are not classic melodramas such as *All that Heaven Allows* (Douglas Sirk, 1955) and *Written on the Wind* (Douglas Sirk, 1956), in which social pressure often plays a more important role than terminal illness or physical limitation, which seems to be the card that many contemporary melodramas play. That is to say, unless of course the film is a melodramatic pastiche, such as Todd Haynes's *Far from Heaven* (2002). "Weepies" as diverse as *Terms of Endearment* (James L. Brooks, 1983), *Philadelphia* (Jonathan Demme, 1993), *Autumn in New York* (Joan Chen, 2000), *Moulin Rouge!* (Baz Luhrmann, 2001), *Open Hearts* (*Elsker dig for evigt*, Susanne Bier,

2002), *My Life without Me* (Isabel Coixet, 2003), *Finding Neverland* (Marc Forster, 2004), *Griffin & Phoenix* (Ed Stone, 2006) and *The Fountain* (Darren Aronofsky, 2006), serve as ever so many examples of films in which the characters feel pain about their misfortunes due to an illness of some kind. However, the films I have chosen are more exemplary of the general point about melodrama and trauma that I wish to make here, in that they all enact trauma in ways that do not require empathy or sympathy as affective responses on the part of the spectator, despite their generic and stylistic differences.

Death as Entelechy: *The Sea Inside*

The first film in my "*irrealis* threesome" is Alejandro Amenábar's *The Sea Inside* (*Mar adentro*, 2004). Already its opening is particularly suggestive of the operational structure of trauma. The story revolves around the quadriplegic Ramón (Javier Bardem), traumatized by his condition and denied any sense of real resolution apart from death. The film starts off with a black screen and a female voice-over giving what seem to be meditation instructions: "Calm . . . you feel more and more calm." Slowly a small movie screen opens that gradually expands and eventually fills the whole screen, first out of focus and then fully in focus. The scenery of a beautiful seashore now opens before us, with turquoise waves splashing onto a white sand beach against a glorious blue sky. The voice-over instructions continue as the camera circles around a man walking on the beach. It is clear that the sea and the beach only exist in somebody's imagination. The scene of mental subjectivity is then abruptly cut to an establishing shot of a gray, rainy Galician landscape. In this way the opening scene of *The Sea Inside* enables transition between imagination and the reality in which the main character is confronted with tragedy, and thus it establishes trauma as the emotional core of the film. In other words, the stratification of indicative (what-is) and conditional (what-could-have-been) embodies the symptoms of trauma, upon which the melodramatic character is unable to act.

Linda Williams has characterized the essence of temporality in melodrama as that of "too late," since in melodramatic fantasies our eternal (and futile) search for absolute love "is always tinged with the melancholy of loss. Origins are already lost, the encounters always take place too late, on death beds or over coffins."[5] This is why temporality of melodrama also has an element of regret, since it is characterized by bad timing, missed opportunities, and sadness about personal past or present actions. As Steve Neale points out, melodrama is best defined not only as a genre of "too late" but also as a genre of "if-only." In melodrama:

> we are led to wish "if only:" if only this character realized the other's worth, if only she or he were aware of the other's existence, if only they had met in different circumstances in a different time, in a different place, *if only* you could have recognized what was always yours.[6]

In *The Sea Inside* this traumatic condition is aligned with the contradiction between Ramón's past expectations and his future prospects. The legal proceedings to obtain permission for euthanasia, involve Ramón recollecting his youth on tape. However, he is reluctant to do so: instead of looking back into the past, he only wants to see the future and death, which he eagerly anticipates. For him the past represents the realm of *irrealis* (what-could-have-been), and the present represents the unbearable actuality (what-is), from which only a future death can free him. When actually Ramón's past does come in and haunts him in the form of repressed memories that surface against his will, he experiences those memories as reminders of a missed opportunity to die in the past, a death which he now hopes to achieve in the present with the help of his lawyer Julia (Belén Rueda). In a telling scene Julia listens to Ramón's tape recording, while going through some old photographs of his. Upstairs Ramón lies distressed, his past haunting him. As Julia looks at the first photo, the image dissolves into a flashback of Ramón just about to dive into the sea. After this the sequence crosscuts between different temporal layers, Julia flipping through the photos, Ramón floating in the water with the whole of his past life passing before his eyes. Then it ends abruptly with Ramón being rescued and gasping for air. The organization of this sequence has several functions. First it establishes a parallelism, a spiritual connection even, between Julia and Ramón. As Julia is terminally ill, she can understand Ramón's death wish from the inside. Secondly, it shows how inextricably Ramón's past and present are intertwined: the past events define the present in a most dramatic way.

This is how *irrealis* as an operational logic works: it both alienates individuals from and simultaneously imprisons them in their own presence. Ramón is alienated from his presence, because it is not the presence that was meant to be, but a presence that has come into existence only as a consequence of one defining, regrettable moment. If only he had not dived into the water at the moment of a withdrawing wave, he would now have had the life he always dreamt of. It is this discrepancy between Ramón's past before the accident and his current state that is the traumatic core of the film, engendered by *irrealis* as an operational structure. This is a discrepancy of which Ramón is painfully aware. From a cognitive perspective traumatic memory is often characterized as inaccessible due to psychogenic amnesia, resulting from repression or dissociation, even though trauma is actually remembered on the level of bodily or sense memory. Jill Bennett defines this experience as follows:

> In the normal course of events, experiences are processed through cognitive schemes that enable familiar experiences to be identified, interpreted, and assimilated to narrative. [. . .] Traumatic or extreme affective experience, however, resists such processing. Its unfamiliar or extraordinary nature renders it unintelligible, causing cognitive systems to balk; its sensory or affective character renders it inimical to thought. [. . .] Trauma is not so much remembered as subject to unconscious and uncontrolled repetition [. . .] the subject is often incapable of making the necessary narrative which we call memory regarding the event.[7]

By contrast, Ramón's memory is unimpaired, since he has memories of the accident that he has always had. However, although this might seem paradoxical, this does not render his memory less traumatic, since the accident itself harps on its own unhealthful remembrance. Ernst van Alphen defines trauma as "failed experience" that is characterized by the impossibility of memorizing and narrativizing the painful event.[8] I propose that Ramón's trauma is remembered, but not memorized, because it does not have the narrative dimension that would enable him to work through the trauma. His trauma is remembered at the level of pre-reflective consciousness (affectivity), not memorized at the level of reflective consciousness (emotion). This is why his trauma "remains somehow fundamental to his existence, and to his unfolding or enfolded conception of himself."[9] Therefore the tragic, defining moment from Ramón's past is constantly at hand in the present as a traumatic repetition which Ramón is unable to let go of or work through. In other words, Ramón's memory is a form of traumatic remembering, a Nietzschean fixed and untransformable eternal return of the same.[10] Ramón is literally trapped inside his own past of which he can only escape through death, and the ultimate catastrophe embedded in his accident, is not necessarily the accident itself, but the tragic and traumatic experience of both dying and surviving at this defining moment—in other words, the emergence of the state of "if-only." Take for instance the scene discussed above in which a flashback of Ramón floating in the water is crosscut to a series of close-ups of Ramón's photographs that Julia is going through. The scene seems to suggest that Ramón's death wish is not merely a desire to end his current suffering, but also a wish to erase his whole life after the accident as well, since his life has not been the life that could have been, if only he had not been distracted before his dive.

In various ways the scene that soon follows is also illustrative of the *irrealis* logic of trauma. Again, Ramón is alone in his bedroom, while José Manuel Zapata sings the aria "Nessun Dorma" from Puccini's *Turandot*. A breeze through an open window waves the white, translucent curtains and Ramón rises from his bed. From the hallway he stares ahead at the opening vista of the landscape behind the window, then breaks into a run and jumps. A breathtaking sweeping camera ride follows, a sequence that Ed Tan and Nico Frijda would call "awe-inspiring,"[11] soaring high over the wild Galician landscape: wooded hills, dramatic moors, rocky cliffs, and the blue sea. Ramón flies. When finally he slows down, he raises his gaze up to the blue sky before he lands next to Julia, who is strolling on the beach, in a movement that resembles the original diving maneuver from the flashback scene. This is a bittersweet scene that embodies simultaneously Ramón's repressed desire to seek love and intimacy, and the impossibility of its fulfillment. Roland Barthes has said that at the heart of all love lies a similar fallacy, and that there is by and large no other basis for love than *irrealis*:

> Similarly, it seems, for the lover's anxiety: it is the fear of a mourning which has already occurred, at the very origin of love, from the moment when I was first "ravished". Someone would have to be able to tell me: "Don't be anxious anymore—you've already lost him/her."[12]

Yet eventually Julia becomes the almost inevitable reason why at least momentarily Ramón's death wish is outweighed by a desire to love and to touch. Throughout the film Ramón's traumatic condition is epitomized in his incapability of physical touch, creating an unbridgeable distance between himself and others. Now sharing a cigarette with Julia becomes a mode of reaching out and touching her. Later they start a book project together, which brings them into contact with each other in the reciprocal mode of touching and being touched—by words, by writing. Finally they fall in love with each other. There is another defining moment in the film that does not only mark Ramón and Julia's falling in love, but also signifies the transformation of if-only into what-is. In this scene Ramón shares with Julia his fantasy of kissing her, while on a visual level the spectators have access to this fantasy in a form of mental subjectivity. The fantasy sequence ends with a close-up of their kiss, and in a very fast dissolve this shot is cut to the kiss that then actually takes place. The outcome is almost a jump-cut effect, and it takes an extra second to register on what level—imaginary, conditional, or actual—the event in the scene is really meant to happen. Metaphysically speaking this is what Aristotle terms entelechy, as opposed to potentiality.

For many reasons love between Ramón and Julia is paradoxical, and therefore once more traumatic. First, the prerequisite cause for their love is Ramón's intolerable condition, which in his own words, prevents him from loving. Secondly, in a more favorable situation Ramón and Julia's paths would never even have crossed. Niklas Luhman has said that love is a matter of "increasing the probability of the improbable."[13] By contrast, Ramón and Julia's love is a matter of increasing the improbability of their probable affair, in such a way that finally it can only exist beyond the boundaries of the imaginable. I mean this to be literally the case and not only figuratively. Julia suffers from an incurable, degenerating disease, and has decided to take her own life and Ramón's too, if he wishes her to. Overjoyed, Ramón agrees and they make plans to commit suicide together on the same day Ramón's book will be published. This means that Ramón and Julia can only unite in love through death, and that the "being" of their love can only be found in "nothingness." This is traumatic, because the ontology of this situation consists of an eternal Ferris wheel of *irrealis*.

Then, as Julia withdraws her promise to assist Ramón with euthanasia after all, he sinks into despair, deeper than ever. Visually this is represented in a sequence analogous to the previous "Nessun Dorma" episode. But this time the whole room is moving uncontrollably through the now darkened and gloomy landscape, only abruptly coming to a halt by hitting the bottom of the sea, in parallel to Ramón's accident. This is depression, the merciless bleakness of the world stripped of anything worth wanting, aside from the acute desire not to be.[14] Julia Kristeva has written that depression is a living death, and that therefore suicide can become a refuge for those suffering from it.

A devitalized existence [. . .] is ready at any moment to plunge into death. An avenging death or a liberating death, it is henceforth the inner threshold of my despondency, the impossible meaning of life whose burden constantly seems unbearable, save for those moments when I pull myself together and face up to the disaster. I live a living death, my flesh is wounded, bleeding, cadaverized, my rhythm slowed down or interrupted, time has been erased or bloated, absorbed into sorrow.[15]

In this light, it might be more accurate to claim that the origin of Ramón's death wish does not lie in his reluctance to live, but in the possibility that he has already died. Potentially, Ramón is essentially dead. The physical act of dying would merely render this potentiality into entelechy, as Aristotle would have it, fulfilling his actuality. At the same time Julia has already developed severe cognitive deterioration due to her illness, and she does no longer know who Ramón is. This is why Ramón's letter handed to her from beyond his grave, never actually reaches her. Returning to the temporality of melodrama as "too late," it could be said that this final "encounter" between Ramón and Julia does not take place too *late,* but in the dimension of frozen and impossible temporality. As a result, love between Ramón and Julia collapses and evaporates, canceling itself out. However, it must be kept in mind that parallelism is inherent to the contrary-to-fact structure of *irrealis.* Next to the tragic universe of actuality, there exists another potentiality, the universe of "if-only." This raises the possibility that the evaporating love between Ramón and Julia did not merely vanish, but was channeled unto that parallel universe, as suggested in the final line of the film:

> But I always wake up
> and I always wish I'd be dead
> to have my lips
> entangled in your hair.

Thomas Elsaesser states that this kind of archetypical melodramatic ending can produce a very strong emotional response in the spectator, since it activates the "desire to make up for the emotional deficiency, to impart the different awareness."[16] In fact, the ending of *The Sea Inside* does not merely activate, but it actually embodies the desire to make up by suggesting the existence of a parallel universe where Ramón and Julia can unite in love. For this reason, the special ending of *The Sea Inside* is bittersweet, in that it actually consoles the spectator despite its apparent tragedy.

Psychosis as Refuge: *Elementary Particles*

The themes of illness and death uniting lovers, are also central to the course of events of the film *Elementary Particles* (*Elementarteilchen*, Oskar Roehler, 2006) based on the controversial novel *Les Particules élémentaires* by Michel Houellebecq (1998). The narrative focuses on two half-brothers, Bruno (Moritz Bleibtreu) and Michael (Christian Ulmen), both devoid of love and life. Emotionally adrift due to their having been abandoned by their hippie mother in childhood, both brothers seem incapable of either seeking, retaining, or regaining intimacy or proximity, nor are they capable of loving other people. Michael, the scientist, does research on cloning with the aim of removing love from the process of reproduction. Bruno, a failed writer who now teaches literature in high school, has no emotional access to his wife or their child, as shown in one disturbing scene where he gives the child a tranquilizer dissolved in milk. After his divorce he finds himself in a mental institution suffering from a nervous breakdown after a failed attempt at seducing one of his students. Both Michael and Bruno long for the life they never had, or gave up, and they have respectively escaped into science and insanity. Or rather, they deliberately avoid any favorable turns in their personal lives, perhaps in order to protect themselves from disappointments. Even though Bruno has a talent for writing for instance, he writes texts that he knows will never be accepted for publication because of their subject matter. Michael, on the other hand, creates outrageous scientific hypotheses on cloning that he assumes are impossible to validate.

Like *The Sea Inside*, the film *Elementary Particles* is full of "defining moments," when time almost comes to a halt in anticipation of which direction the course of events will develop. The first such moment is the earliest flashback in the film, in which Michael is lying on a couch, reminiscing about an early event in his adolescence. In this recollection the young Michael looks at his childhood sweetheart Annabelle dancing with another boy. Then Annabelle walks toward Michael, asking whether he would like to dance with her as well. Paralyzed by such a prospect, Michael refuses. Just like all the other flashbacks in the film, this one is characterized by an unnaturally deep color saturation, signifying the way in which the air is thick with opportunity at such defining moments. For Bruno there is such a moment when he recollects a summer with his mother in a hippie community. In this flashback Bruno tells his therapist about an incestuous incident with his mother and a cat. These defining moments connect the lives of the two brothers, which are now on a parallel course, characterized by the interconnectedness of sex and death. Bruno suffers from impotence and therefore declares that he feels like "being already dead," while Michael is a virgin whose goal as a scientist is to separate sex from reproduction altogether. When successful, Michael's project would be nothing less than a suicidal act of the whole of humanity. Later Michael reunites with Annabelle, as they both realize that they had never stopped loving each other. Michael loses his virginity to Annabelle and afterward she finds herself pregnant. In the light of Michael's scientific research, it is especially ironic that Annabelle has a complicated pregnancy that leaves her infertile in the end, making natural conception a complete impossibility for them.

Above I have argued that, comparable to Ramón in *The Sea Inside*, Bruno is already dead, due to the way he has anesthetized himself when it comes to emotions in everyday life. After his nervous breakdown Bruno really becomes suicidal. Having been released again from a psychiatric hospital, he disappears to a new age holiday resort in the hope of indulging in an orgy. But instead he falls in love with Christiane (Martina Gedeck), a sexual libertine who regularly practices indiscriminate sex with anonymous men. In Christiane Bruno finds a new and unexpected meaning for his life, but what he does not know is that she suffers from an incurable disease that will eventually cause necrosis in her spinal column, leaving her permanently paralyzed from the waist down. The medical crisis takes place at the swinger's club they frequently visit. Christiane is penetrated from behind by a stranger she does not even glance at. Instead her gaze is fixed on Bruno's eyes, who is simultaneously fellated by another woman. This is their form of intimacy. In fact they make love to each other through their anonymous sex acts with other people. Suddenly Christiane's agonized face tells Bruno that something is terribly wrong and she collapses. When she is discharged from hospital, Bruno is waiting for her with a bunch of flowers. "Now you can move in with me," he says. "Are you sure?" asks Christiane. A trace of hesitation shows in Bruno's face and he does not answer. After a short silence Christiane sarcastically releases him of his promise: "You've still got your life ahead of you, you don't have to spend it looking after a cripple."

In the next scene Christiane sits in a wheelchair in her apartment at night, waiting by the telephone for a call that will not come. While Christiane's realization of this situation becomes clearer, the film crosscuts to Bruno's apartment, where he is lying unconscious on the floor, an almost empty bottle of vodka in front of him. Some time passes and then it is dawn. Christiane sits on her balcony, eyes fixed on the multi-story buildings at the horizon. She then directs her gaze at her useless legs and finally at the telephone. The crosscutting sequence that follows next draws a parallel between the scenes at Christiane and Bruno's separate apartments. Bruno wakes up and makes the phone call, but has the telephone only ring once. Meanwhile Christiane sips wine, fully made-up and wearing a beautiful cocktail dress. Bruno goes out into the street, returns and makes another phone call. Again, the phone only rings once. To the sound of escalating music (by Martin Todsharow), the editing rhythm intensifies, marking Christiane's decisive moment. She first stares ahead at the open balcony door and then, fully determined, she rolls her wheelchair onto the balcony. Bruno still tries to reach Christiane, and this time he leaves the phone ringing. Ignoring this, Christiane leans against the balcony railing and climbs over with some difficulty.

This is a moment of potentiality in Gilles Deleuze's sense, a defining moment when life opens itself to multiple possibilities. All possibilities exist simultaneously until the final decision is made. Time stops once more when Christiane listens to the telephone ringing, struggling between two options: the certainty of death or the uncertainty of life with Bruno, and she lets herself drop. Traumatized and dysfunctional after Christiane's suicide, Bruno is readmitted to the mental institution. Walking in a hallway, Bruno suddenly sees a woman moving away from him in a wheelchair, rolling through an open door. In disbelief Bruno calls Christiane's name, the woman turns around and yes, she is Christiane. It is as if the universe had split in two at the moment of Christiane's fall. There is this traumatic universe that denies Bruno any way out except the escape into psychosis. This engenders the universe of if-only, in which opportunities could have been seized and the right decisions would have been made. Consequently, it is the very psychosis itself that provides Bruno access to this parallel universe, where he can be with Christiane forever. In this way, psychosis becomes a choice, instead of a mishap, which Bruno prefers to the traumatic reality of his life.

The parallel existence of the traumatic and the psychotic universe is visually presented through shifting between objectivity and mental subjectivity. When Bruno and Christiane hold each other close during their first "encounter" after her suicide, the shot is cut to a disheartening long shot of Bruno kneeling in a long hallway, his back toward camera, embracing emptiness. The film ends with Michael and Annabelle visiting Bruno at the hospital, and taking him to the beach in their car. Bruno's hallucination of Christiane's presence in the car is shared with us through

IMAGE 3 Presence as absence: *Elementary Particles*

a "point of view" shot that represents Bruno's psychotic universe. Once at their destination, there are four beach chairs, but we only see three people lying in them, until once more we share Bruno's mental point of view of Christiane (image 3). On the one hand the ending is traumatic, because "Christiane" can be seen as a "traumatic image"[17] that haunts Bruno in the form of a hallucination, resulting from his feelings of guilt. He feels responsible for her suicide, and both Bruno and the spectator suspect that he is being haunted by Christiane for his guilt. Perhaps it could even be said that Bruno has both merged with and distanced himself from Christiane's death in order to "re-create" her as being alive for himself. The ending is also traumatic though, because it suggests that such guilt-ridden trauma can only be overcome by escape into psychosis and self-deception, instead of by working it through by means of conscious remembering and acknowledging. On the other hand there is a strange sense of tranquility in this ending, because it merges the realm of if-only with the realm of what-is in such a way, that Bruno is guaranteed access to an alternative realm of happy endings through his psychosis. Therefore, the ending of *Elementary Particles* serves the same purpose as the ending of *The Sea Inside*, consoling the spectator with the establishment, instead of the elimination, of the realm of if-only. But whereas in *The Sea Inside* Ramón and Julia's love is an event in the improbable past, *Elementary Particles* embodies *irrealis* in the present, as love between Bruno and Christiane is presented as an ongoing, albeit equally improbable possibility.

Psychosis as Entrapment: *Reprise*

As we have seen, in *The Sea Inside* and in *Elementary Particles* (implicit) parallelism was created by emphasizing certain defining moments (Ramón's dive, Christiane's fall). In the Norwegian film *Reprise* no such *moment* can be found, but instead the narrative is structured in an if-only mode throughout. *Reprise* is the 2006 feature debut of Joachim Trier. It tells the story of two best friends, Phillip (Anders Danielsen Lie) and Erik (Espen Klouman-Høiner), who are both aspiring novelists, but it is also the story of Phillip's relationship with his girlfriend Kari (Viktoria Winge). The narrative of the film is a mixture of different layers of conditionality. There is no such thing as a universe of if-only created through inherent parallelism, which renders *Reprise* a temporally complex film. The present (what-is) characterized by coincidence, is constantly in collusion with the future (if-only), which is characterized by fate. Therefore in my view the film is about the coexistence of fate and coincidence.

The film opens with a preface sequence that consists of a series of future scenarios of Phillip and Erik after they have sent their manuscripts to a publisher. These black and white shots are brief "flash-forwards" not into the "real" future, but into a future seen as the destined realm of if-only. First their manuscripts would be accepted immediately. Then their books would sell poorly, but this would make them cult classics. All this is told to us by a voice-over on top of a shot of "living" authors' photographs, in which Phillip and Erik are laughing or gesturing nonchalantly, as if they were nonverbally commenting on the voice-over. Then Phillip would lose his faith in literature, first due to the shock of his success, and then due to love that finally would lead him to collapse mentally, as the authoritarian voice-over tells us after a brief hesitation. He would be suffering from the "Stendhal syndrome." However, all this proves to be a kind of premonition to forthcoming events, and the episode illustrates the way in which fate and coincidence modify each other, constantly enfolding into and negotiating with each other.

Erik, on the other hand, would suffer a writer's block and move to Paris, which throughout the whole film stands for the utopian realm of if-only. There he would finally reunite with Phillip at a café, or in the street, or in the metro, or at an airport, or in the Luxembourg Garden. As the voice-over is struggling to make up his mind about the destined future, we are shown brief flashes of these imaginary re-encounters in all these different places. Phillip and Erik would then realize that they are both writing the same book. The publication of this book would have huge consequences, ranging from shaping the sexuality of the 12-year-old son of a pastry chef to triggering a revolution in South Africa. At this point both the voice-over and the flash-forward sequence end abruptly with the appearance of the title card, after which Phillip and Erik truly do mail their manuscripts and the opening credits roll on top of the footage of national day celebrations.

Immediately after the opening credits Erik finds out that his manuscript has been rejected, while Phillip's will be published as a book. In the next brief scene, Phillip is preparing to read extracts from his book to a live audience and this is followed by a scene of him pushing his hand against a window through which the sun shines brightly. No explanation is given of these two apparently unconnected and random scenes, and the following title card indicates a temporal jump to events six months later, namely Phillip's release from a psychiatric hospital. In Chapter 2 I discussed the opening of *Don't Look Now* as an example of a condensation of the feature film as a whole. Similarly, the opening of *Reprise* functions as the complete film in a nutshell, so that Phillip having been admitted to a mental institution comes as no surprise to the spectator. As he takes Phillip home together with their friends, Erik's flashbacks unfold the events leading to Phillip's hospital admittance. First we see Erik's POV, looking at a scar on Phillip's hand in real time. This shot is followed by Erik's "remembrance POV" of Phillip in an emergency room, fresh cuts and blood all over his face and body. In another flashback Phillip cordially greets Erik in his apartment, even when he has just broken a window with his bare hands. On their way home the friends stop by the seashore, where Phillip suddenly grabs Geir and jumps into the cold sea with him, be it only in his imagination. This is not a "real" flashback nor a flash-forward, though, but once more a "peek" into the realm of future if-only when Phillip would be his former self again.

This "peek" is followed by a real flashback of Erik's remembering a past get-together with the same group of friends. The sound of the waves in the present continues uninterrupted over the flashback, then merges into the sound of a record being played in the past. The sound of the record becomes a sound bridge to a longer flashback sequence, combining film footage with still photography as well as non-diegetic inserts. This sequence starts with a punk rock concert, after which the past events start unfolding in more detail, once more accompanied by the explanatory voice-over. This temporally and stylistically complex plot organization ensures that the unfolding of the past not only enfolds the present, but also the future realm of "if-only." The explanation for Phillip's psychosis, rendered by the voice-over as well as given by his doctors, is that it was triggered by his obsessive romance with Kari. But I think that Phillip's psychosis was actually triggered by his inability to separate the present from the future, and coincidence from fate. For instance, during Kari and Phillip's destined and/or coincidental encounter at the punk club, we first see a reaction shot of Phillip looking at Kari, and then, from Phillip's perspective, the camera zooms in on Kari, while the voice-over explains:

> Phillip later told Kari he knew they were destined for each other. In ten seconds, she will look at him. Ten, nine, eight, seven, six, five, four, three, two, one, zero.

This counting backwards has a specific function in the film. As Gilberto Perez points out, counting and storytelling are related acts, since things are counted like a story is told: in succession.[18] Therefore it is significant that Phillip counts backwards. It is an act of telling the story of Kari and himself as always already happened, as an overdetermined course of events. Later on Kari and Phillip meet in a café and then they take a walk in the park. This sequence reminiscent of Godard cuts randomly back and forth between the walk and their rendezvous in the café. The dialogue and the location are torn apart, and it is impossible to say in which location, or in which chronological order the spoken lines were actually said. Phillip recalls tricking Kari into falling in love with him in Paris by counting similarly from ten to zero. Later in the film Phillip and Kari replicate their journey to Paris, on the exact same date as they went the previous time. They stay at the same hotel, go to the same places, repeat the same actions, conversations, thoughts, and emotions, and Phillip even repeats his counting trick. But it is only the first time, that is to say at first sight, that Kari can fall in love with Phillip wholeheartedly. The second time around, at "second sight," the feelings are always weaker, if not impossible. Again, the sequence in Paris is edited with the dialogue and the location torn apart, which suggests that however hard Phillip attempts to re-create what is meant to be, he cannot defend himself against haphazardness, which by necessity takes priority over fate. The more Phillip attempts to be in charge of haphazardness, the more powerfully it grows out of his control. While Phillip was in the hospital for instance, his mother had thrown away all the photos that Phillip had taken of Kari during their last stay in Paris. Phillip now wants to reproduce those photos, but this only causes discomfort and irritation with

Kari, which makes the gap between future "if-only" and present "what-is" wider than ever.

In the fall Phillip experiences his second mental collapse after visiting a house party, which at first seems to be a source of newly found inspiration for his writing. He rides his bike down a hill, counting backwards as he does with his eyes closed so that the passing cars have to dodge him. This is Phillip taking fate to the proof: if only he got through this "test" alive, he would be able to write again. He does get through it alright, and consequently writes a short story in only a couple of hours, which nevertheless does not get Erik's approval. Before his definitive lapse into psychosis, Phillip is seen walking between tram rails, again counting backwards. First he is shot from a high angle with his back toward the camera, then from a low angle looking up at the office building where Kari is working as a telemarketer. The organization of the shots suggests that it is fate itself, and not any intentional action, that has brought him there. "Everything is in synch now," Phillip tells Kari, suggesting that for him there is no distinction anymore between haphazardness, intention, and fate. This is psychosis. And when this "synch" appears to be nothing but a delusion, Phillip is left totally disoriented, with no support whatsoever from his surroundings, and consequently he is readmitted to hospital.

The film ends in the same way as it begins, with an epilogue that consists of a series of scenarios told in the contrary-to-fact future conditional mode, envisioned by Erik. Erik would leave for Paris to write, without saying goodbye to any of his friends. After a year abroad he would return home where he would meet Phillip again at a wedding party. All his friends, including Phillip, would now be settled with their girlfriends. Kari would take care of Phillip and make sure he would take his medicine. Kari would be back at the university, studying psychology, but Phillip would have given up writing, though. The film ends with Erik's "POV" of Phillip and Kari sitting together at an outdoor café with Phillip counting backwards. When his counting ends, the final title card appears. We have seen that in *The Sea Inside* and *Elementary Particles* the protagonists had at least some degree of agency in the course of events, Ramón through his imagination and poetry, Bruno through his self-induced hallucinations. Thus eventually the ending of these two films yielded consolation. Totally lacking this element of agency, the ending of *Reprise* does not console but shatters the spectator.

Furthermore, unlike in *The Sea Inside* and in *Elementary Particles*, in *Reprise* mental illness does not ensure access to, but it blocks out the realm of if-only, since the last scenes of the film in the future are only visions from

Erik's imagination in the present. The tragedy in the ending of *Reprise* is due to its multilayered structure, in which one parallel universe can never interact with or even come across another parallel universe, as happens in *The Sea Inside* and in *Elementary Particles*. In this operational structure the alternative realms of present what-is and future if-only do not "communicate" with each other, but inaccurately replicate each other—hence the title of the film. Phillip's psychosis does not lead to some spiritual enlightenment, as could be said of Bruno's psychosis, however delusional this is. Phillip's psychosis leads to emotional paralysis, a loss of the self and inability to act in the world. Phillip suffers from a lack of agency, because he is trapped in the reprise that looks forward to a false and improbable future destiny. This highlights the ending of *Reprise* as traumatic, insofar as trauma is linked with the impossibility of action, enforced passivity, and disempowerment. Since in the ending of *Reprise* action, in the sense of intentional agency is blocked, the spectator is left inconsolable, imagining the gap, instead of the bridge between the improbable future realm of if-only and the probable present realm of what-is.

Compassionate Participation

In addition to the operational structure of *irrealis*, what the three films discussed have in common, is that they all deny the spectator experiential access to the trauma of their protagonists. As has been argued by Ruth Leys, Jill Bennett, and many others, in trauma art the emotional response must necessarily respect the otherness of the trauma victim. This is what Kaja Silverman maintains in discussing "heteropathic identification," that it keeps its distance to the other who remains "stubbornly exterior."[19] In other words, the emotion that results from heteropathic identification is not grounded in the empathetically putting yourself in someone else's shoes, but in "fissural" participation in the other's suffering. Cinematic parallelism seems to be a successful operational logic in this process. It maintains tension between the self and the other by creating a conditional loop, in which the narrative aligns the spectator with the character and simultaneously separates them. Thus, the films discussed in this chapter are best understood as emotional displays, not predicated on transitional empathy (feeling with), but on the spectators participating in the protagonists' deadlock of identity.[20] This involvement must be characterized as compassionate. Martha Nussbaum makes a clear distinction between compassion and empathy: the latter designates an "imaginative reconstruction of another person's experience," while the former contains no disposition of sharing the experience.[21] Instead,

> Compassion takes up the onlooker's point of view, making the *best* judgment the onlooker *can* make about what is really happening to the [other] person, even when that may differ from the judgment of the person herself.[22]

The words "best" and "can" in Nussbaum's description suggest distance between the experience of the "onlooker" and the "sufferer," even if phenomenologically speaking their emotions were the same. In other words, "com-passion" involves no empathetic fusion, but it has parallelism as its operational structure, not between "what is" and "if only" as with trauma, but between "the self" and "the other." In "com-passion" we feel for the other as if running along on a parallel track. Our emotion remains separate and detached from the emotion of the other, and our focus is on the assumed duality between our own situation and the situation of the other. Compassion always entails judgment that "belongs" to the onlooker only, so it incites emotional proximity with experiential distance. What is needed for compassion is "twofold attention"[23] for the experience of the other, and for the awareness that the other's experience is insurmountably remote. In the three films discussed in this chapter, for instance, most spectators will never share the protagonists' experiences (quadriplegia, psychosis), nor can they confidently imagine what it is like to be in their situations, but they may nevertheless feel compassion for their traumatic plight.[24]

It is through compassion that all three films enable the spectators to reach a stance inside a multilayered time sphere, from which they can participate in them as emotional events. This is a conditional mode of compassionate involvement, in which the spectators inhabit both the level of if-only and the level of what-is. In the films, the only reciprocal modification in-between such levels that allows coming to terms with trauma, is found in escape into death, or into psychosis. But for obvious reasons these are not conceivable options for the spectator. The spectator's stance corresponds to the operational structure of trauma, in which a traumatic event lies outside a victim's ordinary existence. If this person is unable to process and work through the affective meaning of trauma, it will become enduring, and the trauma victim remains stuck in a vicious circle, from which only amnesia, emotional numbing, denial, and delusion can bring relief.[25] It is this inability to process, rather than the traumatic experience itself, which the films discussed in this chapter convey through their parallel narrative structure based on *irrealis*. Or again, the films do not "narrate" trauma, but they embody that aspect of trauma which resists narrativization, that is the conditional dimension of if-only. All three films seem to suggest that only by accepting the inaccessibility of the if-only dimension one may come to terms with trauma, but then none of their traumatized protagonists succeed in doing this.

As Bennett would argue, this is the reason why (visual) art produced in the context of trauma, is transactive rather than communicative. And why it touches the spectator by means of immediate emotional engagement that does not necessarily convey the "reality" of traumatic experience.[26] Despite that all three films immerge the spectators into their characters' psychology through the narrative techniques of perceptual and mental subjectivity, they do not invite identification or empathy. Rather, they affect the spectators through parallelism that conveys upon them the effect of conditionality, which is the operational structure of trauma. It is not at all difficult to raise objections to this claim, especially when it comes to Ramón in *The Sea Inside*, a textbook example of an empathy-evoking, admirable character that does not deserve misfortune. Yet I insist that such response would be a form of misconceived empathy. In fact, the film itself seems to agree with this claim in the scene where Ramón reacts furiously to Rosa's (Lola Dueñas) offer of friendship. He considers her empathy to be a way of giving meaning to her own life, and not to Ramón's. It is only after Rosa has learned to let go of her "false empathy" that she can encounter Ramón as an autonomous subject, instead of merely as a victim of circumstances. Only then is she able to assist him with euthanasia. To summarize: what triggers our emotion in melodrama is not so much empathy with the suffering cinematic characters, but our compassionate participation in their inability to cope with the rift between the conditional spheres of what-is and if-only. Furthermore, it is the film's operational structure itself that highlights this, and induces participation in its parallelism, for which the characters may sometimes function as a vehicle. In this sense the spectator is related to the anxious lover in the Barthes quotation cited above, who always

> . . . holds vigil over the other's absence, as if over a dead body. He or she waits for love or the loss of love as one waits for death: with anxiety, in anticipation and already in mourning. [Either] one waits for an other to arrive with whom he can fall in love, an arrival that always

comes unexpectedly despite its being anxiously awaited. Falling in love offers no reprieve: now the lover awaits the other's loss.[27]

The bittersweet pleasure of watching melodrama is similar to this lover's anxiety. In this context Steve Neale has drawn attention to the disavowal of happy ending, as happy endings are always already absent as the signified, even when present as the signifier.[28] But there is more. We may also feel pleasure because our negative emotions function as an *atonement* for the fictional characters' suffering that challenges us intellectually, emotionally, and ethically.[29] This solution is related to trauma, insofar as such negative emotions also convey respect. Respect for the other's trauma, a positive emotion, through which the spectators can expand their consciousness "productively" without appropriating the traumatic experience of the other as their "own."

In conclusion, a conditional mode of spectatorship can be found at the heart of *The Sea Inside, Elementary Particles,* and *Reprise.* The three films embody *irrealis,* which enables alternation between possibility and improbability. This in turn conditions their emotional eventfulness. Trauma circulates as a discerned inability to act upon the tension between possibility and improbability, which is also felt by the spectators when they participate in the affective operations of the films based on parallelism. This participation is not perceived as a haunting sense of regret, but as a self-reflective acknowledgment that they, the spectators too, are vulnerable to trauma, which for them could also result in seeking refuge either in self-destruction or in self-deception.

Chapter 4

Anguish

Becoming Rhythm

In his 1960 book *The Theory of Film*, Siegfried Kracauer wrote about the "resonance effect" between the spectator and cinema that provokes "in the spectator such kinesthetic responses as muscular reflexes, motor impulses, or the like" and causes "a stir in deep bodily layers. It is our sense organs which are called into play."[1] In this process, "images begin to sound, and sounds are again images [. . .] bringing [the spectator] closer to poetic emotion."[2] Even before Kracauer, Sergey Eisenstein, too, was intrigued by this kind of synaesthetic sound-and-image experiences:

> For the musical overtone (a throb) it is not strictly fitting to say: "I hear." Nor for the visual overtone: "I see." For both, a new uniform formula must enter our vocabulary: "I feel."[3]

Both quotations suggest that not only is there a relation between (musical) sounds and visual images, but also between "sound-images" and emotions, a relation that is based on mutual resonance and permeability. This chapter aims at exploring the ways in which sound in cinema can express and transmit emotion by conveying a sense of affective atmosphere, into which a listener can "tune in" by opening up to this resonance. More in particular, the same can be claimed about music: that it both expresses emotion and induces sharing of the emotion by means of mutual resonance between the music and the listener. This idea is captured beautifully in T. S. Eliot's much-cited verse from *Dry Salvages*: "you are the music while the music lasts,"[4] as well as in Friedrich Hölderlin's statement: "All is rhythm; the entire destiny of man is one celestial rhythm, just as the work of art is a unique rhythm."[5] As I hope to be able to show, this "becoming rhythm" or "resonance" is how both musical and non-musical sound functions in the cinematic experience as well. Every sound, musical or non-musical, can carry emotional information that is resonant in nature and to which our ears are attentive. This is why our ears help us get the "feel" of every sound we hear, and our emotions often arise in response to something external that enters into us like sound and music. Through resonance, through the oscillation of sound waves at certain frequencies that correspond to our "emotional frequencies," the emotional "atmosphere" of every sound (and every sonic environment, for that matter) literally invites "tuning in" from the listener. The resonating materiality of sound "sculpts" our entire being, giving rise to emotions, and by doing so undoes clear boundaries between the self and the world, the inside and the outside. This is possible because we are both "within" and "outside" ourselves corporeally, emotionally, and intellectually, always responding to the affective resonance of the world. A film, too, resonates affectivity, not only through sound, but through its materiality as an emotional event.

The two films discussed in this chapter, Lars von Trier's *Dancer in the Dark* (2000) and Ingmar Bergman's *The Silence* (1963) embody the functioning of resonance in particularly suggestive ways, since in both films resonance signifies something larger: namely, that others are indispensable as sounding boards for our own existence, as well as for our knowledge about our selves. However, it may not be a very obvious choice to draw a comparison between *Dancer in the Dark* and *The Silence*. The former deals with unconditional love (between a mother and her son, but also between the mother and her best female friend), while the latter is about a troubled relationship between two sisters who are incapable of love. At least to a certain extent, the former can be categorized under what has become known as dogma-style, with the exception of its musical sequences. This style is characterized by on-location filming, pronounced handheld cinematography, natural lighting, and the avoidance of optical work and special effects, among other things. By contrast, Bergman's film is dominated by static, compositional arrangements, especially with regard to the facial close-ups that dominate the most crucial scenes. Both films have a young boy that has been abandoned by his mother as a central figure, but in *The Silence* the boy has been abandoned out of negligence, while in *Dancer in the Dark* Selma "abandons" Gene out of love. Nevertheless, I do consider the films to bear similarities, insofar as they can both be seen to embody anguish, an emotion that carries both intense fear and excruciating distress. Through the musical and aural resonance of the films, the spectator is invited to participate in that anguish. The difference is that Bergman's anguish comes into being at the moment when people become emotionally deaf to each other—hence the title of the film "silence." Furthermore, Bergman's silence is a particular kind of silence, since it is full of noise. By contrast, von Trier's anguish comes into existence through the realization that one is the source of one's own choices. In *Dancer in the Dark*, anguish is the condition in the Sartrean sense that overwhelms one at the moment when one becomes conscious of one's freedom of choice, uninhibited by necessity.[6]

Synaesthetic Tactics: *Dancer in the Dark*

The third film in von Trier's "Golden Heart Trilogy,"[7] *Dancer in the Dark* tells the story of a hard-working Czech immigrant and single mother Selma (Björk) who suffers from a hereditary degenerative disease that gradually causes her going blind. When her neighbor Bill (David Morse) steals all her savings meant as payment for an operation that would prevent her son Gene (Vladica Kostic) from inheriting her blindness, Selma is forced to take his life in an ensuing struggle, and is eventually sentenced to death. Critical responses to the film's story line have often, and perhaps not undeservingly, defined *Dancer in the Dark* as overtly sentimental and emotionally manipulative. In his review for *The New York Times*, A. O. Scott, for instance, writes: "[von Trier] seems rather to be conducting a diabolical experiment, to determine if the virtuosic brutality of his style can manipulate the audience into feeling what it cannot believe."[8] As this quotation suggests, the "virtuosic brutality" has less to do with emotional identification with Selma than with the emotional "parameters" of the film itself. I propose that the reason we feel anguish in *Dancer in the Dark* is explained by how we are "enveloped" by its musical sequences that sensitize us emotionally and kinesthetically through an intimate connection.[9] Whether or not this is a question of emotional manipulation is not so much the main issue here as is the way in which the film confronts spectators with their own vulnerability to anguish and their own proneness to escapism and self-deception. Although musicological issues are being addressed in this chapter, my attempt is not so much to propose a new theory on how film scores evoke emotions, as to explore the resonating relationship between the film and the spectator, an endeavor in which anguish operates as a guide.

Dancer in the Dark has an overture, a musical strategy that in cinema is used to set the mood of the film before, during, or instead of the opening credits, as for example in *Gone with the Wind* (Victor Fleming, 1939), *How to Marry a Millionaire* (Jean Negulesco, 1953), *2001: A Space Odyssey* (Stanley

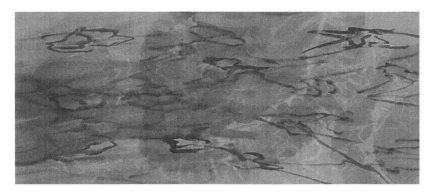

IMAGE 4.1 Synaesthetic overture in *Dancer in the Dark*

Kubrick, 1968), and *Manhattan* (Woody Allen, 1979). In *Dancer in the Dark*, the overture is best characterized as synaesthetic (image 4.1), which Richard Cytowic defines as a "joined sensation [. . .] wherein two or more senses are coupled such that a voice, for example, is not only heard, but also felt, seen, or tasted."[10] The overture sequence consists of abstract, colorful images that dissolve into each other, thereby conveying an affective progression that emerges through the crossing of senses. In the beginning, only a white frame can be seen with some randomly arranged dark spots on top of it. This image dissolves, through many different layers as it seems, into a warm-toned image of childishly drawn, shellfish-like abstract figures, while the harmonious brass music slowly starts off on the soundtrack with an earthy timbre but a sublime melody. The dissolving of images continues throughout the overture sequence, as if we were to penetrate through layers that change their color scale in a range that runs from bright red and yellow through green, purple, and light blue and back to white. The figures in the images, too, change their shapes from "shellfish" and "poppies" through "lipstick traces" and "chrysanthemums" to "leaves blowing in the wind." These colors and figures are comparable to the afterimages that remain on our retinas after we have first looked into a bright light source and then close our eyes tightly. The changes in color and graphics correspond with the changing resonation of the musical "valence,"[11] which begins with a peaceful tone, but soon develops dark timbres as the tone becomes more pompous in its energy before fading away.

In Chapters 2 and 3 I have already shown how the opening of a film can often be read as a "condensed narrative" of the whole feature. The overture in *Dancer in the Dark* can also be seen as a condensation of the complete movie, but not on the narrative level. Instead, the overture is a condensation of the film's emotional progression in which we participate through the resonance conveyed in color and music and which is taken in by our senses.[12] I have already mentioned that the *Dancer in the Dark* overture makes use of synaesthetic tactics that invite us to hear the colors and see the music. In theories of synaesthesia, music and color are often linked through their corresponding wavelengths. In the same way as music is conveyed by acoustic waves, the product of light waves is perceived by our brain as color.[13] But the "synaesthetic perception" of music-color is connected to emotions as well, since emotions too have an intervallic nature. This is the tendency of emotions to oscillate at certain "amplitudes" (intense/mild) and at certain "frequencies" (pleasant/unpleasant), rather than at others. Admittedly, when we talk about emotion we do not usually speak of waves like we do in connection with sound and music, yet this "affective interval scale" nevertheless provides an explanation for the correspondence between resonance of music and resonance of emotion. In the overture of *Dancer in the Dark*, the overall resonance is a condensation of the complete emotional span of the film. It starts off with modest hope and joy, only to become more cautious and dark in its ominous climax, after which a lonely trumpet repeats the melody once more before bringing it to an end.

In addition to the overture, the musical sequences in *Dancer in the Dark* consist of seven "Selmasongs" entitled "Cvalda," "I've Seen It All," "Scatterheart," "In the Musicals" (Part 1 and 2), "107 Steps," and "New World" (during the end credits). They all have something in common which is characteristic of Björk's "regular" songs as well, that is the lack of harmony between their primary and secondary musical parameters. It is generally acknowledged that emotion, such as sadness, can be induced through music by manipulating its primary musical parameters, the musical phrases, melodies, harmonies, and motifs that are culturally determined and as such recognizable as emotionally sorrowful. Albinoni's "Adagio in G Minor," for instance, is often considered as sorrowful because we have culturally learned to associate it with grief, as the piece is frequently performed at memorial services, such as Lady Diana's funeral in 1997. Yet according to Bill Thompson, a more effective way to induce emotion through music is to manipulate its secondary musical parameters, also called its basic acoustic properties, such as rhythm, pace, loudness, timbre, intonation, pitch, and tone of voice.[14] So, Albinoni's "Adagio in G Minor" can be experienced as sorrowful not only because we have learned by culture to associate it with sadness, but also because the piece has the contour of sorrowful human gestures and speech, such as the slowness of rhythm, the softness of timbre, the unenergetic dynamics, and the harmonic sequence of tones.[15]

Both the primary and secondary musical parameters can be emotionally charged in ways that make a piece of music joyful or sorrowful, aggressive or romantic, unsettling or consoling. "Cvalda," the first musical sequence[16] in *Dancer in the Dark* consists of primary musical parameters that are best characterized as full of childlike simplicity with an airy timbre in the major key. The line "Listen, Cvalda, you're the dancer, you've got the sparkle in your eyes," for instance, has a fluid, metrical harmony that conveys a sense of naivety and optimism. But this simplicity is effortlessly transformed into subtlety in the following line "Look at me, entrancer!," which is more irregular in its melody. The melody produced by the harp at the background, too, commences metrically but soon becomes more sparkling, while the wind section blows away at swinging jazz. The beat in this musical sequence is produced by the "factory machines" and "tools" that become percussion instruments, starting to "clatter, crash, clack, racket, bang, thump" and "rattle" rhythmically. All these emergent musical properties of "Cvalda" are non-emotional in themselves, but they gain emotional charge as they become similar to the qualities of human emotional states. This has to do with the three-dimensionality of music as found in the properties of valence (pleasant-unpleasant), energy (alert-weary) and tension (tense-relaxed). In music, any form of valence may occur together with any energetic or tension level, and there is an infinite number of combinations and sequences that determine the fluctuation of emotion through the progression and development of musical valence, energy, and tension.[17]

This means that the sense of emotional progression that music often conveys cannot be explained by its single one-dimensional qualities, that is valence, energy, and tension disjointed from each other, since emotion is a process in which different elements flow into each other, thus influencing its development.[18] The concepts of valence, energy, and tension are particularly appropriate in the exploration of emotional qualities in music, since they occur in time. Or better yet, these concepts are suitable for exploring the emotional resonance between the music and the listener, since human emotions as processes also emerge as a result of changes in the individual's affective valence, energy, and tension as he or she engages with the environment. Both human and musical emotional processes originate in energetic arousal and tension that can be high versus low, vigorous and activated versus sluggish and lethargic, or anxious and jittery versus calm and relaxed. In addition, these processes can be described in terms of their valence, positive versus negative, pleasant versus unpleasant. Happiness, for example, can be high in energy (excitement) or low in tension (serenity), combined with positive valence (pleasure). "Cvalda," for instance, is high in its energy but easy-going in its tension and pleasant in its valence. This is joy. Glen Mazis would say that in this sequence Selma has a "dancing connection" with the world, picking up and joining the energetic resonance of the world, attuning to its rhythmic, shape-shifting, and reverberating qualities, where emotion and resonance are one.[19] Furthermore, this being a film, the music relates to other cinematic elements enhancing their emotional dimension.[20] For instance, the rhythm of the music corresponds with the rhythm of the editing, the movement within the frame, and the framing of the image. The colors are bright and vivid, especially compared to the saturated muddiness of the non-musical sequences, which renders the "Cvalda" sequence reminiscent of the synaesthetic overture in the beginning of the film.

The second musical sequence, "I've Seen It All," takes place right after Selma's love interest Jeff (Peter Stormare) has found out that Selma is practically blind. The lyrics assure that Selma has come to terms with her blindness:

> I've seen what I chose and I've seen what I need,
> And that is enough, to want more would be greed.
> I've seen what I was and I know what I'll be
> I've seen it all—there is no more to see!

Yet both the primary and secondary musical parameters in this sequence influence the spectator's emotional appraisal of its valence, energetic arousal, and tension in an opposite way. The operative analogy between the musical emotional process conveyed in "I've Seen It All" and the human emotional process contradicts the emotion that is expressed in words.[21] Like in "Cvalda," the melody in the minor key is strongly patterned, consisting of a simple theme combined with a more complex movement at the end of the first, the third, and the fifth verse. On the other hand, the strings remain asynchronous with respect to the vocals throughout the whole sequence. The secondary musical parameters consist of a rhythm that starts off with rhythmical clacking of trains on tracks, and then progresses into downtempo breakbeats with a delicate timbre that are characteristic of trip hop artists such as Massive Attack,

Portishead, and Tricky. All in all, the pace is tranquil and the volume is low all throughout the whole sequence. The valence of this sequence is ambivalent and bittersweet due to its sluggish energy on the one hand and its serene tension on the other, bespeaking the melancholy of coming to terms with a situation that cannot be helped.

The third musical sequence, "Scatterheart," takes place right after the murder of Bill. This sequence begins as a lullaby, with the sound of a damaged record playing a simple, repetitive melody produced by a musical box. The record gets stuck and its sound is exchanged for an electronically produced buzzing rhythm. The dead Bill wakes up "alive" and performs a recitative duet with Selma in which they both forgive each other.[22] Gene's repeated song line "You just did what you had to do" comments on the recitation. As the sequence progresses, Selma's singing melody develops from a soothing lullaby into a guilt-ridden song. There is a complicated emotional progression here. On the level of primary musical parameters there is progression from consolation conveyed by the soothing melody of the lullaby to guilt conveyed by the dramatic movement at the end of the musical sequence. Furthermore, there is progression on the level of secondary musical parameters from an initial shock conveyed by the repetitive scratching of the needle on the record to the panicky pulse of the electronic percussion. The spectator relatively effortlessly "tunes in" into this emotional progression, since the music is not experienced being somewhere "out there," but simultaneously inside and outside of the self. We literally feel these emotions conveyed by music in our flesh, the whole body being caught up in the process of listening, capturing, and repeating the variations in musical valence, tension, and energy. Michel Serres describes this process of listening as follows:

> We hear through our skin and feet. We hear through our skull, abdomen and thorax. We hear through our muscles, nerves and tendons. Our body-box, strung tight, is covered head to toe with a tympanum. [. . .] Sometimes dissonant, often consonant, disturbed or harmonious. Resonating within us [. . .] as though our bodies were the union of ear and orchestra, transmission and reception. I am the home and hearth of sound, hearing and voice all in one, black box and echo.[23]

I propose that we also resonate within the film *Dancer in the Dark* and that the film resonates within us. In both sequences of "In the Musicals," this resonance consists of energetic joy originating from the high-pitched rhythm of the xylophone, the clapping, the finger snapping, and the tap dancing to the beat, as well as from the fast tempo of the melody. This escapist joy is in harsh contradiction with the context of events: part one of "In the Musicals" takes place during Selma's arrest, and part two during her murder trial. During these sequences, the musical valence, tension, and energy operate directly on the spectator's body and the senses.[24] As a result, the spectator experiences the development in the emotional process that the music conveys, instead of the narrative development. In a similar vein, sound designer David Sonnenschein argues that music moves us because musical patterns correspond with our ultradian biorhythm, a short-termed cyclic pattern of alteration in our physical and mental makeup that regulates our emotions, among other things. Emotions are produced for instance when there is a harmonic dissonance between the rhythmic forms of the body and the rhythmic forms of music.[25] This is the reason why we can be saddened by sad music even if we were not in a sad state of mind before we started listening.

This is exactly what *Dancer in the Dark* does. On the narrative level the film confronts its spectator with Selma's tragedy, and on the musical level it resonates an opposite effect, bringing the spectator into a state of emotional dissonance. This is most clearly seen in the death row sequence "107 Steps," in which the prison guard Brenda (Siobhan Fallon) leads Selma to her execution. Paralyzed by fear, Selma is able to walk by herself only to the rhythm of Brenda's footsteps, which enables her to imagine performing in a musical. This musical sequence with its uplifting, flowing string movements, and the tuneful vocals has an airy quality. Of all the musical sequences in the film this is the one that resembles most the classical Hollywood musical tunes, especially in films starring Fred Astaire, Ginger Rogers, Gene Kelly, or Cyd Charisse. At the same time Brenda's counting the footsteps in time to her marching continues uninterrupted at the background, which prevents the spectator from forgetting the inevitability of Selma's fate. The spectator becomes the receiver of contradicting resonances and experiences anguish as a result. This anguish is constitutive of hope that the film will generate a happy end for us, as in musicals, and also of the certainty that this will not happen. This makes us participate in Selma's awareness that she herself is the cause of her imminent death, due to the unpredictability of her actions.

The most anguish-evoking scene in the film is that of the execution itself, in which the hysterical Selma collapses and has to be tied up to a board. Screaming piercingly in agony, Selma is unable to escape from the situation into a musical, since there is no rhythmical sound until her friend Kathy (Catherine Deneuve) rushes to her aid and places Gene's (now useless) glasses into her hand. Now Selma can produce the necessary rhythm by rubbing the arms of the glasses against each other, and she sings what she calls "the next to last song" until the hatch is opened abruptly and she drops to her death. In this scene the film does not depict the musical that goes on in Selma's head. Instead, only her singing voice is there as evidence for an orchestra and dancers. Most of the time Selma's (Björk's) voice could be characterized as childish in its charming awkwardness, but when her voice reaches its highest pitch, it slashes like a knife. In addition to its raw emotional impact, the scene has synaesthetic quality, since it invites the spectator, by means of cross-sensorial processing, to "envision" not only the missing musical elements, but also the accompanying colors. At the same time the spectator is made painfully aware of the impossibility of further escape into the realm of the musical. The conflict that resonates in "Selmasongs" is precisely that between freedom and necessity, which confronts us with our own proneness to choose escape instead of the unbound possibilities in the world, as verified through the ease by which we allow the musical sequences to do its resonating work for us. For it is in the musical sequences that the spectator can escape from the film's implicit "diabolical cruelty" toward Selma, away into the joy that these sequences convey too. But ultimately the last scene leaves us shattered with anguish that functions as a reminder, an accusation even, of an attitude that Jean-Paul Sartre calls bad faith, a self-deceptive flight from freedom and responsible self-determination.

Resonating Sonic Space: *The Silence*

Even though both in popular opinion and among those trained in music theory it is generally accepted, that the association between music and emotion is a psychological fact, the debate on whether or not, and in what way, music actually expresses emotion, is exceptionally broad and complicated. Some theorists, such as Eduard Hanslick, argue that there is no significant relationship between music and emotion. Music can merely express the dynamic aspects of an emotion but not the emotion itself.[26] Other theorists, like Susanne Langer, agree with Hanslick but add that the dynamic aspects of emotion are sufficient to express this emotion, and argue that music symbolizes emotion by means of structural similarity between its dynamics and the dynamics of our "inner life."[27] Still others, such as Peter Kivy, accept Hanslick's conclusions to a certain extent, but modify his arguments by asserting that music can be expressive of emotion without expressing emotion, comparable to the head of a Saint Bernard dog that is expressive of sadness (and can be recognized as such) without actually expressing sadness.[28] In my opinion the above views do not seem to apply to *Dancer in the Dark*, because it is the film itself—and not its emotional "content"—that bashes the spectator into agony by means of its resonating modality. As I have already argued, music does not only express emotion by embodying the development of affective progression, but it also enables sharing of the emotion by means of sonic resonance between music and the listener. The same can be argued about sound in general, as each sound embodies an affective environment to which the listener can "tune in" by opening up to the resonating sonic space. With regard to *The Silence*, it is interesting to pay attention to how Bergman himself describes the film as bearing similarities to Béla Bartók's music:

> My original idea was to make a film that should obey musical laws, instead of dramaturgical ones. A film acting by association—rhythmically, with themes and counter-themes. As I was putting it together, I thought much more in musical terms than I'd done before. All that's left of Bartók is the very beginning. It follows Bartók's music rather closely—the dull continuous note, then the sudden explosion.[29]

I think that the above especially applies to the sound design of the film. The most striking aspect of sound in *The Silence* is that with few exceptions, it is almost entirely diegetic and simultaneous. The exceptions to this pattern are the sounds of the clock ticking and of the ominous "wail" toward the end of the film. Regularly the film effectively uses the distinction between the onscreen and the offscreen sound,[30] thereby creating an omni-dimensional space that is characterized by simultaneity and mutually shaping resonance. The film opens with a black frame over which the title sequence appears, accompanied by the ticking of the clock that signifies some kind of emotional urgency that gradually builds into full-blown anguish in the course of the film. In the opening scene two sisters, sickly Ester (Ingrid Thulin) and overtly sensual Anna (Gunnel Lindblom), as well as Anna's son Johan (Jörgen Lindström), are traveling in a train compartment, in an unknown (Eastern?) European country on the brink of war. The particular use of sound is striking from the very beginning. The prominent sounds inside the compartment, together with the dominating humming sound of the train in the background, emphasize the emptiness of the situation. Ester has a seizure and they shut Johan out of the compartment. The boy wanders through the empty corridors of the train. The train enters a tunnel and then passes war tanks standing off the side of the train tracks, which causes impulse noise. The opening sequence ends with Anna and Johan staring out of the train window, shot from outside, while the inside noises (the humming of the train) blend with and transform into the outside noises (the screeching of the brakes). As Ester, Anna, and Johan have now entered into the foreign city, we have literally entered into the film.

The play between the inside and the outside continues into the following sequence that opens with an establishing shot of street life with all its appropriate sonic details: traffic noise, newspaper boys shouting. The next shot shows Johan staring out of the window at the hotel where he is staying together with Anna and Ester, shot from the outside. After that the outside noises are muffled, and finally silenced altogether, as the camera moves inside the hotel room. However, the "silence" of the hotel is not really silent, but full of noises of running bath water, Johan imitating an aircraft, Ester coughing, music from the radio. In this way, Bergman's silence actually consists of noise, but the difference between inside and outside noises is striking nonetheless, since the latter are characterized by their penetrating quality, while the former are best defined as enveloping sounds. Therefore, as soon as the penetrating sound of the real aircraft approaches, Johan escapes from this sound into the "protective," "uterine" sounds of the hotel hallways.[31] He fires a shot from his toy gun at the caretaker (with no effect), and then imitates the sound of the approaching aircraft.[32] On the one hand, Johan wants to be where these sounds are, but on the other hand these sounds threaten to come all too close. In this configuration where Johan stands as the central figure, the inside and the outside close into each other, but leave the inside/outside arrangement intact, with the consequence that everything inside the hotel is like a graveyard, dead to the rest of the world, with the circus performers' room as the only exception.

The use of sound in *The Silence* could be imagined in spatial terms, as three concentric acoustic circles with their own emotional landscapes. The outer circle is city life with all its vivid sounds: the sounds of traffic, lively jazz music played at a bar, the clinking of glasses, the blast of a jackhammer, the clang of church bells. This is Anna's emotional landscape, full of vivacity. In one crucial scene Anna goes out to a bar. The male waiter kneels before her with a longing gaze, pretending to pick up something. She then enters a cabaret where the circus dwarfs perform. On a seat next to hers a couple makes love. Anna, observing the scene, is perplexed at first and then leaves. The reason for Anna's leaving the scene is that it confronts her with her sexual frustration, from which she can only get temporary relief in a quick affair with the waiter from the prior scene. Here the lively jazz music may resonate cheerfulness with its bubbly xylophone and glitzy piano sounds, but the nervousness of the saxophone underneath the melody suggests that something distressful is bubbling under Anna's nonchalant appearance.

The middle circle is the hotel as an aural and emotional vacuum, since even though there is sound, this is not truly "heard" by anyone. Any sound without a receiver is an impossibility, due to the ontological nature of sound, as will be duly explained. It is a well-known scientific fact that physical sound is a pressure wave which results from a resonating energy that is absorbed and transmitted by the mobile particles of a medium through which it moves. Thus the production of sound involves changes of pressure in the matter surrounding it, such as air or water. In the words of Rick Altman, this leads to a concept of sound as a three-dimensional material event that offers itself to be heard. In other words, the changes of pressure are detected by our sense of hearing, be it not in a straight line, and this process guarantees the spatial nature of sound:

> [Resonance] creates pressure, which is communicated through a medium. At the other end of sound's path, the human ear collects that pressure and transforms its mechanical energy into electrical impulses that the brain understands as sound. This is not a direct process, but it involves a great deal of reflected sound or reverberation, produced by the sound that reaches the hearing ear only after bouncing off one or more surfaces.[33]

If a tree falls in a forest and no one is around to hear it, does it make a sound? The sound theorist's answer to this famous philosophical riddle is an unambiguous no. There is no sound, because sound ontologically requires a receiver, a human ear at the other "end" of the sound that collects the resonating pressure, which the brain understands as sound. In Jean-Luc Nancy's thinking, too, sound can be understood in terms of event as a shared space of meaning that consists of . . .

> . . . a totality of referrals: from sign to a thing, from a state of things to a quality, from a subject to another subject or to itself, all simultaneously. Sound is also made of referrals: it spreads in space, where it resounds while still resounding "in me."[34]

This is why sound in *The Silence* is silent, especially in the middle circle. It lacks the aspect of event or resonance. Sound in *The Silence* is silent, because it offers itself to be heard but not to be listened to. The hotel as an acoustic vacuum is Johan's emotional landscape that signifies his inability to be listened to even though he is heard, with the grotesque dwarfs being the only exception here. In his book *Listening*, Jean-Luc Nancy writes that to "hear" is to understand the sense of sound, whereas to "listen" is "to be straining toward a possible meaning, and consequently one that is not immediately accessible."[35]

Thus, there is a functional difference between listening and hearing. Listening is "the opening of the world in resonance, a world taken away from the arrangements of objects and subjects,"[36] while hearing is "merely" a linear apprehension of sound without resonance, as in sound passing through the person who hears without effort. Therefore, listening is necessarily a sonorous event that requires resonance between elements. In other words, listening requires an effort to "tune in to" and resonate with each other, something the characters in *The Silence* are not prepared to do. Language in *The Silence* is a form of silence for instance, since it functions to set up barriers instead of bridging distances between individuals. For one thing, the people in this strange country speak an unrecognizable language that Anna and Ester cannot listen to, and neither can they be listened to in any of the languages they do command. For Anna this is a pleasant situation, a way of avoiding all effort: "How nice that we don't understand each other," she says to her one-night lover, the waiter from the previous scene in the café. Secondly, despite the fact that Anna and Ester share the same language, they have become deaf to each other. Or better, Anna and Ester can only hear, but they cannot listen to each other in the sense of "straining towards a possible meaning [. . .] where sound and sense mix together and resonate in each other, or through each other."[37] The only words that gain resonance are the words *written* down by Ester in a foreign language as a farewell present to Johan. The film ends with Johan reading Ester's letter aloud on the train, while Anna opens the window, letting in the impact noise that smothers his voice, so that once more it cannot be listened to.

Finally, the inner circle is the hotel room as a subjective soundscape of raw emotion: unreciprocated love and sexual jealousy. This room is full of suppressed shouting, gagging, wheezing, moaning, panting, crying, hysterical laughter, pain, and suffocation. This is Ester's emotional landscape that is marked by a disturbing intimacy. According to Nancy, sound has always to do with contagious or shared participation in the process of "opening oneself up to the resonance of being, or to being as resonance."[38] Sound is by necessity a form of intimacy since its "sense is supposed to be found in [mutual] resonance, and only in resonance."[39] Therefore, hearing sound has much to do with touch as a form of sensory perception, for how otherwise can such sounds as the scratching of nails on a chalkboard give us goose bumps? We literally feel the sound in our flesh, our whole skin caught up in the process of listening, capturing, and repeating the variations in sonic valence, tension, and energy. This relationship between sound and tactility has been acknowledged by many sound theorists, such as Michel Serres in the quotation cited in the *Dancer in the Dark* part of this chapter. Sound designer Philip Brophy also speaks of the ways in which sound can attain a tactile presence that can resonate with the skin of the listener.[40] And within a psychoanalytic framework, theorists such as Guy Rosolato, Didier Anzieu, and Kaja Silverman speak of the sonorous space that envelops the listener in a manner akin to the uterine bath.[41]

For Michel Chion the tactile significance of sound is the effect of its "material heterogeneity," the effect of feeling associated with the sound source. The sonic details that signify the tactility of sound are "materializing sound indices" that are often exaggerated in cinema or even recreated by a Foley artist in order to "render" to the sound source its "true" qualities—the strength and bestiality in the roar of the bear in Jean-Jacques Annaud's *The Bear* (*L'Ours*, 1988), the sensual sound of rustling silk in François Truffaut's *The Bride Wore Black* (*La mariée était en noir*, 1968):

> The materializing indices are the sound's details that cause us to "feel" the material conditions of the sound source, and refer to the concrete process of the sound's production. They can give us information about the substance causing the sound—wood, metal, paper, cloth—as well as the way sound is produced—by friction, impact, uneven oscillations, periodic movement back and forth, and so on.[42]

In this way the process of rendering sounds conveys the materiality of sound as tactile sensation, and therefore it might be said that sounds affect by means of touch, our whole skin being a hearing organ. In addition the small irregularities that are often present in the material sound indices aid us in sensing the concrete presence of sound. By contrast, if sound is "too pure," it is often experienced as ethereal instead of substantial. For instance, Ester's masturbation scene in *The Silence* consists of impure sounds that develop through bodily obstacles: breathing out

IMAGE 4.2 Sound as intimacy: *The Silence*

through the bitter taste of strong liquor, Ester's cotton pajama resisting the cotton sheets, her breathing in through a blocked nose. These sounds feel almost too intimate (image 4.2), because they have their origin in private bodily functions and the "frictional impurities" of the body.

As stated above, what is remarkable about these concentric spatial circles is the way in which they constantly intertwine and penetrate each other through sound. The sounds of approaching war, fighter planes, the entire city evacuating, threaten to enter the zone of stillness throughout the whole film. In one scene the fighter planes draw so near to the hotel that their rumbling even shakes the water carafe inside. And there is Anna, arranging a meeting at the hotel with her waiter, who is an outsider. Their lovemaking disturbs the state of static idleness which the hotel and its residents have drifted into. After their sexual climax, Ester's gentle voice and quiet sobbing reaches Anna's ears off screen, and Ester herself enters the room where the lovers are. In rage, Anna then insults and attacks Ester verbally and Ester responds with apparent gentleness, which in turn drives Anna further into a state of hysteria that only ends when her lover penetrates her once more. In the next scene Anna is seen dressing up, faraway church bells clanging ominously in the background, while Ester lies unconscious outside the room. Later on lying in bed, Ester commences a painful but "euphoric" account of penetration to her "own" age-old waiter, who obviously cannot understand a word she is saying:

> Erectile tissue . . . it's all a matter of swollen tissue and secretion; a confession before extreme unction. Semen smells nasty to me. I've a very keen sense of smell and I stank like rotten fish when I was fertilized.

As soon as this monologue is over, the real pain comes, first combined with the empathic ticking of a clock and then with the only non-diegetic sound in the entire film, a howling noise that both wails in alarm and penetrates and suffocates everything else.

Therefore it seems to be penetration that lies at the centre of *The Silence*. On the one hand it is present as a banal metaphor for sexual assault. In fact, many critics have paid attention to the incestuous, self-destructive, and promiscuous themes in the film. On the other hand the theme of penetration has a far wider meaning in *The Silence*: it is the extension and the expansion of the source of sound (the "self") to include the listener (the "other") and *vice versa*. Nancy writes:

> To listen to is to enter that spatiality [of sound] by which, *at the same time*, I am penetrated, for it opens up in me as well as around me, and from me as well as toward me: it opens me inside me as well as outside, and it is through such a double, quadruple, or sextuple opening that a "self" can take place. To be listening is to be *at the same time* outside and inside, to be open *from* without and *from* within, hence from one to the other and from one in the other.[43]

Between the characters of *The Silence* this process is blocked—hence, the "silence"—and, as a result affective circulation between them is blocked as well. A similar "emotional urgency," as Thomas Elsaesser calls this, is present in many films of Bergman, but in *The Silence* it takes the form of a crisis, in which Anna and Ester cannot help but seal their ears and thicken their emotions to the point where listening as openness to penetration is no longer possible. In other words, Anna and Ester have failed in the "togetherness" (being-with) of the self with the other, the inside with the outside, in the process of listening. Anguish emerges as a consequence of this failure, not only for the characters but also for the spectator. Anna and Ester have cut off the emotional circulation in which they should participate, both as suppliers of affective interest toward the other and as receivers of reciprocal affection from the other. Again, the spectator feels this distressful urgency as transmitted by the film itself, since *The Silence* is not an easy film to "take in." At first the film's violent resonance disrupts the listening process and produces resistance instead of mutual resounding. Thus, a certain amount of effort is required from the spectator in order to gain insight into the film. Yet it is precisely this effort that renders *The Silence* a sounding board for the spectator. By forcing upon the spectator the distressful effects of emotional deafness through unsolicited sonic penetration, the film leaves the spectator with two choices. One either closes oneself up, in which case the film will remain silent forever. The alternative is to open oneself up to its resonance regardless of its dissonant properties. The latter option requires effort and results in anguish, but the anguish will not go unrewarded. While in *Dancer in the Dark* the anguish cannot find an outlet and hence becomes enduring, in *The Silence* it comes as an invitation to gain insight into listening as a form of being-with, the only protection mechanism against agonizing human loneliness.

Chapter 5

Shame

Self-awareness lies at the heart of shame, an emotion that is organized along the axis of seeing and being seen. In this context Ruth Leys has coined the phrase "spectatorial logic of shame." This notion refers to the feelings of shame that an individual experiences as a result of being conscious of negative exposure to other people, even if this exposure is only imagined. This phenomenon is part of our fundamental condition of simultaneously being subject and object in the world. We are capable of observing an "objectified version" of ourselves in anticipation of how we would be viewed by the other in a particular, shameful situation. The triangularity of shame equals first the awareness of our actions, secondly the awareness that our actions can be interpreted by others, and thirdly the awareness of who we are and who we want to be. In cinema there is also the possibility of the spectators' awareness of their own looking, the awareness that their viewpoint has already been incorporated in the film, the awareness that all the time their "desire to look" is reciprocally observed by the institution of cinema itself. This happens for instance when the film explicitly directs the spectators' attention to its own artificial status, the way in which it is constituted. Moments like these can be awkward for the spectators, not only because they are threatening to their personal space, but also because they suggest that the spectators are constituted for the film and not *vice versa*.[1]

In this chapter I will discuss two films that both embody the operational structure of shame along the axis of seeing and being seen: *American Beauty* (Sam Mendes, 1999) and *Borat: Cultural Learnings of America for Make Benefit Glorious Nation of Kazakhstan* (Larry Charles, 2006). Both films contain the possibility that shame will be acknowledged by the spectator as a mode of self-reflection. In turn this becomes a question of moral agency and of multiplicity of coexisting viewing positions. Furthermore, in neither of the films "substitute shame" (shame by proxy) is immanent, since the spectator's emotion is not based on the process of identification. Through self-reflection both films enable a triangular viewing position for the spectator, through which shame can be passed on transculturally. Such in spite of the fact that both films explicitly deal with American culture, as epitomized in a bourgeois, suburban nuclear family in *American Beauty*, and in the cultural ideal of Americanness in *Borat*. The way in which shame can transpire through cultures has to do with its contagiousness. It affects anyone who has ever internalized the cultural concept of shame, regardless of how shame functions within various specific cultures.

Suburban Rebellion: *American Beauty*

American Beauty opens with the sound of a camera shutter whirring. A teenage girl called Jane (Thora Birch), filmed in her underwear, confesses to the camera her shame about being forced to live with a father who is not a role model but "some horny geek-boy who's gonna spray his shorts whenever I bring a girlfriend home from school." This cinematic prologue establishes an interplay of feelings between being disempowered and being exposed in the experience of shame, which is the driving force of the whole film. There is a triangle that consists of the shamed (Jane), the one who shames (her father) and the observer (the camera), illustrating the operational structure of shame in particularly suggestive ways. The camera shutter whirrs again, clicking as the title card appears. Then the opening sequence starts off with an establishing long shot in which the camera flies over suburban America, until gradually descending, it gets closer to a peaceful and idyllic tree-lined street called Robin Hood trail, a name that says it all. Next, with his voice-over narrating the events from death, we witness Jane's father Lester Burnham (Kevin Spacey) waking up and going through his morning routines, the best part of which is "jerking off in the shower." Thus mercilessly exposed, it becomes clear to the spectator that nothing in the lifestyle of this particular suburban family is what it seems to be when seen from a distance. Or as the tagline of the film says: "Look closer." The shower scene is cut to Lester's wife Carolyn (Annette Bening) tending her beautiful red roses in the garden lined by a white picket fence, which establishes a perfect décor into which her grungy daughter and her loser husband just do not fit.

American Beauty casts a darkly satirical eye on this supposedly perfect, but actually dysfunctional nuclear family, by establishing that lack of

control over self-image is at the center of their interpersonal relationships. This lack of control manifests itself in the emotion of shame. It
is generally acknowledged that shame is an interpretive process. Seeing
oneself from other people's position is combined with the experience
of being unable to take control of one's self-image and to organize a
response.[2] In *American Beauty* Lester is a disappointed copywriter, stuck
in a loveless marriage and confronted by the meaningless of existence
in an early mid-life crisis. Inspired by the brazen, "existentialist attitude"
of Ricky Fitts (Wes Bentley), a boy who has just moved opposite the
Burnhams, Lester starts to take active measures to free himself from all
social responsibilities. First he deliberately provokes his employers into
firing him, shamelessly blackmailing his boss for a year's salary while at
it. Then he starts doggedly pursuing Angela (Mena Suvari), the girl of
his desires, without taking into consideration that she is also Jane's best
friend. "I feel like I've been in a coma for about twenty years, and I'm just
now waking up," Lester's voice-over elucidates while fantasying about
Angela lying on a bed of roses, rose petals falling on top of him.

Yet in his quest for freedom from shame, Lester damages all his personal relationships by his unabashed behavior. As a result the members
of his family feel ashamed on behalf of him, but all of them in their
own way, that is to say depending on their personal values and on how
they want to be seen in their own social context. Naturally, for insecure
Jane Lester's behavior toward Angela is an enormous cause for shame.
A father who desires his daughter's best friend, is just too Oedipal, or
incestuous even, to keep on living with. But in addition to her father's
behavior, Jane's self-loathing and her painful self-awareness of how she is
exposed to others, is fed by her friendship with the beautiful and (seemingly) self-confident Angela, who only seems to use Jane in order to feel
better about herself. The only person who truly sees Jane is her school-
mate Ricky, the boy next door, be it only through the lens of his video
camera at first, which is rather paradoxical. However, in the end Jane is
able to expose herself to Ricky without shame.

By contrast, Carolyn is an ambitious real estate agent, for whom only
appearances matter. This is obvious for instance after Jane's dance performance when Carolyn is proud of her for "not screwing up once"
(in front of others), rather than for actually performing well. Carolyn
believes that appearance is more important than substance, as it is only
the way she is seen by the people she admires that confirms her sense
of identity as a successful businesswoman, wife, and mother. And it is
especially "Real Estate King" Buddy Kane's opinion she heeds. Buddy,

played by Peter Gallagher, believes that "in order to be successful, one must project an image of success, at all times," and Carolyn enters into an adulterous affair with him, in the hope that his success will reflect on her. But Buddy ends their relationship coldly and abruptly, after Lester has caught them out at a hamburger bar where he is working behind the counter ("Smile! You're at Mr. Smiley's!"). Carolyn understands that Buddy's reason for ending their relationship is not that he is afraid of an expensive divorce, but that Carolyn does not "project an image of success," as her husband appears to work at a hamburger bar.

Thus the whole film circles around shame of being seen, and Lester functions as a catalyst for such shame, after he has freed himself from his emotional paralysis. The way in which *American Beauty* embodies the feeling of disempowerment serves to demonstrate an important feature of shame. People who are ashamed experience themselves as objects, instead of subjects, as they are in the world of the other. When in shame, the self is experienced as taken over by social forces beyond one's control, because in shame the other can offer a (contemptuous) point of view on oneself that one cannot influence positively.[3] Lester's behavior causes that the other characters in the film are unable to keep up the façade of suburban life that symbolizes the American Dream, and thus keep shame out of the picture. Especially Carolyn is constantly concerned how both she and her nearest and dearest will appear to other people in their social environment. Carolyn's shame is shame by proxy, grounded in her marital alignment with Lester. As soon as shame renders the family's unfulfilled desires visible, as well as the underlying social structures that stifle those desires, the film turns from a satirical comedy into a hysterical, twisted nightmare, and even the pace of narration changes from sleepy to hectic. A good example of this "discontent of civilization" is the case of Ricky's father, Colonel Fitts (Chris Cooper), who appears as a homophobic ex-marine collecting Nazi-memorabilia. As later on we find out, his homophobia and this role of marine, which he so painstakingly plays out, are just a masquerade to hide his own suppressed homosexuality. He mistakes Lester for a gay and makes a pass at him, only to find out that he is not. This is so emotionally disturbing for Colonel Fitts that he kills Lester, in order to avoid that he would have to live with the feelings of shame that the humiliating episode caused him. Lester has become an incarnation of the social eye that Colonel Fitts imagines watching him in disapproval for his failed masculinity. By getting rid of Lester, who is the only person who knows about his homosexuality, Colonel Fitts attempts to get rid of shame.

In her book *From Guilt to Shame*, Ruth Leys has coined the phrase spectatorial logic of shame, which refers to the feelings of shame that individuals experience as a result of their being conscious of negative exposure: "shame is an emotion that is *routed through the eyes* and the logic of shame is a *scene of exposure*."[4] In a situation in which somebody is exposed negatively to others, that individual's humiliation can become contagious as it were, affecting the observers through the emotion of shame, but without their identifying with the individual as such:

> In taking on the shame, I do not share in the other's identity. I simply adopt the other's vulnerability to being shamed. In this operation, most importantly, the other's difference is preserved; it is not claimed as my own. In taking on or taking up his or her shame [. . .] I put myself in the place of the other only insofar I recognize that I too am prone to shame.[5]

American Beauty embodies feelings of disempowerment that not only evoke shame in the characters of the film, but also in the spectator. The spectatorial logic of shame turns the viewers into observers of the characters' mortifying and uncontrollable public exposure. Consequently this turns the viewers' gaze back upon themselves so that they feel exposed too. The viewers feel the shame of Lester, Jane, Carolyn, and Fitts, not because they share these characters' shame, but precisely because they do not. What the viewers share is the vulnerability to shame as an interpretive process in which one feels exposed, seen from the standpoint of others, experiencing the inability to regain control and organize a response.

The masturbation scene from the opening sequence shows a living (present) Lester in the shower, while a dead (future) Lester comments on the proceedings sarcastically: "Look at me: jerking off in the shower. This will be the highpoint of my day. It's all downhill from here." Lester's voice-over has a double function here that is characteristic to shame. It demonstrates how the self can shift between the viewpoint of the exposed actor, and that of a critical, detached observer. Both these aspects of the self continue to perform simultaneously, even though the voice-over actually belongs to the deceased Lester. In the next scene Lester makes a fool of himself when he clumsily collects his documents after they have dropped out of his briefcase, the voice-over commenting: "Both my wife and daughter think I'm this gigantic loser." In the last shot of the opening scene Carolyn is in the driver's seat, queen of the road, while Lester is napping in the backseat. Next to Carolyn in the front seat is Jane, both looking in opposite directions, as if there were an unbridgeable distance between all three of them. Furthermore, the way in which the frame is composed suggests an intersubjective triad inherent to the emotion of shame, in which the spectator's position can shift from the shamed (Lester) to the one who shames (Carolyn) or to the observer (Jane) in all possible combinations at any given moment.

These are embarrassing scenes to look at, not because the spectator identifies with Lester and therefore shares his feeling of shame, but because the spectator participates in the intersubjective triad that connects Lester, Carolyn, and Jane, and that reflects larger sociocultural structures by analogy. The spectator simultaneously holds the position of the shamed, the one who shames, and that of the external observer, in the triangular structure characteristic of a shameful situation. As Sartre shows in his *Critique of Dialectical Reason*, an intersubjective consciousness based on a dyadic self/other relationship can only be an individual feeling, rather than a social feeling of "we." A socio-cultural identity is necessarily depending on the "third other" looking.[6] In shame, it is the third party that makes the intersubjective triad visible to itself, providing the social context and the perspective which allows the emotion to emerge in the first place. In shame, the shamed and the one who shames can only recognize themselves in their roles through their awareness of another third who sees them as such. The intersubjective triad in the car establishes Carolyn as the one who shames, Lester as the shamed one, and Jane as the external observer that confirms these roles—and all parties involved, including the spectator, share this awareness.

Lester's meeting with Brad, the efficiency expert, suggests a hierarchical triad of employee, supervisor, and the (invisible) employer, of which Lester is the most vulnerable to negative exposure, because of his lower rank. This is epitomized in the way the scene is filmed: Brad from low angle in medium close-up, Lester from high angle in long shot and with a wide-angle lens, while the abstract painting behind his back silently observes the scene. In the Dancing Spartanettes scene a halftime entertainment dance performance during a high school basketball tournament turns into a private fantasy of Lester's. Here Angela is portrayed as an object-to-be-looked-at in Laura Mulvey's sense, as an erotic object for Lester's gaze only. The rest of the audience and the other dancers disappear, the lights darken as Angela steals the spotlight, moving sensually and now filmed in slow motion. She unzips her cardigan, a gesture that is repeated three times, from the depths of which rose petals fly toward the astounded Lester. However, something in Angela's performance—her "returned gaze" perhaps—refuses to accept the position of "to-be-looked-at-ness," since her body is "a body so secure in its power to dazzle the gaze of others that it can count on not being observed."[7] As a result Lester suffers lack of spectatorial power and is reduced to being an object himself. Lester is degraded, because his overwhelmed gaze is not active but passive, and because he is unable to become the agent of his own desire. Indeed, in this later scene in a parking lot, where to Jane's immense embarrassment he imposes himself on Angela, again Lester seems to exercise little control over his behavior. As a result Lester strikes us as a man who both degrades himself and is degraded by others as a sexual, professional, paternal, and marital subject.

In the parking lot scene it is the editing instead of the composition of the frame which again suggests triad intersubjectivity between Lester, Jane, and Angela. At this moment it is Jane that is shamed, as she feels the shame that she believes Lester should be feeling but does not, painfully aware of how both she and her father are seen by Angela, who in turn acts as a catalyst to this shame. Jane's shame is another example of shame by proxy, this time as a result of her filial connection with Lester. This scene makes the spectators' toes curl too, because the triangular viewing position that is simultaneously opened up for them is that of the exposed, the one who exposes, and the observer, thus rendering the emotion of shame painfully palpable. But unlike in the previous scene in the car, this time Jane is both the one that is ashamed and the one who shames, absorbing the shame that she attempts to put on Lester in vain.

This is about to change, though. Already in the first part of the film Lester's ironic way of being-in-the-world is in stark contrast to how his family feel about him and how he feels about himself. Already in the opening scenes Lester's ironic personality is revealed, for example in a telephone conversation about his client who is never in, in his overenthusiastic greeting of Brad, and in his sarcastic comment to Buddy: "I wouldn't remember me either." When finally he becomes determined to change the state of affairs, this results in shamelessness. He masturbates lying next to Carolyn who is asleep, and refuses to get intimidated by her disgusted comments after she wakes up and realizes what has been going on. Instead, Lester now thinks that offence is the best defense and he strikes back: "Well, excuse me, but some of us still have blood pumping through our veins." Now he is perfectly aware of, and also deliberately indifferent to, how he is seen by Carolyn and Jane, or by his colleagues and neighbors. His false pride in his "degradation," which is the opposite of shame, becomes the source for his brazen expression and transformational energy. His pride is "false," because it is a conceited defense against basic neediness, and associated with narcissism and infantile omnipotence. Only toward the end of the film does Lester develop a sense of self, along with a sense of shame that materializes in the presence of others. Indeed, shame often leads to the self-reflective realization that one's sense of self is embedded in intersubjective relationships,[8] a realization one can deny by escaping into false pride. But such a realization can also lead to acceptance of one's inadequacies and of people's "reciprocal neediness." Lester reaches this state of realization when a disgusted Jane shouts at him: "You stare at [Angela] all the time like you're drunk," and he finds out later that seemingly experienced Angela is still a virgin. But for Lester this realization comes too late. By contrast, Fitts' shame is solely devastating, with murderous consequences. These two characters embody two aspects of shame. Its transformational power is shown in the figure of Lester, and the capsulate, traumatic shame that loops back upon itself, characterizes the figure of Fitts.[9] At first it may seem illogical that Fitts kills Lester and not himself, but regarded from the logic of shame it actually makes perfect sense. First, there is the simple reason that Lester might tell others about the humiliating incident and thereby publicly shame Fitts. But in fact Fitts' shame has already been public all the time, insofar as it is "seen" by the imagined marine community that constantly looks at Fitts and defines Fitts, even when nonexistent in reality.[10]

In her book *Stiffed: The Betrayal of the American Man*, Susan Faludi examines the so-called masculinity crisis that has emerged out of the experience of being controlled in a competitive culture, which expects men to be in control themselves. According to Faludi this is the prevailing American image of masculinity, based on the myth of the loner untouched by society, and epitomized in the figures of Jesse James and Dirty Harry.[11] I feel tempted to add Lester Burnham to this list, even though I am aware of the obvious objections, since Jesse James and Dirty Harry are archetypical antiheroes, whereas Lester is "merely" a suburban man in midlife crisis, a "loser" similar to William Foster, the character played by Michael Douglas in Joel Schumacher's *Falling Down* (1993). But perhaps the addition is justified after all in the light of the postwar cultural shift in American consideration of masculinity, where the antihero has had to give way to the suburban rebel. Thus Warren Susman holds the suburban culture of abundance responsible for "spoiling" the American man. In his words the "instinctual" concept of masculinity as a restless individual had to be repressed in order for the "civilized" man to flourish.[12] Whether or not this concept is as "instinctual" as Susman

makes it sound, is not my main concern here. Nevertheless, the change
that Lester undergoes can be seen as the quest of a suburban rebel.
On his very own "Robin Hood trail" he is up against those who have
deprived him of his masculine agency: his family and his employers, to
be more specific. Lester believes that he can cure himself from his emotional numbness by getting removed from the domestic world that he
once believed he was meant to build. He gains false pride from being
downsized, trades the sensible family sedan in for a Pontiac Firebird,
as a symbol for his newly found male virility, and takes up running and
weight training. Furthermore, Carolyn becomes the designated culprit
of Lester's prior demasculinization, so she has to be re-disciplined even
with violence. Although Lester does not actually hurt her, he expresses
his physical rage toward her by aggressively throwing a plate of asparagus
into the dining room wall, thereby re-establishing his role as king of the
table. He meets Carolyn's adultery with indifference, which can also be
seen as exercising control over her, insofar as indifference implies rejection of interest in Silvan Tomkins's sense, a total lack of commitment and
respect toward the other, to which concept I will return below.

But Lester's newly gained masculine control is based on the adornment
of his outward appearance, a new car, new muscles, and a new youth-
ful job. It is not drawn from internal qualities such as emotional integrity. Thus, by re-establishing his position as head of the family without
reassuming social responsibility as a husband and especially as a father,
Lester is faced with constant disorientation: lack of support from the
world in return. In other words, the problem with Lester's choice is that
it is based on wanting to eat his cake and have it too. This is a "choiceless
choice" in a negative sense insofar as it expresses desire to exist outside
societal pressure, while benefiting from society at the same time. He sees
himself as a center of choice and freedom, without acknowledging that
he is in need of others too, and without being aware of others and the
positive possibilities this condition of dependence can bring along. As
I said before, Lester only realizes this possibility toward the end of the
film, when first he sees himself through Jane's eyes, and then through
the eyes of a larger social community, after which he regains his sense of
what is "right." In one telling scene Lester picks up an old family photo
of himself, Carolyn, and Jane, and examines it with affection, a gesture
that may well express his desire to retrieve family life as a means of "prov-
ing himself" as a man. A few seconds later Fitts shoots a bullet through
Lester's head. In many ways the characters of Lester and Fitts reflect each
other, even though Fitts' vulnerability to exposure is very different from

Lester's. Consumed by fascination with homosexuality and his simultaneous fear of it, Fitts' shame comes from his suspicion that the world will discredit his claim to masculinity, whereas Lester had never been under the illusion that such a claim could be made for him in the first place. In addition to this Fitts fears that Lester would destroy his carefully constructed presentation to the world as an archetypal military officer, which is the ultimate cause of his violent act.

Again, understanding all this does not necessarily mean that the spectators share the exact same emotions with either Lester or Fitts. What the spectators share is their vulnerability to exposure, either to an imagined or to an actual observer, because they are invited to occupy any position in the triangle between the shamed, the one who shames, and the observer in a shameful situation. It is this very same position that Lester and Fitts find themselves in. Especially Fitts' situation demonstrates an important feature of shame, which is that in the scene of exposure no actual observer is necessary in order to feel shame. One may feel shame being alone and knowing this to be so. Thus, the role of the observer is metaphorical, and "being seen," or "being exposed" is emblematic for being at a disadvantage and suffering loss of power. This recognition of disadvantage and disempowerment is what is central to shame. Fitts does not shoot Lester because he is afraid that Lester will expose him, as it clear that Lester does not care. It is an attempt to undo his experience of being shamed in the above sense.

Unruly Sociology: *Borat*

The same spectatorial logic of shame that underlies the tragic elements in *American Beauty*, also serves very efficiently in creating comedy. Its triangular structure lends the satiric elements in *American Beauty* self-reflective status, that is to say it enables the spectators' conscious self-perception, which potentially has a transcending effect on them. This strategy is perhaps nowhere more effective than in the so-called comedies of embarrassment such as *Borat: Cultural Learnings of America for Make Benefit Glorious Nation of Kazakhstan*.[13] In *American Beauty* all characters eagerly strive to maintain at any cost what psychoanalysis terms an "ideal ego," an attempt that is ultimately doomed to fail. By contrast the character of Borat actually overcomes his disempowerment by yielding to degrading exposure, giving in to the shaming presence of others in a manner that belies defeat through surrender. This is how shame in *Borat* differs from shame in *American Beauty*.

In *Borat* British comedian Sacha Baron Cohen plays the role of a fictitious Kazakh journalist Borat Sagdiyev, traveling around the United States to make a documentary. With its Candid Camera aesthetics, the film is partly improvised, partly performed, and most of its "characters" are random individuals that Borat just happens to come across during his trip. The reception of the film was steeped in controversy: it was denounced as racist, sexist, homophobic, anti-Semitic, xenophobic, fraudulent, insulting, politically incorrect, and anti-American all at the same time. But I think that in fact the "intention" of the film might be to cancel out such controversial elements through transparency, exposing them in broad daylight, so that potentially spectators will see through such notions and reject them. But it is difficult to say whether or not the film is actually successful in undoing its own "bad values."

Often defined as a mockumentary, the film commences with a prologue that depicts Borat's home village in Kazakhstan (actually filmed in Glod, Romania) as dilapidated, deprived, boorish, and incestuous. In this prologue Borat arrives on the scene in the same way as he conducts his interviews. His presence is marked by assertive energy and an air of intimidation due to his bluntness, his relentless grin, and his penetrating gaze directly into the camera. Borat's presence is intimidating, because it does not live up to the Western viewers' conventional expectations of documentary reporting. Borat's ignorance of this fact exposes him negatively, but as he obviously does not realize this, the viewers get confused, uncomfortable, and embarrassed as a result. And eventually shame sets in, at the very latest during the scene in which Borat goes sunbathing by the river in a lime green thong swimsuit. Again, this experience of shame is based on the discrepancy between Borat's lifestyle and the easygoing trendiness portrayed in American media. Borat tries to live up to that trendy image without much success, and without realizing what is wrong with the picture. Borat in his swimsuit is a hilarious image, but at the same time the image is also very sad, because it bespeaks otherness (albeit staged) in the context of the American Dream. Sad and hideous images are often the funniest ones, their hilariousness inseparable from the threat of evoking shame. But why do *I* consider this image shameful rather than, say, contemptible or aesthetically repugnant? I think the answer is best formulated in Silvan Tomkins's definition of shame:

> Shame operates only after interest or enjoyment has been activated; it inhabits one, or the other, or both. The innate activator of shame is the incomplete reduction of interest or joy. Such a barrier might

arise because one is suddenly looked at by another who is strange; or because one wishes to look at, or commune with, another person but suddenly cannot because s/he is strange; or one expected him to be familiar but he suddenly appears unfamiliar; or one started to smile but found one was smiling at a stranger.[14]

In terms of this definition shame is not necessarily related to some violation of social norms, even though it often is. But Tomkins postulates that shame can only appear when an individual has actively shown interest or joy in someone or something, and when subsequently that interest is frustrated. For spectators looking at Borat's swimsuit with interest based on their background knowledge of Western fashion, the recognition of his fashion failure functions as a reduction or even rejection of such interest. In other words, the discrepancy between the frame of "fashionable coordinates" and Borat's representation of it makes that he is exposed to the spectator in his boorish nakedness, but not to himself. Here the triangular structure consists of Borat, who demands to be recognized as fashionable, the fashion system that rejects Borat's demand, and the spectator-observer that witnesses Borat's ignorance of his failure. As a result, it is the spectator who feels an awkward moment of surprise and experiences an interruption in the circuit of looking.

In discussing Diane Arbus's photograph *Masked Woman in a Wheelchair*, David Benin and Lisa Cartwright talk about this work of art as an "elicitor of the affective surge [through which] emotions are privately negotiated and brought into check before we look around again."[15] I think something similar happens when we watch Borat in his swimsuit. After an initial "shock" we need to adjust our viewing mode and our emotions before we can look again, but then this time with amusement. It is particularly interesting that one can be perfectly aware that Borat is a staged figure, deliberately designed to elicit embarrassed reactions, and still respond precisely in the way that is demanded, that is to say with feelings of shame. Once more this demonstrates the contagiousness of shame, for regardless of the spectators' awareness, the image insists on being shameful. The image is shameful, because it refuses to be recognizable for, or show recognition of the spectator, who relates to the image with certain cultural expectations. Borat in his swimsuit violates the "contract of looking" by first inviting the spectator to look, and then rendering himself into an unrecognizable, strange object of look that threatens the "established order," not unlike the grotesque body in the Bakhtinian sense. As a result the spectators are left with two options: to look away in embarrassment, or to renegotiate their relationship with the image through laughter. Eve Kosofsky Sedgwick has noted that one of the strangest features of shame is how easily someone's humiliation can be transferred to an observer, even when these two have nothing to do with each other.[16] In Borat's case, humiliation enters the spectator even though that is not what Borat feels himself. Again, this has to do with the intersubjective triad of somebody who is exposed, an "exposer" and an observer, which in this case the spectator is forced to imagine on behalf of Borat.

Upon his arrival in New York City, Borat introduces himself to other passengers on the subway by kissing them on the cheek, but he is faced with indifference, skeptical glances, and even open hostility, especially after his suitcase tumbles open and a living hen flies out. This is a reversal of the rejection of interest put forward in the Tomkins quotation above. It is an abundance of proffered interest that is rejected as a threatened invasion of personal space and thus experienced as shameful. In other words, not only the rejection of one's activated interest or enjoyment causes feelings of shame, but the imposition of unsolicited interest can be equally shameful, because for its recipient it often leads to lack of control of a situation and inability to organize a response. In this case the spectatorial logic of shame ensures that the recipients of Borat's unsolicited interest are exposed to the observers of the situation in a disempowering manner. They are aligned with Borat at random as it were, if not by proxy, and they know this to be so. Here, the triangular structure is "reversed" in that it is the one who shames that actually feels the emotion rather than the shamed (Borat) or the observer. In this case the spectatorial logic functions as a "shame multiplier" that "depends on the subject's consciousness of exposure [. . .] that the [subject] would not be able to control."[17] The hostility in such a situation is a protection mechanism against shame, a manner to regain control of one's agency in a bizarre situation.

Once out on the street Borat soon causes commotion again by overcordially greeting pedestrians, relieving himself in a flowerbed, or masturbating in front of a Victoria's Secret shop window. By disempowering and degrading himself, Borat actually degrades the passersby through whose eyes he is qualified in degrading terms. The subway scene raises various questions, such as why did the true nature of the situation go unnoticed for these passengers, and how did they react when they realized that they were made into participants in a comedy act without having given consent. Did they feel embarrassment, anger, amusement?

Furthermore, while watching this scene it is tempting to convince one-self that one would not get befooled in a similar situation. Reacting in any other way than the passengers in the subway scene is highly unlikely, though. In other words, when witnessing such scenes from a safe dis-tance, not only do we laugh at Borat, but also at the discomfort of the unwitting participants.

In fact, the use of spectatorial logic as a shame multiplier invites the spectators to participate in humiliation through laughter, which empha-sizes their feelings of "social superiority" toward the participants in the film. Laughter enables to take distance from the scene of humiliation. It is an opportunity to occupy a safe spectatorial position in the intersub-jective triad, which is not accessible for the "victims" of the joke. For the force of our laugh "emerges as a transformation out of another force already in progress, a force in this instance that presses towards embar-rassment or shame."[18] This means that not laughing would equal admit-ting to one's own vulnerability to the spectatorial logic of shame, which we already share with the participating victims. But in fact laughter is an unsafe strategy here, insofar as laughter always comes to an end, often by transformation into some other emotion. True laughter cannot be forced or faked, and especially in comedies of embarrassment it always contains the dreadful possibility that the joke is on oneself instead of on the other. Among other reasons this is why I feel that experiencing humor in *Borat* is far from inevitable. Instead its spectators must "work" in order to construct the emotion of amusement and be on the safe side. By rendering the triangular structure of a potentially shameful situation spectatorially unstable, *Borat* constantly threatens to throw the spectator off balance as it were. This is a dreadful possibility, which can only be overcome by "doing laughter" before "being done by humor."[19]

A large part of the film consists of Borat interviewing unwitting American experts on humor, feminism, politics, and high-society etiquette. In addi-tion Borat is filmed getting a driving lesson, participating in a gay pride parade, visiting a television studio, trashing an antique store, hitchhiking a ride in a camper with three drunken fraternity brothers, taking part in a Pentecostal camp meeting, and finally attempting to kidnap Pamela Anderson. During these interviews and the encounters Borat violates and knocks over nearly every social taboo in the book, insulting his inter-viewees and random acquaintances with his seemingly unintentional vul-garity and his bigoted statements about gender relationships, ethnicity, and sexual orientation for example. At first Borat's over-the-top loutish-ness is generally tolerated, as the participants in the film are under the impression that he is socially challenged, due to his unfamiliarity with American customs. Posing as Borat, Baron Cohen takes full advantage of his victims' mistaken belief that he is sincere and legitimate. Again, this raises numerous questions, such as why did the participants in the documentary take Borat's sincerity for granted so easily, and to what extent does this have to do with their truly believing that his ethnic origin was genuine? In order to see through Baron Cohen's act it seems that one first needs to see through one's own cultural prejudices. And then again the same questions actually need to be asked about the spectators themselves, rather than about the participants.

Among all the toe-curling scenes in the film the rodeo sequence is one of the most painful to watch. In this scene Borat, wearing a triumphantly serious facial expression, addresses a loudly cheering rodeo audience as follows:

> Can I say first, we support your war of terror. May we show our support to our boys in Iraq. May U.S. and A. kill every single terrorist. May your George Bush drink the blood of every single man, woman, and child of Iraq. May you destroy their country so that for the next thousand years not even a single lizard will survive in their desert.

This speech is followed by an instrumental version of the American national anthem, to which Borat sings off-key the fictitious anthem lyrics of Kazakhstan. For this he receives an outraged reaction from the audience. In the rodeo scene the spectator is actually more ashamed on behalf of Borat than on behalf of the unwitting audience. The reason for this is that Borat first seems to proceed along the lines of a "legitimate" American patriotic discourse, before he takes it over the top. The opposite is true for another, equally painful moment in the film, the agonizingly long naked fight scene between Borat and his "producer" Azamat Bagatov (Ken Davitian) in their hotel room. The scene, which according to one *Washington Post* film critic "makes a sumo wrestling match look like Anna Pavlova performing 'Swan Lake,'"[20] is mercilessly graphic in its nudity. Every inch of wobbly flesh is filmed "up close and personal" in every possible position, often with sexual connotations (image 5), until still in the nude the two finally invade a real-life annual banquet of mortgage brokers at the same hotel. It is clear that emotional identification or shame by proxy are not at stake here for the spectator. What makes the spectator uncomfortable in watching these scenes is not so much what Borat and Azamat do, but rather that they do not feel ashamed about

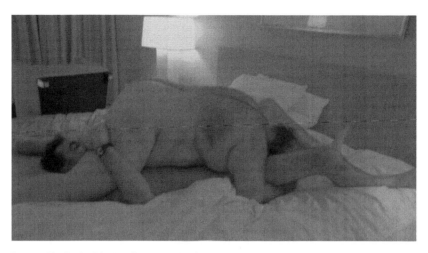

IMAGE 5 : Intimidation by raw nakedness in *Borat*

what they do, as they break the general Western code of conduct regarding (male) nudity. The scene intimidates by its raw nakedness, and it is here that we encounter the function of shame at its purest. Slavoj Zizek writes that shame functions thus that it "opens up with the prospect of the total 'transparency' of the human being."[21] The nude men are "transparent," because they are unbound by any institutionalized social rule, becoming Bakhtinian unruly, grotesque bodies *par excellence*.

Yet the most troubling, and perhaps also the most controversial scene in the film is the sequence in which Borat gets a ride on a camper with three fraternity students, making their way to California. They cordially welcome Borat on board and start pouring drinks. The scene is (in)famous for the constant flow of bigoted statements made by the students and evidently uncensored by the filmmakers. This led to an unsuccessful court case filed against *Borat*'s producers by two of the participants, claiming defamation and requiring an injunction against DVD release of the film. Here are a couple of highlights of the things said:

So you like the bitches out there in the fucking old Russia, there? [. . .] The fucking ho's baby! [. . .] You fuck the shit out of them, then you never call them again. [. . .] They don't have my respect, you know.

We should have slaves. [. . .] Our country, the minorities actually have more power. [. . .] Anyone that is minority has the upper hand. We have the Jews. We have anybody that's against the mainstream.

It is interesting to note how Baron Cohen's performance in this scene differs from that in the rest of the film. While normally Borat is assertively present in the situations he creates, in this scene he actually stays in the background and allows the situation to develop almost without his own influence. Furthermore, while almost all the other participants in the film at least try not to betray suggestive opinions when talking with Borat, these students are remarkably outspoken. According to the lively Internet discussion on the subject, many viewers have just appreciated this as an example of plain stupidity typical for fraternity boys, who therefore deserve all the defamation that is coming to them. But I think that these students actually expose themselves for the simple reason that they are not conscious of being looked at through the eyes of the rest of the world, since they welcome Borat as an exotic version of one of their own. A more open-minded form of the fraternal system of institutionalized masculinity seems to exist, in which social equality for women, ethnic minorities, and homosexuals is included. But many sociological studies demonstrate the existence of apparent misogyny and racism in all-male, all-white fraternities.[22] Whether or not such is the case, is not the main point of my argument, though. Ethical considerations of Baron Cohen's approach aside, I maintain that it is interesting to note that he exercises control over this situation precisely by letting go of control, as the students' statements are brought forward in spite of, rather than due to Borat's provocation.

We have noticed that in the subway scene the spectators were prompted to laugh as an expression of their feelings of social superiority toward the victims of the joke. By contrast they are denied such a spectatorially safe position in this camper scene. This camper scene is not "safe," because the whole situation is so overwhelmingly shameful, that it becomes nearly impossible to distance oneself from it. This is the "double movement" in shame that Sedgwick defines as

> . . . not a discrete intrapsychic structure, but a kind of free radical that [. . .] attaches to and permanently intensifies or alters the meaning of [. . .] a prohibited or indeed a permitted behavior, [becoming] a script for interpreting other people's behavior toward oneself [and *vice versa*].[23]

In the camper scene it is this "free radical" that compels an immediate assessment by the spectator, because we are intensely and involuntarily confronted by its shameful effects of misogyny and racism. As a result the spectatorial logic of shame in this scene collapses, the intersubjective triad of the shamed, the one who shames, and the observer merge into one. This renders *Borat* sociologically interesting, dialogic even in the spirit of Mikhail Bakhtin, since it produces "double outsideness,"[24] which enables the spectators to view the event from the perspective of shared concern. In other words, the spectators are invited to "exit themselves," which enhances conscious self-reflection on their part. Yet such self-reflection does not equal scrutinizing their viewing position from an objectified third-person point of view. Rather, through an organic relationship with the film, the spectators experience this double outsideness as subjectively lived. What the spectator is subjectively exposed to, is how particular social relations are objectively organized by shame. In turn this reveals the affective dimension of shame in divulging cultural values, whether these are bigoted or not.

Chapter 6

Anger

It is popularly believed that one cannot understand evil unless one feels empathy for the victims, as in "putting oneself in someone else's shoes."[1] It is an equally popular assumption that spectators faced with scenes of victimhood in cinema, will automatically identify with the victims, not with the perpetrators. This may be so, but as Susan Sontag has brilliantly pointed out in her *Regarding the Pain of Others*, such identification constitutes an ethically problematic audience reaction. Writing about the dubious feelings of "sympathy" that are evoked in viewers saturated by shocking realistic television images of faraway victims of "war and murderous politics," she concludes:

> So far as we feel sympathy, we feel we are not accomplices to what caused the suffering. Our sympathy proclaims our innocence as well as our impotence. To that extent, it can be (for all our good intentions) an impertinent—if not an inappropriate—response.[2]

To her such a response is problematic, since it diffuses the spectators' moral obligation to think about their own privileged position as a political cause for the suffering of the victims they sympathize with. However, what is interesting for the purpose of the argument in this chapter, is that Sontag's approach corroborates that observers confronted by realistic or fictional images of evil, will not truly identify with the victims, or that at least this is a multilayered phenomenon. The three films discussed in this chapter resist straightforward victim-identification and oblige the spectators to try and understand the suffering of others from a multifaceted viewpoint. All three films appeal to the spectators' justified feelings of anger, embodying emotions that reflect on the power relationship between the protagonists and the political systems in which they live.[3] In analyzing these relationships I have found Robert Solomon's three feature phenomenological definition of hatred particularly useful. In this context "hatred" serves as a common designator of nasty human attitudes. Within hatred Solomon distinguishes between the emotions of hate, contempt, and resentment. According to him contempt is an emotion that looks down on those considered inferior for whatever moral or social reasons, whereas resentment is the emotion of the weak looking up at those considered oppressive. Hate is an emotion of equality though, directed toward individuals one is opposed to, but who are regarded as equals.[4] This is how Tom Doniphon (John Wayne) opposes Liberty Valance (Lee Marvin) in John Ford's *The Man Who Shot Liberty Valance* (1962) for instance. In this chapter I will reiterate Solomon's emotional threesome in discussing Gus Van Sant's *Elephant* (contempt), Steve McQueen's *Hunger* (hate), and Cristian Mungiu's *4 Months, 3 Weeks & 2 Days* (resentment). The emotions embodied in the aesthetic systems of each of these films appeal to our justified anger, as they epitomize the crushing effect of power institutions upon individuals. And in each case this anger is central to our ethical reasoning and political compassion, which is beyond identification with the protagonists or the acceptance of their actions. Finally I will state as my view that all three films have ethical significance, insofar as they endorse our responsibility to consider what it means to be social subjects in the world of "unlimited interdependence."[5]

Looking Down with Contempt: *Elephant*

As I see it, *Elephant* (Gus Van Sant, 2003) is a film that denies the spectator any sympathetic or empathetic identification whatsoever. Instead it foregrounds anger as an objectified emotion that has its source in the perception of injustice. Based on the tragic reality of the 1999 Columbine High School massacre, the film depicts the events in a suggestive, rather than a straightforward manner. The treatment is void of any attempt to offer an explicit psychological motivation or rational explanation for the shootings. Instead a feeling of senselessness is maintained throughout the film. As a result the spectators are not provided with a source for catharsis that would reduce their anguish in a manner of "emotional cleansing."[6] On the contrary, the spectators' torment becomes persistent, mirroring the traumatic effect of the violent events. At the same time the film establishes contempt as its powerful emotional core by focalizing the narration through the killers. In turn this intensifies the emotional experience of the film, because the spectators are compelled to "sync" their emotions with the killers' sentiments, rather than with those of the victims who flee in terror.[7] In fact, this "forced participation" in the film's contemptuous core does function as an implicit explanation for the tragedy it depicts, for without contempt the massacre would indeed have been impossible to commit. As a result our emotional experience of the film becomes ethically complicated and anger sets in, directing itself at this hidden cause of the tragedy.[8]

The film opens with time-lapse footage of sky and clouds before a storm: the sky gradually grows darker while playground sounds that are hardly audible in the background slowly fade away. The interlude in the killing sequence later in the film consists of similar footage of a nightly storm with thunder rumbling at a distance and wind blowing ominously. The film's ending is similar to its opening, with footage of a storm clearing up and birds calling. Yet this is accompanied by a disturbing sound effect that suggests that the storm is not yet over. These are shots that function as a powerful symbol for the impending disaster, but they are also suggesting the presence of a superior, spiteful being, looking down with contempt at others without any respect whatsoever for human life. The opening sky footage is followed by a high-angle shot of a car swinging from side to side on the road, until the teen in the passenger seat, John (John Robinson) instructs his drunken father to let him take the wheel. Since the film predominantly uses straight-on, shoulder-height sequence shots, such (extreme) high- and low-angle shots convincingly visualize the suggestion of looking down contemptuously. After this structure of looking down has been established, the narration is focalized through another teenager Elias (Elias McConnell) taking pictures of a punk rock couple. Next the narration is resumed through John, getting into trouble with the school principal for being late.

There are a few stylized moments in slow motion such as when Michelle (Kristen Hicks) discontinues her jogging exercise to stare at the sky, as if she were expecting a new (symbolic) storm, while John is playing with a dog. But otherwise the first part of the film almost entirely consists of observational sequence shots, reminiscent of *cinéma verité*, as the camera follows different high school archetypes in action, often from behind their shoulders: the skater boy, the artist, the nerdy girl who is insecure about her body, the quarterback and his beautiful girlfriend, the bulimic gossip girl, the political activist. The sequence shots have an overlapping temporal structure, as the same actions are repeated from different focal points many times. But even more interesting is the way in which the shots relate to each other spatially. It is as if the camera were drawing a floor plan of the school area for us. The sequence shots continue until 20 minutes of the film have passed, when John encounters Alex (Alex Frost) and Eric (Eric Deulen), the killers under arms at the school entrance. At this point the plot moves back in time to show events that took place before the massacre, focalized through Alex. We witness him getting bullied by his classmates during a science class, while the unconcerned teacher pays no attention. The next scene shows Alex as he seems to ponder about cafeteria servings, but in reality he is studying the area for the purpose of compiling his floor plan. The sounds of the cafeteria are gradually more amplified and become cacophonic, reflecting Alex's growing rage inside.

After these flashbacks there are more sequence shots, but this time the cacophony that is Alex's persistent rage, is carried over into the shots that take place in the present, lending the scenes a menacing atmosphere. The narration is now "doubly focalized," through Alex and through his future victims. Or rather, although the narration is focalized through Alex's schoolmates, it is simultaneously distanced from them, so that even though we witness the events from his schoolmates' focal point, our imagination stays with Alex. From this menacing viewing position the students' doings gain a new significance: the noise of the film processing tank that Elias is swinging about, suddenly resembles a ticking clock. The sound of the preparation line in front of the dishwasher in the cafeteria kitchen resembles the rustling of removing a firearm safety catch, and the slamming doors sound like gunshots. These noises lend the scenes a sense of inevitability. These sequence shots carry on until the moment right before the first bullet will be fired, after which the narration again moves back to a previous day, showing Alex in his basement room at home, playing "Für Elise" and "The Moonlight Sonata" on the piano and browsing the Internet for weaponry. In this scene the camera makes a circular movement, panning the walls of Alex's room covered with his paintings and drawings. It is clear that this basement is the all-important "safe haven" where Alex can express himself artistically, out of everyone else's sight apart from Eric's. But creative expression without an audience is like that famous image of a falling tree in the forest. It shows Alex's inability to reciprocal connection with others, to which I will return shortly. The circular movement continues as Alex is playing "Für Elise," until he gets to the third development in this composition. Then the circular camera movement stops, and the camera zooms in on Eric playing a shooter game, after which we get to share his viewpoint watching the computer screen. It is no coincidence that Alex plays the popular piece by Beethoven. It starts off harmoniously, but has a very dark and anguished third development that symbolizes the calm before a storm just like the film's opening sequence.

In the third section of the film the spectator specifically stays with Alex and Eric, planning their attack at home on the morning before the massacre. The action is interspersed with disconcerting flash-forwards of students running away in terror from the perceptual point of view of the killers, resembling the single player's perspective in the shooting game shown earlier in the film. The way in which Alex and Eric studying the floor plan are filmed in worm's eye view from below, again suggests the contempt the boys feel for their soon-to-be victims (image 6). Here the change in temporal structure from flashbacks to flash-forwards and the different range of story information align us with the killers, not the victims, which is ultimately the most disturbing effect of the film. Furthermore, this alignment is far more disturbing, as the film successfully eliminates all possibilities of sympathy for the victims, who are either portrayed as not very likeable or shown in a manner that puts them at a distance. The only exception is John, a friend of the killers, who even receives a warning from Alex and who in turn tries to warn the others, but in vain. The film ends without resolution, showing Alex tauntingly reciting eeny, meeny, miny, moe to two students he discovered hiding in a freezer, one of which we recognize as one of the students bullying him earlier in the film.

As mentioned before, the film does not intend to provide the spectators with unequivocal answers as to why the tragedy happened, which might have lured them into a false sense of security. Instead the overall motif of senselessness combined with the double focalization of the film through the victims and through the killers, induces anger and frustration. I propose that the double focalization aligns the spectators' emotional participation with the killers, rather than with the victims. Through this structure of double focalization, the film embodies contempt as an emotion that establishes an unbridgeable distance between the "superior" qualities of the self and the "inferior" qualities of the other.[9] In other words, the operational structure of *Elephant* distances itself from those Alex is contemptuous of, first of all from his bullies, but also from the teachers and other students who tolerated the bullying. Regardless of our genuine concern for the (future) victims, the film precludes any sympathetic alignment with them. At the same time it is clear that the origin of Alex's contempt lies in the unfairness of his situation. His situation is unfair, because it is

IMAGE 6: Contemptuous gaze: *Elephant*

brought about intentionally and not by random events. As a result the spectator starts to experience anger, but this does not direct itself toward the killers as such, but toward the situation at large: the school system that condones a climate of bullying, and that ignores the psychological problems of individual nonconforming students.

This means that Alex's actions originate from conditions for which he cannot be blamed, in a world that presents itself to him as hateful and in which he has not been able to become human in the sense of "getting outside the self," as he has been met with hostility only. For Martha Nussbaum this "getting outside the self" is a precondition for empathy, and Alex's complete inability to empathize with others, leads to his failure to recognize that it is wrong to kill other human beings.[10] This is why I think we are not supposed to see him as innately bad, even if he is fully responsible for his actions, as the rage and contempt that make him a killer, are induced by bullying. Even though he is simply defined by rage in the end, this stems from outside causes for which he cannot be blamed, as his only fault is that he is different. Our anger is an acknowledgment that Alex's rage and contempt are produced by the misfortune he suffered and the injustice that denies him the social support that human dignity requires. Philip Fisher explains this connection between anger and dignity as follows: "[Anger] sponsors a fundamental claim for a model of human worth and dignity, [. . .] nearly equal to the worth and dignity of reason."[11] It might also be said that the operating radius of Alex's agency is marked by his rage. The school is the place where he wants his agency to be operative but where he strongly experiences that it is not. About such deprivation Jon Elster writes:

> Beyond a certain level of satisfaction of material needs, our need for the esteem of others is more important than anything else, except perhaps our need for self-esteem; and their withholding of esteem can be intensely painful.[12]

Axel Honneth defines this denial of social recognition as a form of disrespect that

> represents an injustice not simply because it harms subjects or restricts their freedom to act, but because it injures them with regard to the positive understanding of themselves that they have acquired intersubjectively.[13]

As a consequence of such disrespect, a person's physical and moral integrity are affected. Alex being thrown "spitballs" at, feels defenseless and at the mercy of another person. His being "restricted" to his basement results in the feeling of being structurally excluded from certain basic rights of recognition within society. In addition, as he lacks confidence that his circumstances will change, the course of events drag Alex even more deeply into rage and despair. Therefore it could be claimed that Alex's rage originates from his being a target of disrespect of others (bullies, teachers), and that his consequent act of terror is an act of retaliation, an attempt to restore his intrinsic and social self-esteem by making others suffer the consequences of their contempt for him. Needless to say, this strategy does not justify his actions, but it does deny the spectator the easy solution of exclusive identification with the victims. As argued, *Elephant* embodies contempt as its emotional core, in which the spectator participates through double focalization. However, this is not a matter of identifying with the killers either, or sympathizing with them, since there is a clear asymmetry between the spectator's emotions and those of the killers. We do not share Alex and Eric's contempt, even though we experience its existence.[14] What we share is anger aimed at a system that generates (self) destruction in outsiders, as it fails to direct their agency otherwise. This lends the film its disturbing tone of senseless inevitability. Here double focalization functions as a device that moves the self of the spectator toward the other, thereby epitomizing mutual responsibility as a basic human requirement.

Hate as Positive Liberty: *Hunger*

It is not too difficult to draw comparisons between *Elephant* and Steve McQueen's *Hunger* (2008). Both films are inspired by true events and based on the lives of real people. *Elephant* contains the story of Eric Harris and Dylan Klebold, whereas *Hunger* is based on the life of Bobby Sands, an Irish Republican Army activist. Serving a fourteen-year sentence during the Northern Ireland Troubles in 1981, he initiated the notorious second hunger strike in Maze prison that resulted in his own death after 66 days.[15] Both films are structured episodically and they do not introduce their central characters in the beginning of the film, but at a later point, in *Hunger* even at approximately the 25-minute mark, after one-third of the film. In both films there is multiple focalization, which complicates the unfolding of the films as emotional events. But whereas in *Elephant* the focalization is polarized in various characters, *Hunger* gradually penetrates the inner recesses of the protagonist's lived experience, so that in the end we find ourselves inside Bobby Sand's embodied mind. There is another important distinction, though. In *Elephant* the emotional core of the film consists of contempt and feelings of superiority, which is also the driving force behind the psychological makeup of the protagonists, whereas *Hunger* embodies hate as an emotion of equality, as Solomon would have it.

After a brief glance at a scene of protest by imprisoned female IRA activists, banging their aluminum tableware against the concrete floor in a frenzy, the film starts off with a prologue, in which we first stay with prison guard Raymond Lohan (Stuart Graham), going through his morning routine before heading off to work. He plunges his bruised fists into a hot water bath, almost without any facial expression, before putting on his perfectly ironed clothes that are neatly arranged on the edge of his bed. Next he eats his neatly arranged breakfast at his spotless dining room table, before carefully checking for the presence of snipers in the street and for bombs under his car. Even the cinematographic composition of these shots bespeaks calm symmetry and the suppression of emotions, as opposed to the shots in later scenes in which we stay with the activists. Furthermore, during this prologue any violence that the guards exercise against the activists, is only hinted at and not depicted graphically. We are only shown the effects of this violence afterwards, and not on the activists, but on guard Lohan, who is later witnessed to cool his freshly bruised knuckles in cold water.

Explicit visualization of violence commences only when the plot moves back to show earlier events. In the transition to this flashback a Margaret Thatcher speech accompanies the images in voice-over. A newly convicted activist is brought in, and the events start unfolding *in medias res*, showing the so-called no-wash and blanket protests. In support of their demand for political status imprisoned IRA activists refuse to wear prison uniforms like regular convicts, and wear blankets instead. Now the spectator is brought to witness the inhuman, repulsive conditions under which the activists in prison live, as the narration is focalized through two nonconforming prisoners Gerry (Liam McMahon) and Davey (Brian Milligan), who share the same cell. They smear their excrement over the walls of their prison cell, build dams with the leftovers of their supper to divert their urine so that it floods the corridor, as part of the "no wash" protest, and smuggle messages to and from the outside world in their rectums. This is truly disgusting. Carl Plantinga, among others, has argued that disgust in cinema is often too close to the real-life emotion to be considered an "aesthetic" emotion, and that as a result the difference between the fictional and the actual experience becomes a matter of "degree and not of kind."[16] In his discussion of Pier Paolo Pasolini's *Salò, or the 120 Days of Sodom* (*Salò o le 120 giornate di Sodoma*,1975) Julian Hanich has further argued that the function of such obtrusive cinematic disgust is to "humiliate" the spectators into viscerally experiencing the consequences of—in the case of *Salò*—"unabashed, unleashed power."[17] It could be argued that likewise in *Hunger* disgust is there to humiliate the spectators. However, in contrast to *Salò* disgust in *Hunger* does not align the spectator with the prisoners, but with the guards, who are at the receiving end of the protest. Or better yet, the film establishes an exchange of humiliating acts between the guards exerting violence and the protesting imprisoned activists, in which neither party can gain the upper hand.

Based on the juxtaposition between the symmetrical neatness of the prologue and the filthy images that follow, it would be easy to conclude that the power relationship between the activists and the guards is based on inequality, rather than equality, as the prisoners are apparently at the mercy of the inhumane guards. But I think that the juxtaposition actually does communicate equality, and that the "no wash" protest scenes are there to justify the activists' demands in a situation where they ostensibly have no rights. Therefore the emotion that *Hunger* embodies is (reciprocal) hate, the emotion of equality, in contrast to contempt that is the emotion of superiority as epitomized in *Elephant*. Furthermore, from the uncompromising, resolute manner in which the IRA activists endure their conditions in order to achieve their goals, a sense of pride ensues that protects them from feelings of inferiority that the guards' violent and humiliating actions would otherwise evoke.

Perhaps one might even claim that the IRA activists and the guards are equal because they are all victims, or "prisoners" of the Thatcher government. This is strongly suggested by the appearance of Margaret Thatcher as a voice-character, not as an embodied voice, but as a female *acousmêtre* that functions as "a master of ceremonies" according to Michel Chion.[18] But there is also the aspect of their own positive liberty, a notion coined by Isaiah Berlin in his 1958 essay "Two Concepts of Liberty." This refers to the power of an individual to act as a member of a community in order to achieve a certain end, in contrast to negative liberty that refers to individual agency free from communal restraint. According to Berlin positive liberty can lead to a situation in which a (political) community determines how, when, and what individuals should desire, regardless of their own free will.[19] I am not qualified to argue to what extent this was valid for the real IRA activists or the Long Kesh prison guards. Nevertheless, victimization as a result of "positive liberty" is what the film communicates to me. For instance, it is group solidarity that causes the activists to compromise their basic human rights to physical and mental health, and even to endanger their lives. But on the other hand the guards also have to compromise their sense of security, their emotional bravery, and even their basic humanity in order to be able to fulfill their communal potential in "Her Majesty's Service." If they started questioning the justification or the morality of their actions, they would lose their ability to function as guards.

In the cinematic event this dilemma is represented on the level of affectivity, rather than on the level of narration. There is the opening sequence with guard Lohan for instance, whose body seems to be restrained by its own orderliness, in which we participate by means of sensation rather than signification. In another more painful scene later on in the film, the activists are forced to crawl naked in between two lines of military policemen who beat them mercilessly with their truncheons.

An astounded younger policeman stands among them, and it is his scream that sets off their collective, rhythmical beating of their shields. Here the noise is the element that confronts us "with the violence of sensation that occurs before any figuration of violence results,"[20] a reality we share with the younger policeman. The scene ends with a pregnant image of the young policeman in tears leaning against a blue wall on the right, while the activists are beaten to pulp on his left, the wall of humanity separating him from his colleagues. Following Marco Abel, one might claim that the violence of sensation in this scene gives rise to the ethics of "response-ability" that depends on bodily necessity instead of on rational (cerebral) choice,[21] as the sound functions as an immediate assault on our senses, being affective in a very primal way.

The "no-wash" protest is abruptly brought to a violent end, as the activists are herded from their cells by brutal force. Their long beards and their hair is cut, they are thrown into a bathtub and cruelly cleaned with a scrubbing-brush. Until that moment in the film violence was only hinted at by images of open wounds and bruised knuckles, but now it is shown in a viciously graphic form. At the same time the narration gets more locally focalized, as it is mostly restricted to the treatment Bobby Sands (Michael Fassbender) undergoes. Then the shot of guard Lohan cooling his fists is repeated, and we realize that what we have witnessed so far, were only flashbacks introducing Sands's decision to go on hunger strike. In this way the film juxtaposes two political positions, epitomized in the figures of Lohan and Sands, while the narration is doubly focalized through the positions of both characters. Furthermore, this double focalization emphasizes to what extent hate functions ambivalently. It becomes the substance of individuals, a validation of their sense of self, but it also provides them with an identity in the social world. This holds for both Lohan and Sands. As Sara Ahmed points out, not only is hate in this sense a form of equality but it is also a form of intimacy:

> [I]t is an investment in an object (of hate) whereby the object becomes part of the life of the subject even though (or perhaps because) its threat is perceived as coming from outside. [. . .] [T]he subject becomes attached to the other through hatred, as an attachment that returns the subject to itself.[22]

Shortly after the bathroom scene Sands receives a message that the government has agreed to the prisoners wearing civilian clothing, but the apparel that the activists receive, are not their own clothes, but sets of

ridiculously colorful, mismatched garments. The guards shake with fur-
tive laughter while handing these over. This incident causes the final
escalation of violence before the hunger strike. The activists smash their
cells and order is restored by brutal force, while guard Lohan is shot
through the head when visiting his elderly mother in a nursing home.
Why is this clothes incident particularly highlighted, although seemingly
insignificant? First, it represents a moment of contempt, a moment of
emotional inequality in the otherwise equally structured configuration
of cinematic emotions. It is striking that just as in *Elephant*, such inequality is visualized in an extreme high-angle shot of Sands in his cell, sitting next to the offensive pile of neatly folded civilian clothes: a bright
red shirt, green tartan trousers, and a yellow sweater. This moment of
contempt disturbs the emotional balance between the prisoners and the
guards, and consequently it triggers a riot. Secondly, the incident gains
importance when one realizes that clothes are often anything but neutral. Dressing consciously is a way to exercise one's agency, to lend meaning and identity to one's body actively, in contrast to "receiving one's
identity" passively from some abstract cultural entity.[23] Even political
values can be expressed through clothing by both empowered and disempowered groups, as shown in *Hunger* by the activists wearing blankets
for example. Withdrawing the right to control, to frame one's own body
image in the field of vision, removes the body's rhetorical and expressive
potency. This is exactly why the activists in the film refuse to wear the
prison uniforms in the first place. In this context Gerard Hauser writes:

> Political prisoners often use their bodies as their rhetorical means of
> last resort, but often also as their most (perhaps only) effective rhetori-
> cal weapon to confront and beat the state.[24]

According to Hauser, a hunger strike is a final attempt at overpowering
the oppressor by submitting oneself to the oppressor's power: a defeat
through surrender. Furthermore, Chris Yuill points out that this particular hunger strike by Sands was a powerful means of mobilizing emotion,
fuelled by "a rage against British Imperialism"[25] and aimed at evoking
anger in the public sphere. This is what *Hunger* does too. By embodying
hate as an agent of pride, the film evokes anger in the spectator, whose
emotional experience is shaped by a sense of justice and the film's dis-
playing the causality of evil through double focalization. The final section
of the film shows the last few weeks of Sands's life and this is introduced
by a long take of a janitor mopping the urine-flooded corridor floor,

again accompanied by a (non-diegetic) radio speech by Prime Minister Thatcher who declares:

> Faced now with the failure of their discredited cause, the men of violence have chosen, in recent months, to play what may well be their last card. They have turned their violence against themselves through the prison hunger strike to death. They seek to work on the most basic of human emotions, pity, as a means of creating tension, and stoking the fires of bitterness and hatred.

This Thatcherian discourse appears both mistaken and belittling as regards the activists' cause. As argued in Chapter 3, pity always involves looking down upon the pitied and as such it is an emotion of inequality. Pity involves lack of esteem, and both the person who pities and the person pitied know this—nobody wants to be pitied.[26] This film does not seek to evoke pity in its spectator either. Sands hardly strikes us as pitiable, but rather as a virtuous man, due to his "Grecian" qualities of resoluteness, courage, and stamina.[27] Furthermore, his decision to go on hunger strike is not taken under pressure of "hot" emotions, but it is based on his emotional "cool," characterized by disenchantment and reason. This means that the spectator does not have to agree with Sands's arguments in order to appreciate the motivation for his actions. In a scene that is almost entirely done in one extended shot, uninterrupted by editing or camera movement, Sands underlines to Father Moran (Liam Cunningham) that a course of action being "right" does not depend on its likely consequences (Sands's death), but on its intrinsic qualities:

> My life means everything to me. Freedom means everything. [. . .] This is one of these times when we've come to a pause. It's a time to keep your beliefs pure. I believe that a united Ireland is right and just. [. . .] Having a respect for my life, a desire for freedom, an unyielding love for that belief means that I can see past any doubts I may have. Putting my life on the line is not just the only thing I can do, Dom. It's the right thing.

In the final scenes of the film Sands's body has become strongly emaciated, and it is obviously more likely than not that he will die. The voice-over of his physician provides a medical discourse on the physical consequences of his hunger strike, while we watch close-ups of Sands's withered body, his skin damaged by bedsores. Platters filled with aromatic dishes are placed at his bedside, and then taken away untouched. These scenes are again affective in a very primal way, as focalized through the physician who has to witness Sands's voluntary self-inflicted violence without being able to intervene. Finally the film gets focalized inwardly, which is introduced by a scene in which Sands writhes in pain. The shots are superimposed by images of flying birds that flutter and beat their wings in frenzy, symbolizing the vitality that now escapes his body. The perceptual and mental subjectivity increases, as the narration shares with the spectator Sands's worsening condition and his hallucinations of himself as a teenager. There remains a form of double focalization though, which places us simultaneously at an inside and an outside position. We are positioned inside Sands's embodied mind, while we simultaneously observe his condition from an external position that we share with his physician, with the prison guards, and with his grieving parents who come to visit.

Toward the end of the film there is a scene that illustrates particularly well in which way the hated other can become an intimate part of the self, thus contributing to the core of a person's subjectivity. In this scene Sands is bathed by a nurse who has a UDA tattoo across his knuckles, which he deliberately places within Sands's field of vision. We witness this from a point of view shared with Sands. An enraged Sands raises himself from the bath, but his emaciated body collapses onto the bathroom floor. After this the nurse carries him back into the hospital room in a gentle embrace. In the spectator's experience the nonconforming and the conforming attitudes now become entwined, instead of juxtaposed. As a result anger sets in, directed at the inevitability of the events represented, but this inevitability is not experienced as entirely meaningless, at least not to the same extent as in *Elephant*. Sands's hunger strike is not merely an act of (self) destruction, but an act of knowingly rendering oneself unintelligible in the Thatcherian system of absolutism, thereby severely resisting it from an opposite, but equal standpoint. This is precisely why inevitability in *Hunger* is not devoid of purpose, as it is in *Elephant*. Yet, in both films the double focalization also conceptualizes coexistence, which would include all political systems however brutal and unsettling, urging us to think about what it means to live alongside one another.

Friendship as Resentment in Solidarity:
4 Months, 3 Weeks & 2 Days

Originally part one of Cristian Mungiu's *Tales from the Golden Age* (*Amintiri din epoca de aur*) series, the acclaimed *4 Months, 3 Weeks & 2 Days* (*4 luni, 3 saptamâni si 2 zile*, 2007) is a powerful drama film about two friends, the university students Otilia Mihartescu (Anamaria Marinca) and

Gabriela "Gabita" Dragut (Laura Vasiliu). The two girls try to arrange
for an illegal abortion for Gabita in Communist Romania under Nicolae
Ceaucescu in 1987, when the regime maintained a strict pro-birth policy.
Stylistically the film is dominated by static sequence shots filmed from
a straight-on angle, combined with handheld aesthetics especially in its
outdoor takes. From the very beginning of the film the narration focuses
on Otilia, who is followed running around town. However, the story line
does not explain what is actually going on until more than 30 minutes
after the opening scene, when there is a dialogue between the abortion-
ist, Mr. Bebe (Vlad Ivanov) and the girls. Only then it becomes clear
what the title of the film stands for: the exact amount of time Gabita
has been pregnant. The film opens with a medium shot of a messy table
that apparently serves both as a dining table and a desk, with a small
aquarium containing two goldfish in the middle. The camera tracks out
and we meet the two girls in their room, Gabita onscreen and Otilia off-
screen, in the middle of a conversation, reviewing the items they need
for the day. Then the camera follows Otilia from behind her shoulders,
as she runs around the college dorm, trying to barter and buy soap and
cigarettes for herself and Gabita, as well as milk powder for the newly
born kittens found in the boiler room.

From the very beginning the film gives a powerful impression of a highly
regulatory society in which bribing and underground economy thrive,
and in which customer service is an unknown concept. However, rather
than the plot-based elements, it is the organization of sound and cinematography in particular that is responsible for the creation of an overall
atmosphere of oppressive tension throughout the film. Reminiscent of
The Shining discussed in Chapter 1, the camera frequently follows Otilia,
only to stop abruptly as though letting her "escape" from the grid. In
Romania's reality though, escape seems impossible from a regulatory
social framework that keeps everyone captive behind its invisible fences.
This system is panoptic in the Foucauldian sense. All functionaries, from
ticket wardens and hotel receptionists to social authorities, exercise control over each other as disciplinary parts of a societal network.[28] In this
system individual agency belongs to those who are not locked away in the
corridors of the panopticon, such as people that work outside the legal
economy, or those that practice illegal medicine.

The framing of the film embodies this panoptic vantage point too,
defining the image as a power system, in which Otilia and Gabita are
totally powerless, except for the "power" to submit themselves to it. At
the same time the narration is strongly focalized through Otilia's point
of view, although there is hardly any perceptual or mental subjectivity in

the film. Instead focalization is achieved through the handheld aesthetics that carry us into the film as carnal, haptic subjects. However, this does not align us with Otilia, but with those that exercise authority over her. Even when physically absent, such forces touch her, tangibly and force-fully constraining her gendered body within the boundaries of the estab-lished order. In other words, the camera functions as a pure point of view, as discussed in Chapter 1, suggesting the panoptic presence of a disem-bodied, authoritative subject. The camera functions as a perceiving and a touching subject that polices and disciplines Otilia, an invisible and dis-embodied, but nevertheless tangible presence in a prescriptive force field that keeps her captive within the discourse of what the political system considers the norm. The handheld aesthetics in *4 Months* align us with this force field haptically, while the film forces us simultaneously to par-ticipate in the effects of Otilia's captivity from the inside. In one forceful scene Bebe yells insults at Otilia, the camera jumping into a close-up of his raged face. At this moment Bebe does not only attack Otilia, but also the spectators, who suddenly become very much aware of the effects, if not the conditions of her entrapment. As a result of this double focalization we are simultaneously inside and outside the panoptic function, disciplin-ing and being disciplined, touching and being touched. The operational structure of resentment is one of double focalization too, involving an awareness of wrongdoing to oneself, as well as of acceptance of that wrongdoing without protest. This is why Friedrich Nietzsche, among oth-ers, defines resentment (or "ressentiment") as a self-destructive strategy through which the "weak" deprive themselves of free will and agency.[29]

In *4 Months* Otilia and Gabita also adopt a self-destructive strategy, accepting their disempowered position when they reluctantly give in to Bebe, who blackmails them into having sex with him. Viewed from the perspective of politics of touch, one could say that in analogy to the political system Bebe confirms his position as the one who chooses to touch. Otilia and Gabita do not have this choice and they cannot even choose not to be touched. In the end Bebe has sex with them, while the camera stays in the bathroom first with Gabita and then with Otilia, as the girls take turns. At some point after her return from the bedroom Otilia's back is shot in close-up, as she faces the wall opposite the camera, her upper body slightly hunched over, as if pressed down by some invis-ible weight. In the next shot she is in front of the mirror washing Bebe's touch from her face, when sobbing Gabita rushes in. Otilia directs her gaze in the mirror at Gabita, but her eyes do briefly seem to meet us, acknowledging our presence, the presence of the camera, reminding us that watching always involves the possibility of being watched in return.

In the very final shot of the film there is a similar situation. The camera watches the girls through the window of a hotel restaurant, which has a slightly mirroring effect. Otilia looks sideways and for just a split second she directs her gaze at the spectator behind the camera again, after which the film abruptly breaks away to the end credits played to the cheerful Romanian hit "Te aud mereu."

Through this act of acknowledgment Otilia creates a distance between us and herself. It is a justified rejection, which tells us how her suffering defies representation and narration. Constantin Parvulescu makes a similar point when he writes that it is not possible to understand Otilia and Gabita "emotionally, at least not through identification. There is no such thing as a subjective common denominator that can function as a vehicle of empathy across time."[30] However, in my opinion we can understand the *effect* of their suffering, even if we cannot understand their *experience* as such. This effect is steeped in resentment and anger. But through her act of acknowledging our spectatorship, Otilia also distances herself from the panoptic presence in the film. From this she may gain a form of individual agency with a different kind of potential. Thus, at such moments her resentment does not function as a strategy of self-deception but as one of self-awareness. Generally speaking such eventualities are rare though, and they need special forms of motivation such as solidarity and friendship, as will be argued in the last part of this chapter.

Drawing from Julia Kristeva and Giorgio Agamben, Thomas Elsaesser talks about "abject agents" that are outcasts in a social community. These are located in negative, liminal spaces that are made up of exclusion, of the discarded, the useless, and waste, and their agency is characterized by "active non-activism."[31] All characters discussed in this chapter can be seen as such abject agents, Alex in his basement, Sands in prison, Otilia in the student dorm, which according to Parvulescu functions as a "protective matrix."[32] In this context Kristeva writes about bodies that are at the limits of their condition as living beings.[33] Such characters as Alex and Sands are what Elsaesser calls "posthumous" or "post-mortem" subjects,[34] who subjectively live their bodies as if they were already dead. What is more, the agency shown in both Alex and Sands is conditioned by their "ghoulishness," which renders them into abject subjects. Otilia can be defined as an abject agent too, because the political conditions under which she exercises agency are highly circumscribed, due to her age, gender, and social position. Yet the film does not portray her as a victim, because regardless of her situation, she is not self-enclosed in her resentment. The reason for this is that the ethics of her actions are based on being-with, instead of being-against, as is the case with Alex and Sands. And it is precisely this moral outlook that prevents her from being self-enclosed in resentment.

Resentment has often been considered an emotional strategy that accepts and even celebrates a hopeless life in which one feels helpless. Resentful individuals experience inferiority before a world that has already defeated them.[35] Robert Solomon, for instance, argues that resentment is an emotion that attempts to uphold the very conditions that prompted resentment in the first place.[36] This is the reason why Nietzsche considers resentment a hypocritical strategy insofar as it is circumscribed to the same situation that is dismissed as hopeless out of self-righteousness. It is tempting to maintain that in extreme right-wing or left-wing politics resentment is the key emotional strategy too, since such claims often appear to result from a self-righteous celebration of stasis instead of change, regardless of the message proper. However, the resentment embodied in *4 Months* does not correspond to Nietzsche's philosophical approach or the practice of extremist politics, since it is concretely imposed upon Otilia from the outside and it is not saturated by self-deception. This becomes painfully clear in the scene in which Otilia visits the birthday party thrown by her boyfriend's parents. The scene is filmed from the height of the table by means of a static camera in a medium shot and from a straight-on angle, so that the composition of the image is reminiscent of (a segment of) Leonardo da Vinci's "Last Supper" (1495–8). In this scene Otilia is portrayed sitting slightly to the right of the middle of the frame, while her concerned boyfriend is sitting behind her, slightly to her right. They are both surrounded, suffocated as it were, by the other birthday guests both inside and outside the frame. Otilia is an abject stain in the field of vision, out of place in the picture. The table company is engaged in a vivid conversation, but Otilia is mostly ignored, except when sorted out and insulted by one patronizing male guest. Even though Otilia's face shows almost no emotional expression, the way in which the framing is organized in this scene again betokens suffering and entrapment. There is an obvious analogy with the political power system in which she feels lonely and insignificant. But the birthday party scene can also be interpreted as a moment of potentiality, as a decisive moment almost comparable to the biblical Last Supper, in which multiple options are open. There is a choice between conforming or not conforming to the oppressive political system. In an interview about the film as released on the *4 Months, 3 Weeks & 2 Days*

DVD (Artificial Eye, 2007), its director Cristian Mungiu has said that the dinner table scene:

> . . . is about social classes during the communist regime and the sub-tle influence of propaganda over our education, but also about the following—despite believing we were immune to propaganda, when we quarreled with our friends, we sometimes used the same arguments that the system used to indoctrinate the people. [The scene is also] a vision of the future—it shows how life would be for a girl, if she chose this conventional road in life, by becoming part of the conformist family.

The most disturbing part of *4 Months* takes place toward the end, when Otilia returns from the birthday party and finds Gabita asleep in their hotel room. She has had a miscarriage in the bathroom as a result of Bebe's treatment. Otilia enters the bathroom, while the camera remains fixed on her shocked facial expression. Then it moves into the direction of her gaze, showing us the bloody fetus on the bathroom floor in a viciously graphic manner. The camera stays with this troubling sight, while Otilia searches for a plastic bag off-screen and then carefully packs the fetus into it. After that she heads outside, where night has already fallen. Again a handheld camera follows Otilia very closely, almost threateningly, while an aural close-up of her heavy breathing perceptually aligns us with her from the inside. The scene is filled with menace and peril throughout, but the tension becomes nearly intolerable when a strange male figure suddenly appears from the shadows and enters into our field of vision in the blurry background. The image in this scene is very dark, but from the darkness all kinds of sounds emerge to frighten Otilia, such as a dog barking, glass breaking, a whistle blowing. She finally climbs to the top of a multi-story building and dumps the wrapped fetus into a waste shaft, during which the sounds of her heavy breathing and the bundle falling down the shaft are very loud.

To share a personal anecdote: the first time I saw *4 Months* was in a movie theater in Amsterdam in November 2007, and especially during the disposal scene the atmosphere in the theater was literally filled with anxiety. It was one of those moments when one concretely and tangibly senses and absorbs the surrounding emotional atmosphere. In this case I had the experience in a crowded movie theater, in which the total audience were on the edge of their seats. Why such a strong emotional reaction? Obviously the spectators were concerned for Otilia's safety, as they had all the power to see but no capacity whatsoever to act and help her. Yet, I think that such concern is enhanced by anger, directed at the broader system of oppression that keeps Otilia captive. The lack of light and sharpness in the image together with the handheld camera movement heighten the cinematic presence, which becomes the agent of oppression, and as such is capable of affecting the spectator's exposed sensibilities. This is experienced as anger, which we feel precisely because Otilia does not. Yet it must be stressed that this is not a case of sympathy (or empathy) since, as Philip Fisher points out:

> What happens in these cases is a blank spot where the reader or spectator *volunteers* passion, stepping in to supply the missing fear, grief, shame, or anger. Volunteered passion is a stronger demand on the spectator and a more perfect aesthetic strategy for the eliciting of passion than sympathy, understood in the narrow sense of feeling alongside another's explicit emotional state, can ever be.[37]

Through a "blank spot" the film itself produces an ethical space, which the spectator fills with the justified anger that its protagonists are lacking. This anger is also the key to understanding Otilia's motives, even if it is not her suffering we grasp. Her actions are motivated by friendship and solidarity, qualities through which resentment can gain transformational political power, serving as a catalyst for change, instead of as a self-enclosed emotional deadlock. In this context Solomon claims that resentment also includes an intention for the future, an intention "to act, to change the world and change our Selves [. . .] to destroy [. . .] an oppressor in resentment."[38] But in order for resentment to become a positive emotion triggering abject action in a transformational sense, something extra is needed that enables the emotion to change the direction of its "towardness," and that something is friendship. For it is one thing to feel anger about one's own circumstances as in self-enclosed resentment, and another to feel anger on behalf of someone else, which qualifies as solidary resentment. Erin Manning writes:

> Friendship is political, it is a reminder that all thought, all sense, all touch, all language is for and toward the other. [. . .] Friendship is a movement of sensation, a politics of touch that challenges me to (mis) count myself as other. Friendship is a condition of emergence, it is the fold of experience out of which a certain politics is born.[39]

So, it is friendship that is at stake in *4 Months*, and its operational structure is solidary resentment, in which the spectator participates through double focalization that evokes justified anger and a (perhaps romantic) desire for a rightful world. As a result of this anger the spectators also experience solidarity toward Otilia and Gabita, but this sentiment is not based on empathy or identification, since it presumes and respects the cultural and temporal separateness of the characters. Thus, such solidarity becomes a form of allegiance, in which those showing solidarity "exit themselves" without "appropriating" the other and *vice versa*.

All films discussed in this chapter allow the spectator to participate in the *effects* of suffering caused by a system of oppression, without attempting to convey the *experience* of such suffering. All films in this chapter avoid the experience of shared suffering by complicating the narrative focalization in such a way that it evokes ambivalent emotion. For all emotions discussed in this chapter are ambivalent, that is doubly focalized in themselves. For a person to hate, or to resent, or feel contempt for that matter, is to invest in the object these sentiments are directed at. The effect is an eternal return of that object of hatred, contempt, or resentment, and thereby this object becomes an essential part of this person's life. Thus the object sometimes even becomes somebody's reason for being, as is the case in *Elephant* and *Hunger*. To make the spectators participate in this operational structure, is to appeal to their justified anger, directed at social and political structures that provoke negative emotions in individuals who subsequently become self-enclosed. The devastating consequences of this process are shown in *Elephant* and *Hunger*. The only film in this cinematic threesome that strictly implicitly conveys the possibility of sublimating resentment and rendering it into something positive, is *4 Months*. But ultimately, seeing that the story is set in 1987, two years before the actual Romanian Revolution, the film does not resolve the issue of how successfully Otilia and Gabita might have expanded their mutual solidarity in the direction of communal political action.

To conclude, the emotion of anger in the cinematic experience of *Elephant, Hunger,* and *4 Months* is not some uncontrolled rage, like the emotion Alex feels in *Elephant,* but an essential element in the ethical reasoning beyond one's personal moral codes. For we acknowledge that from a strictly subjective perspective it would be much too easy to dismiss Alex's actions as purely and randomly "evil" for instance. Instead, anger functions as a catalyst of political compassion that has nothing to do with identification or even acceptance of the actions of the protagonists. Such compassion based on justified anger is more a sign that everyone is part of everyone else's world and that therefore oppression concerns us all. It is this sentiment that guides us "truly toward something that lies at the core of morality, and without which any moral judgment is a ghastly simulacrum."[40]

Chapter 7

Love

"What we talk about when we talk about love," asked Raymond Carver in his 1981 short story of the same title. On a different plane, a cultural theorist might ask what we talk about, when we talk about the concept of love in relation to the concept of romance. There is indeed the question to what extent culturally determined narratives about love function as a formative fabric of intersubjective relations, as they are part of our daily existence. On the other hand, how can love be an open strategic game that defies any form of social control telling us who to love, what to love, and when to love? This chapter discusses three very different films about love and romance, approaching them from very different perspectives. These films are less concerned with love as an emotion, as in "being in love with," but they embody love as an intentional attitude on a scale that runs from cynicism through irony to authenticity. They invite the spectator to join into the "game of love" seductively, repulsively, and co-creatively. Thus, all three films actually touch upon ethics, insofar as they encourage evaluative perception of our own love preferences, whether based on sexual desire, romantic fantasies, familial arrange-ments, narcissistic mirroring, or affective reciprocity.[1] Furthermore, the films are characterized by cinephilia of a special kind, which is not an elitist, "elusive feeling of nostalgic attachment to images, stories, and sounds,"[2] but an intellectual curiosity toward affective reciprocity in the cinematic experience.

Cinema as Seduction: *Dangerous Liaisons*

As Christian Keathley has argued, a "curious cinephile" *prefers* a viewing strategy that is best characterized as openness to sensuous and affective encounters with film.[3] As any cinephile of this kind knows, some films only exist to fall in love with, and Stephen Frears's *Dangerous Liaisons* (1988) seduces the spectator like no other. This act of seduction is staged on a battleground between men and women, between love and desire, sincerity and dishonesty, vanity and happiness, revenge and forgiveness. The staging in *Dangerous Liaisons* functions as what Ronald de Sousa would call "love's theater,"[4] where love is merely a performance and where roles can easily be swapped and characters substituted. Furthermore, in this theater of love some people are both actors and directors, as they operate both in front of and behind the scenes, manipulating and deceiving their environment. Like in so many other films discussed in this book, the opening of *Dangerous Liaisons* demonstrates this setup in a nutshell, and especially its mise-en-scene illustrates the workings of love's theater in particularly suggestive ways. The mirror is a central mise-en-scene element here, along with ornamental rococo costumes and makeup, by means of which servants carefully adorn ("mask") both the Marquise de Merteuil (Glenn Close) and the Vicomte de Valmont (John Malkovich). The film opens with Merteuil complacently studying her mirror image, her face still free of makeup, while Valmont's face is only shown to us after his makeup has been completed. The way in which the editing is organized in this opening sequence, suggests that Merteuil and Valmont are mirror images of each other: both are charming, fascinating, intelligent, and devoid of any moral considerations concerning their actions.

In Freudian thinking there are two ways for people to fall in love. There is the attachment model, in which the object of love is parent-substitute, and the narcissistic model, in which the object of love is conceived after the example of one's own self (the narcissistic object-choice). Merteuil and Valmont clearly take the second route. For them love, even the love between themselves, is as calculating, detached, and cynical as is borne out by their characters. It is to be enacted as a staged performance according to a carefully premeditated screenplay based on false impressions and artificial emotions, in which both parties aim at gaining the upper hand. According to De Sousa, the sentiment to be associated with love as theater is irony, but I think it is best defined as cynicism, insofar as it lacks reciprocity and "towardness." As Maurice Merleau-Ponty explains, this kind of "false" love may lead to the belief that one is in love. It may be experienced and enjoyed like "true" love, but it is actually all about the subject, not the object of love as being-in-the-world.[5] Perhaps it could be said that Merteuil and Valmont are aesthetic lovers, "vampires that want their cake and eat it too," according to Glen Mazis. For an aesthetic lover a commitment only means loss of freedom. This approach to life entails:

that the aesthete has no faith that the content of his experience is the key to fulfillment, but rather, it is what he or she can *extract* from the experience of the content while not being "caught up" in it; and [. . .] that all experience, even a purely sensual one like tasting wine, becomes filtered through the mind or becomes an occasion for the mind to savor reality from a distance.[6]

This type of lover can enjoy the loved one aesthetically, as if he or she were a work of art, until the inevitable emotional complications start to ruin the enjoyment. Aesthetic lovers cultivate their ability to be free from entrapment, and experience their love as outside observers and manipulators. It would seem that eighteenth-century France was a perfect setting for aesthetic lovers, an era in which according to Niklas Luhmann, "the code of *amour passion* was developed for extra-marital relations," and when "courting one's own wife would have appeared highly ridiculous as would have any expenditure of passion in order to gain access to one's own conjugal bed."[7] In *Dangerous Liaisons* Merteul candidly advises Cécile de Volanges (Uma Thurman), the younger noblewoman who is under her tutelage:

> When it comes to marriage, one man is as good as the next. And even the least accommodating is less trouble than a mother. [. . .] Provided you take a few elementary precautions, you can [have sex], or not, with as many men as you like, as often as you like, in as many different ways as you like.

Both Merteuil and Valmont are top players in the game of love. Valmont wants to seduce the virtuous Madame de Tourvel (Michelle Pfeiffer), while Merteuil is determined to corrupt the young Cécile in order to take vengeance on a former lover, to whom Cécile is promised in marriage. When Cécile falls in love with Chevalier Danceny (Keanu Reeves), Merteuil and Valmont pretend to help the secret lovers, so that they can stage-manage their affair as they please in their theater of love.

In Chapter 2 I introduced the notion of the spectator being aligned with an immoral character by morbid curiosity. In a similar manner Merteul and Valmont's immoral schemes are actually very enjoyable for the spectator, who is curious about the way their game of love will develop, rather than concerned about its consequences for the morally virtuous characters such as Madame de Tourvel. Furthermore, the sequence in which Valmont seduces Cécile is not entirely unlike the troubling scene with mister Bebe in *4 Months, 3 Weeks & 2 Days*, discussed in Chapter 6. First Valmont tricks Cécile into having a copy of her bedroom key made for him, allegedly to deliver Danceny's letters to her. But once inside her room he blackmails her into having sex with him and in addition ruthlessly enjoys her torment at the breakfast table after their first nightly encounter, sticking his tongue out at her in such a way that it looks like a vulva. For the spectators too, this is a blunt, comic hint at the nightly proceedings. Yet unlike in *4 Months*, such episodes in *Dangerous Liaisons* do not anger but delight the spectator. Why is our reaction so different? I think the answer is to be found in the way the film seduces the spectator. The film makes the spectator willingly or unwillingly fall in love by the sheer beauty of its rococo setting where the actors carry out a well-rehearsed choreography, by its subtle humor, and by the elegance of its plot development. What happens to us, is the same that happens first to Cécile and later to Madame de Tourvel: we give in to the film's and Valmont's charms because, as Cécile avouches, "he just has a way of putting things."

However, Valmont himself falls in love with Madame de Tourvel although he does not realize it, or does not want to admit it to himself. For Merteuil Valmont's love is painfully clear though, and this puts them at an unbridgeable distance. A telling shot of Merteuil in front of a mirror-paneled door conveys the crisis into which she is thrown now (image 7). The image is distorted and shattered, symbolizing how she is left disoriented about love and her own identity, her subjectivity no longer supported by Valmont, as he has ceased to mirror her actions and attitudes. In other words, it is at this moment when mirroring between Merteuil and Valmont has come to a halt, that Valmont is unable to continue his role in the theater of love. In another telling shot, when Valmont informs Danceny, who is now Merteuil's current lover, about Cécile's whereabouts, we witness Merteuil observing the scene through a mirror in the background. At first the reflection is blurry, but then for a brief moment the image becomes more clearly visible, as Danceny expresses his strong concern for Cécile. Here the mirror stands for separation between Valmont and Merteuil, whereas in the beginning it represented their bond. Subsequently, it is at this point at the latest that the film changes from a comedy into a tragedy.

Merteuil manipulates Valmont into breaking up with Madame de Tourvel, offering as a feeble explanation: "It's beyond my control." In this scene Valmont is visibly torn between his vanity and his love for Madame de Tourvel. His struggle, brilliantly performed by Malkovich, is visualized in the contradiction between speech and gesture: Valmont's

IMAGE 7: Crisis mirrored: *Dangerous Liaisons*

words are vicious and merciless, but his trembling voice and his facial expression give him away, at least to the spectator. The gripping scene is strongly affective and leaves the spectators shattered too, and it might be claimed that our hearts too are broken by Valmont, when he breaks both his own heart and Madame de Tourvel's. Thus, not unlike *The Vanishing* discussed in Chapter 2, the film "punishes" the spectators for participating in this game of love, which ultimately could not be taken as light-heartedly as they might have expected in the beginning. First *Dangerous Liaisons* invites us to enjoy love's theater in a cynical, detached mood, as we are indulged by the film, enjoying the delight of "being in love" without having to pay the prize, the fear of rejection, and other such consequences. But then the film undergoes a change of heart, or rather, after having seduced us, it no less than deceives us now, as Valmont likewise seduces and deceives Madame de Tourvel, finally to be deceived in return, beaten at his own game. The cynicism that protected Merteuil and Valmont from moral considerations in the beginning, fails and they are punished too. Valmont gets himself killed on purpose in a duel with Danceny and Merteuil becomes a social pariah. The ending of the film reflects the opening sequence, showing Merteul in front of her mirror image after she has been booed at the opera. She slowly removes the makeup ("mask") from her expressionless face, which is nevertheless full of affectivity which indicates that the final curtain is now drawn on her play of love.

Ironic Abjection: *Romance*

When *Dangerous Liaisons* seduces, Catherine Breillat's controversial film *Romance* (1999) repels. The logic of love in this film comes down to irony, rather than cynicism. Yet like *Dangerous Liaisons*, it presents us with a world in which love and desire are strictly separated, irreconcilable provinces of the mind and body that are only accessible through mutual exclusion. Accessing the domain of love implies exclusion from the domain of desire, which means that one can either be loved or "be screwed" by somebody, but not simultaneously. As a result the interpersonal relationships between men and women are once more reduced to a battlefield. The story evolves around a woman called Marie (Caroline Ducey), who is heavily frustrated, because her egoistic boyfriend Paul (Sagamore Stévenin) has withdrawn any form of sexual attention. Out of sheer frustration, Marie has an affair with Paolo, a stranger from a bar (played by the Italian porn star Rocco Siffredi), followed by an affair with her older colleague Robert (François Berléand), who has a Don Juan complex. Next she gets raped by a random passerby who thinks she is a prostitute, after he has first offered her money to perform cunnilingus. Finally she finds herself miraculously pregnant from Paul after a bed scene, in which they hardly seem to have had intercourse, perhaps a veiled reference to the Virgin Mary's immaculate conception. On the day of the delivery Marie opens the gas tap just before she leaves for the hospital with dearly caring Robert, and at the moment she gives birth to a baby boy, their apartment with Paul still inside, is blown to smithereens.

From the very beginning of the film a conflict develops that is determined by coordinates on the axes of touching and not-touching. The film starts off with a close-up of Paul in makeup before a fashion shoot. Here the attributes that are customarily associated with femininity, such as a pink makeup sponge and powder puffs, stand out pronouncedly against the male face. In his role as a model Paul is made into an utterly masculine spectacle, to be looked at but not to be touched, posing as a matador at a bullfighting arena, while Marie watches from a distance. Later, when they are in bed together, Marie begs Paul to take off his cotton sleepwear. While Paul indifferently stares at the television screen, Marie takes his penis into her mouth, only to get coldly rejected. Robert Nozick writes that in intimacy, "we let another within the boundaries we normally maintain around ourselves, boundaries marked by clothing and by full self-control and monitoring."[8] Paul's refusal to either touch

Marie or to be touched by her suggests that abstinence, not intimacy, is at the basis of his love for her. He wants to be "absent" from her, yet as they practically live together, Paul is forced to create an artificial distance by eliminating all possibilities of touching between them. Touching without affectivity is simply a matter of physical contact, but touching turns into intimacy when affectivity comes into play. Affectivity is the resonance of our skins, separate membranes in touch with each other, resulting in a positive or negative affective valence that becomes an integral part of our experience of touching and being touched. We are intimately "in touch with" through this affective valence which pushes and pulls us into ever-shifting emotional relations.[9] But instead of submitting himself to this form of "being-in-touch" Paul chooses to stay within his bounds by refusing to strip naked. The crisp white cotton of his T-shirt functions as an insensitive membrane, which will not resonate in any degree of affectivity.

This raises the question as to whether Paul is truly in love with Marie, or merely with an image of her. In general, entering into any form of intimate relationship involves a desire to connect, which is a reciprocal interest. In this context Silvan Tomkins points out that such interest has to do with our basic longing for communication and reciprocal attachment.[10] However, relationships always involve being vulnerable to the fear of one's interest being rejected, the fear that the desire to connect is not reciprocated. In other words, all relationships contain the continuous possibility that rejection will occur, and the acceptance of this possibility becomes a necessary condition for "mutual generosity of mind and body" between individuals.[11] But since such generosity is always about taking risks, it can be considered "safer" to fall in love with an image of one's own invention that can be abandoned at will. It is this possibility that Paul openly flaunts in front of Marie by dancing with other women in an intimate, sexually suggestive manner. As a result of his attitude Marie's sexual jealousy, which she originally felt for not being desired, functions as a substitute for being-in-touch. It reflects how Paul's not touching her feeds her desire to be touched, compelling her to reach out to him even more, which in turn provokes further rejection on his part.

A pattern of touching and not-touching returns in the scene in which Marie has sex with Paolo. Out of a sense of emotional integrity she uses affective coldness as a protective shield to eliminate all possible tenderness between them. She holds a harsh monologue that is obviously designed to create distance, while she gives her body to him at the same time. During the act her voice-over declares:

> I don't want to see the men who screw me. Or look at them. I want to be a hole, a pit, the more gaping, the more obscene it is, the more it's me, my intimacy the more I surrender. It's metaphysical. I disappear in proportion to the cock taking me. I hollow myself. That's my purity.

This is cultivation of sensuality devoid of emotional connection, sexual intercourse without "towardness." It is a form of touching without affectivity, by means of which touching would become intimacy. Or rather, it is masturbation, since their intercourse does not contain the "anticipation of sense" that in Jean-Luc Nancy's thinking "is what makes one return to the other and what therefore makes it so that there is one *with* the other."[12] In her attempt to eliminate all touching as "being-with" between herself and Paolo, Marie aims at creating a form of non-affective intimacy that can only consist of pure desire, and has nothing to do with love. Marie's desire is not love, because it "lacks its object—which is the subject—and lacks it while appropriating it to itself. [. . .] [Libidinal] desire [. . .] is foreign to love because it sublates, be it negatively, the logic of fulfillment."[13]

Perhaps it could be said that Marie seeks transience with Paolo, tangible physical encounters, which provide an outlet through fulfillment of sexual desire, whereas with Paul she strives for permanence, an abstract and transcendent relationship with no established way for consummation. But this would be in line with an erroneous dualistic concept of mind versus body, in which sexual passion as "physical eros" is separated from "spiritual eros," the Platonian drive toward beauty and truth in the eternal realm. Similarly Torben Grodal distinguishes between a "spiritual" form of love that is characterized by permanence and a "physical" form of love characterized by transience. According to him *Breaking the Waves* (1996) conceptualizes such a distinction. The heroine Bess (Emily Watson) is torn between her physical, embodied, and romantic "basic" form of love for Jan (Stellan Skarsgård) and her spiritual, disembodied, and authentic "higher" form of love for this same man. In the end, the spiritual form wins, when Bess sacrifices her body in order to save Jan's life. Grodal comments that it is "an extreme position to actively destroy the body and to claim that the Spirit thereby fulfils a higher destiny."[14]

Leaving this aside, I would propose that the non-affective sex scenes in *Romance* carry a meaningful psychological comment on Marie's love, without such a dualistic approach. A cinematographic comparison with conventional porn will make this clear. As Paolo is played by Rocco Siffredi, it seems apt to use material from one of his porn films for this purpose. In *Best of Rocco* (2002) usually more than two people participate in each sex scene. There is kissing, no condoms are used, which suggests intimacy. The scenes show a sequence of all known sexual techniques in the book, and participants in the sex acts frequently change positions during intercourse. The cutting frequency is higher than in *Romance*, there are more (extreme) close-ups of faces, breasts, and genitals, as well as more different camera angles. Throughout the film the overall lighting is harsh. The length of one single sex act is approximately fifteen minutes, but the use of elliptical editing suggests that its entire duration is longer. The character played by Siffredi acts as a typical porn stud with some romantic "soft" traits, but nevertheless entirely in control. Perhaps even more telling is that every act ends with a close-up of his penis, ejaculating on a woman's belly, her face, her buttocks, or her mouth.

This pornographic convention is often defined in terms of voyeurism, in which the act of "pure" watching is an alternative for subjectively emotional, character-centered imagination, for instance. As many psychoanalytically oriented feminist readings of pornography have demonstrated, in conventional porn this voyeuristic viewing position is available to the male gaze only. The female figure in pornography is subjected to this male gaze, but as she simultaneously signifies enigmatic castration anxiety, she poses a problem that needs "to be dealt with" or there will be no visual pleasure for the male spectator.[15] According to Linda Williams, the generic problem-solving function of pornography is to disentangle this enigma of sexual difference, that is woman's lack of phallus, through female orgasm as a form of disavowal.[16] But as in contrast to male orgasm, female orgasm is problematically invisible, fetishizing conventions are used for this purpose. Therefore the disavowing female orgasm is depicted by means of showing women ecstatically enjoying so-called cum shots or money shots, through close-ups of male ejaculation on their bellies, breasts, or faces.

Denying such cinematographic porn conventions, Breillat uses one long take to film Marie and Paolo's copulating bodies in *Romance*, during which there is an almost imperceptible camera movement from medium shot to long shot and finally back to medium shot. The penetration remains off-screen even though the sex act by Siffredi and Ducey is rumored to be non-simulated.[17] During the moment of climax the protagonists' shoulders are in view, relatively irrelevant body parts when it comes to reaching orgasm, although the film acknowledges the climax on the level of sound with Paolo loudly moaning. Other features of this sex scene are the de-eroticized use of a condom, Paolo being portrayed as having a strong need for tenderness, and the overall soft lighting. Most importantly, the scene lacks a cum shot, and as a result the male orgasm suddenly becomes an enigma too. Here the question is not whether her orgasm was "real" but whether his was. In other words, the invisibility of Paolo's orgasm calls the authenticity of his climax into question. By ignoring the cum shot as masculine affirmation of female pleasure, the scene defines male pleasure in feminine terms and not *vice versa.*

Another prominent element in Breillat's film is Marie's real-time voice-over, constantly commenting on the events in the film, in a flatly neutral, almost bored tone. This configuration of voice and image incorporates the logic of shame and exposure. As I have argued in Chapter 5, in shame people shift their viewpoint from the position of an embodied actor to that of a disembodied observer, but in such a way that they fulfill both functions simultaneously. Making out in a car with Paolo, Marie's voice-over declares: "I watch myself giving in, as if it wasn't me." Later when Marie starts an affair with Robert, her voice-over again comments on the act of seduction from an outside point of view: "This kind of embarrassment is desire. It's part of the game . . . that's what this is, a trivial relationship, a very shameful one."

At the same time, Robert exposes Marie to herself, first verbally ("You are amazed that I'm fingering your pussy"), and then literally by forcing her to open her eyes and to look at herself in a mirror, while he caresses her. It is this sense of exposure, and not the physical act of domination that soon follows, which arouses Marie sexually. In this scene her desire is conditioned by shame, but this is a form of liberating shame that enables her to redefine her sexuality beyond the negation of masculinity, from which it gains new meaning and dynamic force. In other words, for Marie shame has the function of deconstruction and it results in reorientation of her sexuality toward a model beyond the normative slut versus virgin polarization. As a result of this she is later able to cry to her rapist that she is not ashamed. After being raped, her tears are no confirmation of humiliation, but a blatant sign of triumph after which she can return to her life as if nothing significant had happened.

Another important feature of *Romance* is its color design and more specifically, the contrasting red and white in the film's mise-en-scene. In Paul's apartment the dominating color is white: white marble, cold white light, plain white walls and pure white cotton—even his cat is white. This is combined with sterile orderliness, shiny surfaces, and taut design in chrome and glass. By contrast Robert's apartment is dominated by earthy colors: taupe backgrounds against which bright, warm red colors stand out. In addition Robert favors antique wooden furniture, heavy fabrics, and different ethnic style furnishings, ranging from Japanese screens to Californian Jacuzzis. Furthermore, Paul himself is a neat, good-looking young man with a firm body, as might be expected from a male model, whereas Robert is more robust and down-to-earth. Not only do these two color schemes represent the distinction between pure, innocent love, and dangerous, shameful desire, but they also refer to a discord between body and mind. At first Marie, wearing mostly white, stays firmly within the sphere of cerebral love, but as she grows more attached to Robert and less fond of Paul, she enters the domain of raw desire and starts wearing red. In her red dress she seems rather out of place in the picture-perfect whiteness of Paul's environment. But paradoxically, after having freed her body from any association with spiritual love, Marie becomes desirable for her "cerebral lover" and they finally have sex.

Toward the end of the film there is an important grotesque fantasy sequence, showing a circular, reservoir-like space divided in two by a separating wall, equally circular in shape. The inner core of this space is a sort of white hospital room with women, including Marie, lying on beds arranged in a circle in such a way, that from below the waist their bodies stick out on the other side of the circular wall. The outer ring is a shabby red corridor where men walk around naked, putting their penises into the anonymous vaginas that are thus made available for penetration and impregnation. This sequence does end with a cum shot, a close-up of a random penis ejaculating on Marie's belly, which is at least strange, considering that the purpose of this extraordinary place is precisely to enable impregnation. This shot is cut to a close-up shot of gel being squirted on Marie's abdomen in preparation of an ultrasound scan. Here the cerebral and the visceral, love and desire, get more and more inextricably intertwined, while at the same time the romance in *Romance* escapes from the realm of "masculinity" into the realm of "femininity."

The delivery scene contains some very explicit close-ups of a real birth. Stylistically these shots stand in harsh contrast to the rest of the film, which can be characterized as stylized and unobtrusive. Watching these images full of blood and slime, a thrill of disgust is hard to avoid. Jean-Paul Sartre has defined slime as a feminine substance that threatens to evoke what the (male) self has rejected in order to protect itself.[18] This carries overtones of what Julia Kristeva says about the excluded abject: "There looms, within abjection, one of those violent, dark revolts of being, directed against a threat that seems to emanate from an exorbitant outside or inside, ejected beyond the scope of the possible, the tolerable, the thinkable."[19] The ending of *Romance* renders Marie into a monstrous pure abject, which to Barbara Creed equals the "archaic mother" that embodies the "primordial abyss, both the point of origin (birth) and the point of termination (death)."[20] Marie becomes the abject mother, but in *Romance* her monstrosity is embraced and celebrated instead of rejected and denied, by which the film gains ironic significance. In my opinion, *Romance* is best viewed as an "ironic love story" that both affirms to deny and denies to affirm the abject-feminine. Addressing the concept of irony, Søren Kierkegaard wrote:

> Irony is a qualification of subjectivity. In irony, the subject is negatively free, since the actuality that is supposed to give the subject content is not there. He is free from the constraint in which the given actuality holds the subject, but he is negatively free and as such is suspended, because there is nothing that holds him. But this very freedom, this suspension, gives the ironist a certain enthusiasm, because he becomes intoxicated, so to speak, in the infinity of possibilities.[21]

In *Romance* abjection is ironic and irony is abject insofar as both these elements complement each other as sources for a critical reexamination of the expectations that especially women seem to hold for their intimate relationships. Yet ironic abjection does not merely determine the internal dynamics of the film itself, but it also constitutes the operational structure through which the film makes itself emotionally intelligible to the spectator. This structure ostensibly embraces, but actually resists the idea of romantic love that "originates from envy, thrives in insecurity and ends in disillusion"—as Toni Morrison puts it.[22] *Romance* creates a discrepancy between content and form, enunciation and reception, even between affectivity and emotion. The irony in *Romance* acknowledges that love has more to do with "the system of intimacy" (Luhmann) that tells us who to love, how to love, and when to love, rather than with our individual agency. One of the central assumptions in Western society's system of intimacy is that romantic love forms a union including both the lover and the loved one, with which they both come to identify. In this concept sexual desire is the arena for celebrating this newly formed "we," a view that Robert Nozick advocates in the following passage:

It is not only the other person who is known more deeply in sex. One knows one's own self better in experiencing what it is capable of: passion, love, aggression, vulnerability, domination, playfulness, infantile pleasure, joy. The depth of relaxing afterward is a measure of the fullness and profundity of the experience together, and a part of it.[23]

By contrast, *Romance* does not celebrate, but rather ironically calls into question this assumption that union should be the central characteristic of love. Marie's voice-over commentary is not "blinded by love" for instance, but knowing and sarcastic. By commenting on her own romantic life, Marie presents piercing remarks about the ideals of love, while at the same time she expresses her frustration at her own inability to fulfill those ideals. By acknowledging her own experience in relation to the system of intimacy, Marie distances herself from it, and she also invites the spectators to question the expectations they might have about their intimate relationships. Therefore, the most appropriate "viewing position" for *Romance* seems to be held by the ironist, whom Richard Rorty has defined as "the sort of person who faces up to the contingency of his or her most central beliefs and desires"[24]—including his or her ideas of love.

Authentic Love: *Eternal Sunshine of the Spotless Mind*

Another central assumption in the romantic system of intimacy concerns exclusive commitment to the loved one, the idea that "true" love is geared to one person only, and cannot be administered in variable degrees. Nozick again:

> It is intrinsic to the notion of [romantic] love, and to the we formed by it, that there is not that willingness to trade up. One is no more willing to find another partner, even one with a "higher score," than to destroy the personal self one identifies with in order to allow another, possibly better, but discontinuous self to replace it.[25]

According to this view romantic love is an attitude that directs the lover toward the loved one, resulting in an entity that might be called a "we." Such an attitude presupposes a capacity for exclusive reference toward a loved one.[26] However, this concept is not part of a universal ontological order, but it is based on cultural propositions, which Luhmann summarizes as love's code. When internalized, this code becomes the exclusive source of identity, meaning, and significance in the lover's world.

In Michel Gondry's contemporary "comedy of remarriage," *Eternal Sunshine of the Spotless Mind* (2004), Joel (Jim Carrey) and Clementine's (Kate Winslet) love for each other has altered their "topology of self." It holds for both lovers that their sense of self has been affected by the loved one to the extent that love has practically caused a "locked-in syndrome." When their love ends in disillusion, they literally have no alternative but to "empty their lives" of each other. A major part of the film plays in Joel's head during a memory-erasing procedure that is carried out on him by a company called Lacuna. Clementine has already undergone a similar "operation" in order to erase the memories of their two-year relationship. First Joel is told to collect every item he owns that has some association with Clementine. Next these items are used to create "a map of Clementine" in Joel's brain, to which both have apparently transferred certain properties during their relationship, resulting in a kind of joint "identity pool." "I cannot remember anything without you," Joel says to "Clementine" at a certain point.

Lacuna's technicians attach the headgear to Joel and start erasing his recollections one by one, starting out with the most recent events. Internal and external diegetic sounds start to mingle, actions start to repeat themselves and the image goes blurry. As soon as Joel starts to think back on his life with Clementine, different layers of time come together, perhaps forming a Deleuzian crystal image *par excellence.* Joel is present in his own memories, inside his own head, but as an outside observer. We, the spectators, are positioned inside Joel's head with him. We alternatively watch internally to the outside and externally to the inside, and together with him we mistake the present for the past. The external world encounters the internal while the past merges into the present, as the house that is Joel's history with Clementine is falling apart. "Oh my God, *déjà vu, déjà vu,*" says Joel, holding his head inside his head. Indeed, *Eternal Sunshine* is reminiscent of the experience of *déjà vu,* the experience when past and present intertwine in a feedback loop. Joel's memories are fed back into his mind as part of his memories. Similarly, Steven Shaviro writes about the film as follows:

> Joel's memories from different periods melt into one another; while aspects of individual memories get torn apart, disaggregated, and redistributed. Scenes that Joel remembers turn into scenes that focus on the act of remembering itself: he tries to wake himself up, in order

to get through to the technicians who are manipulating his sleeping brain.[27]

The procedure eradicates the abstract emotional core of Joel's memory of Clementine, after which his concrete separate memories of her start to fade in a degradation process. That emotional core is romantic love which has evolved into a fusion of two personalities, who have formed a united "we." Although their relationship does not seem to have been very good, one might even say that Joel is stuck with Clementine, because she has "amalgamated" with him and now needs to be erased painfully. At this point the film itself becomes an embodiment of Joel's being-in-the-world, which is saturated by Clementine to the extent that he does not know where "he" ends and "she" begins. Here Joel's originally remembering Clementine is blended with his memory of her as he physically relives their common past during the erasing process. The spectators duly come to participate in this tribulation by means of their mutually possessed intentional bonds with the protagonist.

Joel's physical suffering during the erasing procedure is also part of his own past, while he reads his pain as one of Clementine's attributes in his memory. In this complex process he deconstructs and eliminates her within the bounds of his own body. Thus, while specific coordinates on Joel's brain-map are erased, his entire being-in-the-world is altered too, since memory and body are inseparably embedded in each other. As a result everything falls apart, fades away, vanishes, as images and sounds become transparent, altered, resonant, asynchronous, superimposed, distorted. Objects are misplaced, places get mixed up, sounds are on the wrong frequency. There is bi-location, reversed order, acceleration, and deceleration. Lake Charles turns into Grand Central Station, which then turns into Clementine's grandparents' living room, which finally turns into the Lacuna office. Spatial and temporal specificity are torn apart, while the narrative unfolds from any point in time, and past, present, and future are constantly redeveloped.

But then at some point in this process Joel realizes that Lacuna technician Patrick (Elijah Wood) is now in love with Clementine. Although Joel is unconscious, Patrick's voice penetrates into his "mind-house," calling Clementine by a nickname that Joel has actually given her. Patrick's love for Clementine is a threat to Joel's sense of self, as he is dependent on her for the reciprocity of his love, as in the Nozickian "shared identity." As a result Joel decides to thwart the memory-erasing procedure and to hold on to his memories of her. Inside his own head he has a discussion with "Clementine," who advises him to hide her in memories where she does not belong, which are "off the map." A nursery rhyme that they sing together carries them into a childhood memory, while merging old and recent memories. A childhood summer shower occurs in the living room of "now," while Joel and Clementine themselves become childish adults.

The procedure cannot to be terminated though, and this is when the film becomes even more surreal. Bathing in the kitchen sink, Joel and Clementine get flushed down into a drive-in theater, all soaking wet. The images of Joel's memories become more vague and blurred, as he escapes into memories that have already been erased, of which he only recalls the erasing, not the original content. Soon the image collapses like a house of cards, which is suggestive of Joel's bodily presence falling apart completely, and once again implies his painful reliving the past during the erasing process. The final location in this sequence is a Montauk beach house that played an important role in Joel and Clementine's first encounter. Here the external world, in the shape of wind, sand, and sea enters the building that stands for Clementine and wipes it away. In the final scene before he wakes up, Joel's complete life with Clementine passes before his eyes in normal order, like a landscape from a moving car.

Yet the procedure does not appear to have been 100 percent successful for either Joel or Clementine. When they meet again on the Montauk beach, they experience a bond between them that neither of them can explain. A seemingly absent, but profoundly present residue of Clementine lingers in Joel and *vice versa*. I offer as my opinion that within the logic of the film "artificial forgetting" is a passive intentionality that removes memory on the level of reflection (emotion) only, but not on the level of pre-reflection (affectivity). In other words, memories of love that have been erased from reflective consciousness nevertheless remain preserved in pre-reflective consciousness. Artificially erased memories remain remembered on the level of what Charlotte Delbo calls "sense memory," not on the level of "thinking memory."[28] The memory-erasing procedure does not work, since it only focuses on thinking memory, leaving sense memory intact.

In a similar vein, on the level of reflective consciousness one can decide to end a love relationship instantaneously, but actually falling out of love is a bodily process that hurts the soul and can be painfully long and slow.[29] In this context the open ending of *Eternal Sunshine* poses interesting questions, in addition to demonstrating how a personal interpretation of love can influence the emotions it evokes. For a romantic spectator the second "go-around" for Joel and Clementine could signify their eternal oath, based on the absolute value of their love. But for a Nietzschean spectator the "eternal" aspect indicates the innumerable times that Joel and Clementine will have to live through their past relationship.[30] For an existentialist the ending could be what Jean-Paul Sartre calls "bad faith:" a passive, overwhelming strategy to avoid a life of responsible self-determination, parading as a mode of salvation.

But perhaps the ending can also be seen as a possible origin of authentic love between Joel and Clementine. Simone de Beauvoir defines this as a human interrelationship that assumes "the contingence of the other; that is to say, his lacks, his limitations, his basic gratuitousness."[31] Authentic love avoids the mutual desire for shared identity in favor of affective reciprocity, which *always* "starts over." It opens a vista in which the lovers remain two separate beings, between whom love spans across differences ("i love to you").[32] Here love is a dynamic movement toward the other and "flesh" is inseparable from "soul." That Joel's memories of Clementine get eventually erased from his mind (and *vice versa*), might just be a blessing in disguise. It could grant their love new creative reciprocity, which nourishes autonomous personalities in lovers. The second go-around does not come about because Joel and Clementine desire to share their identities, but precisely because they do not. Instead, they prefer to open themselves up to each other by acknowledging each other's autonomy. Keith Lehrer describes this as follows:

> My autonomous preference for what she autonomously prefers is or can be a form of love for her that is an expression of my autonomy that respects her expression of her autonomy. We are far from the original magic, but also from the disillusion, of extreme love.[33]

Only this kind of total openness makes authentic love possible, emanating as mutually enriching self-determination that has a dynamic force of its own. Furthermore, their love is no longer self-deceptive, as now they even prefer to cherish features of each other that they generally disliked, since such flaws reveal the other's autonomy too. Yet this form of love may be difficult to practice and can even be agonizing, as it demands both strength and vulnerability. It requires the lovers to assume responsibility in life and to give up control about whether or not one is loved back. But reversely, authentic love plays an important role in assuming responsibility in life, because in authentic love mind, heart, and body are intertwined in such a way that they lose their structuring boundaries. As a result the autonomous lovers are opened up to "countless possibilities of influencing and being influenced by something uncontrollably other."[34]

This view takes us from romantic love as bondage to authentic love as wisdom. For here love becomes a tool for self-expression, and thus it carries great possibilities for self-determination, which does not mean, however, that love should be the *only* source of self-determination. Lovers who love authentically, invent, act, and make choices. They see love as something to be actively brought into existence, rather than as a destiny to which one can only passively submit. This results in a greater responsibility for one's life and one's identity.[35] Romantic love may hinder responsible self-determination insofar as it keeps the lovers preoccupied with whether or not they are worthy of love. But authentic love binds the lover to the loved one by leaving him or her essentially independent. Authentic love is not an either/or question between the autonomous or the shared self, but a reciprocal exchange of selves, by which two autonomous subjects enlarge and enhance themselves through the other, in open totality and mutual enrichment.

In *Eternal Sunshine*, the dynamics of authentic love are founded in generosity, which becomes the prerequisite for self-determination and which denies a mystical union between lovers. Already during the erasing process Joel invites Clementine inside his memory "house" to places where she does not belong. By opening himself up—revealing his shame, his painful memories—to Clementine, Joel generates a possibility for creative self-determination, without relying on her for the reality of his existence. The implication is that such generosity is always rewarded through the creative possibilities of self-determination. According to Irving Singer, this is what the creativity of love is all about. Strictly speaking such an attitude is not even generosity, since the lover does not need to lose anything of himself.[36] Similarly, this is what Kaja Silverman calls "the active gift of love," which "implies both idealizing beyond the parameters of the 'self,' and doing so with a full understanding of one's own creative participation with respect to the end result. It means to confer ideality, not to find it."[37] Viewed from this perspective, the erasing procedure paradoxically becomes a creative process for Joel, but only from the moment when he starts to resist it. This moment marks a shift from passively forgetting to actively working over his memories, by which Joel reinvents his past and his own self, overcomes his petty traumas and humiliations. In turn this engenders self-determination, which enables him to deconstruct the previous romantic illusion and to love Clementine authentically.

The spectator's delight in seeing these lovers reunited is also based on the creativity of love. Unlike "romance cinema," *Eternal Sunshine* does not ask its spectators to "passively identify" with the central characters in search for ideal partners, who will supply the tenderness and admiring attention they have learned to expect.[38] By contrast, the film requires the spectators to reflect actively, both on the film itself and on how they are positioned in the midst of the unfolding of events, thereby offering them intellectual and creative delight. The notion of authentic love is significant here, because its operational structure is analogous to the spectator's participation in the passionate and creative production of this cinematic event.

Furthermore, such is the case for film scholars who are "aficionados." They too prefer an affective way of making sense of the cinematic event and to understand the "object" of their study reciprocally, that is to say by acknowledging each other's emotional sensitivities. Throughout this book I have proposed that to "think with" cinema emotionally is to shift the question from representation to affective participation. Such an approach will not reduce a film to an illustration of certain theoretical insights, but it will remain attentive to the inseparability of the "subject" and "object" in scholarly practice. To approach cinema emotionally, is to interact with it from within, as part of the affective event that the film is, which is an attitude that I hope to have held up in my "feeling cinema."

Notes

Acknowledgment

1 Also the subtitle of E. M. Dadlez's *What's Hecuba to Him* (University Park: Penn State University Press, 1997).

Introduction

1 Wendy Cope, *Serious Concerns* (London: Faber and Faber, 1992), 47.

2 Michel Serres, *The Five Senses: A Philosophy of Mingled Bodies*, trans. Margaret Sankey and Peter Cowley (London: Continuum, 2008), 327. On the difference between affective appraisals and emotional evaluations, see especially Silvan S. Tomkins, *Exploring Affect: The Selected Writings of Silvan S. Tomkins*, ed. E. Virginia Demos (Cambridge: Cambridge University Press, 1995).

3 Brian Massumi, *Parables for the Virtual: Movement, Affect, Sensation* (Durham: Duke University Press, 2002); Erin Manning, *Politics of Touch: Sense, Movement, Sovereignty* (Minneapolis: University of Minnesota Press, 2007).

4 Sianne Ngai, *Ugly Feelings* (Cambridge: Harvard University Press, 2005), 27.

5 Antonio Damasio, *The Feeling of What Happens: Body and Emotion in the Making of Consciousness* (San Diego: Harcourt, 1999).

6 "The Object Speaks Back" was the subtitle of the Theory Seminar "Ways of Writing" at the Amsterdam School for Cultural Analysis (ASCA) in 2006–7.

7 Within the paradigm of psychoanalytic film theory, Lisa Cartwright has recently also proposed a model of (moral) spectatorship in which the spectator is "apprehended by the projective force of the image, who may be apprehended bodily, and who may be 'moved' in this process." Lisa Cartwright, *Moral Spectatorship: Technologies of Voice and Affect in Postwar Representations of the Child* (Durham: Duke University Press, 2008), 41.

8 Daniel Frampton, *Filmosophy: A Manifesto for a Radically New Way of Understanding Cinema* (London: Wallflower Press, 2006).

9 For Jennifer Barker too the film does not only express emotion, but it also *experiences* emotion through motion that draws the spectator toward and away from its fleshy materiality. Jennifer M. Barker, *The Tactile Eye: Touch and the Cinematic Experience* (Berkeley: University of California Press), 14–15.

10 Mikel Dufrenne, *Phenomenology of Aesthetic Experience*, trans. Edward S. Casey (Chicago: Northwestern University Press, 1989).

11 Francesco Casetti, *Eye of the Century: Film, Experience, Modernity*, trans. Erin Larkin with Jennifer Pranolo (New York: Columbia University Press, 2005), 138.

12 Needless to say, studying a film's representational aspects also involves questions as to what the film does, that is what its ideological effects amount to. Nevertheless, the difficulty with the representation concept is, that it presumes to mediate in the "ontological gap" between film and spectator as independently existing identities. On this difficulty, see Karen Barad, *Meeting the Universe Halfway: Quantum Physics and the Entanglement of Matter and Meaning* (Durham: Duke University Press, 2007), 47.

13 See also Saskia Lourens, "Writing History: National Identity in André Brink's Post-Apartheid Fiction" (PhD diss., University of Amsterdam, 2009), 79.

14 Rick Altman, "Cinema as Event," in *Sound Theory, Sound Practice*, ed. Rick Altman (London: Routledge, 1992), 4.

15 See, for instance, Ed S. Tan, *Emotion and the Structure of Narrative Film: Film as an Emotion Machine* (Mahwah: Lawrence Erlbaum Associates, 1996).

16 Colin Radford, "Emotions and Music: A Reply to the Cognitivists," *The Journal of Aesthetics and Art Criticism* 1 (1989): 70.

17 See, for instance, Martha Nussbaum: "Emotions [as well as cinematic emotions, as I argue] view the world from the point of view of my own scheme of goals and projects, the things to which I attach value in a conception of what it is for me to live well." Martha C. Nussbaum, *Upheavals of Thought: The Intelligence of Emotions* (Cambridge: Cambridge University Press, 2001), 49. See also David Pugmire, *Rediscovering Emotion* (Edinburgh: Edinburgh University Press, 1998), 63. Yet this does not necessarily mean that all cinematic emotions have to do with a personal worldview. Thus the sublime as an emotional experience is an overwhelmed response to the aesthetic value of the film that has little to do with its relationship to the spectator's own flourishing well-being. Nussbaum, *Upheavals of Thought*, 54; see also Cynthia Freeman, "The Sublime in Cinema," in *Passionate Views: Film, Cognition, and Emotion*, ed. Carl Plantinga and Greg M. Smith (Baltimore: Johns Hopkins University Press, 1999).

18 In this connection Jacques Rancière has coined the notion of "emancipated spectators" who "translate" the work of art "on the basis of their own intellectual adventure [. . .] who play the role of active interpreters, who develop their own translation in order to appropriate the 'story' and make it their own story." Jacques Rancière, *The Emancipated Spectator*, trans. Gregory Elliott (London: Verso, 2009), 21–2.

19 David MacDougall, *The Corporeal Image: Film, Ethnography and the Senses* (Princeton: Princeton University Press, 2006), 1.

20 This is due to the nature of emotions in general: they are "situational and indexical; they point to the ways in which the self is positioned within a particular interaction, and in that respect, they are a sort of shorthand for the self to understand how and where it is positioned in a particular situation." Eva Illouz, *Cold Intimacies: The Making of Emotional Capitalism* (Cambridge: Polity Press, 2007), 38.

21 Serres, *The Five Senses*, 80.

22 Edgar Morin, *The Cinema, or the Imaginary Man*, trans. Lorraine Mortimer (Minneapolis: University of Minnesota Press, 2005), 182–3.

23 Jean-Luc Nancy, *The Birth to Presence*, trans. Brian Holmes et al. (Stanford: Stanford University Press, 1994), 166.

24 Jean-Luc Nancy, *Being Singular Plural*, trans. Robert D. Richardson and Anne E. O'Byrne (Stanford: Stanford University Press, 2000), 83. Casetti, too, talks about a similar phenomenon when he writes that what emerges in cinema is a "mutual interdependence," where the spectator participates in the "destiny" of the film. Casetti, *Eye of the Century*, 143.

25 Philip Fisher, *The Vehement Passions* (Princeton: Princeton University Press, 2002), 2.

26 Noël Carroll, *The Philosophy of Horror; Or, Paradoxes of the Heart* (New York, Routledge, 1990).

27 For instance Janet Staiger describes how she changed her "emotional attitude" when watching Tobe Hooper's *The Texas Chainsaw Massacre* (1974): "By using the intertextual frame 'Tobe Hooper has used Hitchcock's *Psycho* as an intertext for [the film] and I am smart enough to see this,' I am constructing for myself the role of a listener to a joke I am attributing to Hooper. Thus, I become complicit with Hooper in the mechanisms of a tendentious joke, rather than the joke's victim—the 'average' viewer of the movie." Janet Staiger, *Perverse Spectators. The Practices of Film Reception* (New York: New York University Press, 2000), 185.

28 Morin, *The Cinema, or the Imaginary Man*, 107.

29 Ronald de Sousa, "The Rationality of Emotions," in *Explaining Emotions*, ed. Amélie Oksenberg Rorty (Berkeley: University of California Press, 1980), 137.

30 However, this does not necessarily mean that emotions are suffered in a passive mode. Robert Solomon writes for instance how emotions "do not just happen to us, but we are responsible for them. We practice them, cultivate them, and in many cases choose them, even if unconsciously [. . .] we can become self-conscious, reflect on and describe our feelings, make resolutions, and profoundly change our emotional behavior. This is the source of our freedom and our responsibility for our emotions." Robert C. Solomon, *True to Our Feelings: What Our Emotions are Really Telling Us* (Oxford: Oxford University Press, 2007), 190, 231.

31 For instance Richard Shusterman proposes to shift the methodology of studying artistic experience "from analysis to Eros." By stressing the importance of "sensitively feeling intentional consciousness" instead of a "disinterested, distanced contemplation," he argues that the role of a scholar is similar to that of a creative artist and *vice versa*: "As a good creative artist is a critically engaged observer of her work, so an attentive [scholar] is actively (including somatically) engaged in imaginative production of aesthetic experience." Richard Shusterman, "Aesthetic Experience: From Analysis to Eros," *The Journal of Aesthetics and Art Criticism* 2 (2006): 220.

Chapter 1

1 Carroll, *The Philosophy of Horror*, 17–20.

2 Solomon, *True to Our Feelings*, 33.

3 In 2009 for instance *The Shining* was voted the number one most frightening film in the history of cinema by the subscribers of the website *Total Sci-Fi Online*, leaving behind other "possessive" films such as *Psycho* (no. 5), *The Exorcist* (no. 21), *Ringu* (no. 34), and *The Blair Witch Project* (no. 67).

4 In an interview with Michel Ciment Stanley Kubrick is quoted saying: "In every aspect of the decor it seemed to me that the perfect guide for [making *The Shining*] could be found in Kafka's writing style." http://www.visual-memory. co.uk/amk/doc/interview.ts.html, accessed May 20, 2009.

5 Martin Buber, *The Knowledge of Man*, trans. Ronald Gregor Smith and Maurice Friedman (New York: Harper & Row, 1965), 44.

6 For proposed solutions thus far see Colin Radford, "How Can We Be Moved by the Fate of Anna Karenina?" *Proceedings of the Aristotelian Society* 49 (1975): 67–80; Kendall L. Walton "Fearing Fictions," *Journal of Philosophy* 1 (1978): 5–27; Carroll, *The Philosophy of Horror*, and Murray Smith "Film Spectatorship and the Institution of Fiction," *Journal of Aesthetics and Art Criticism* 2 (1995): 113–27.

7 The difficulty with Carroll's solution is that it seems as if the thought needs to be *explicitly* entertained. By contrast, Malcolm Budd argues that a thought "embodied in existence" is sufficient. Malcolm Budd, *Music and the Emotions* (London: Routledge, 1985), 13.

8 Barbara Creed, *The Monstrous-Feminine: Film, Feminism, Psychoanalysis* (London: Routledge, 1993), 22.

9 Solomon, *True to Our Feelings*, 3.

10 Smith, "Film Spectatorship and the Institution of Fiction," 127. According to Martha Nussbaum, this possibility to explore life's possibilities through fiction is the original meaning of Aristotelian catharsis as a source of "illumi-nation and clarification, as the agent, responding and attending to his or her responses, develops a richer self-understanding concerning the attachments and values that support the responses." Martha C. Nussbaum, *The Fragility of Goodness: Luck and Ethics in Greek Tragedy and Philosophy* (Cambridge: Cambridge University Press, 1986), 388; see also Nussbaum, *Upheavals of Thought*, 238.

11 Fisher, *Vehement Passions*, 15.

12 Fisher, *Vehement Passions*, 160, italics mine.

13 Torben Grodal, *Moving Pictures: A New Theory of Film Genres, Feelings and Cognitions* (Oxford: Oxford University Press, 1997), 127–8.

14 Tan, *Emotion and the Structure of Narrative Film*, 55.

15 Neither is this always necessary in real life. For instance according to David Pugmire, a person who does not believe in haunted houses may nevertheless be terrified to enter into an old house with a gloomy and ominous appear-ance. In this case, the person does not believe in haunted houses, but neither does he *disbelieve* in them. Pugmire, *Rediscovering Emotion*, 29.

16 Eva Schaper "Fiction and the Suspension of Disbelief," *British Journal of Aesthetics* 18 (1978): 31–44.

17 R. T. Allen, "The Reality of Responses to Fiction," *British Journal of Aesthetics* 1 (1986): 64–8.

18 Glenn Hartz describes a similar situation: "My teenage daughter convinces me to accompany her to a 'tear-jerker' movie with a fictional script. I try to keep

an open mind, but find it wholly lacking in artistry. I can't wait for it to end. Still, tears come welling up at the tragic climax, and, cursing, I brush them aside and hide in my hood on the way to the car. [. . .] How can someone who forswears any imaginative involvement in a series of fictional events, respond to them with tears of sadness?" Glenn Hartz "How We Can Be Moved by Anna Karenina, Green Slime, and a Red Pony," *Philosophy* 74 (1999): 572.

19 Radford, "How Can We Be Moved by the Fate of Anna Karenina?" 75.

20 Albeit admittedly the emotion that I am describing here can be classified as "phony" insofar as it is more or less "mechanically" constructed out of the "ready-made atoms" of preexisting emotional patterns that is the "Hollywood formula." On "phony" emotions in aesthetic experience see Ronald de Sousa, "Self-deceptive Emotions," in *Explaining Emotions*, ed. Amélie Oksenberg Rorty (Cambridge: Cambridge University Press, 1980), 295.

21 Michael Stocker with Elizabeth Hegeman, *Valuing Emotions* (Cambridge: Cambridge University Press, 1996), 43.

22 Jenefer Robinson, *Deeper than Reason: Emotion and its Role in Literature, Music, and Art* (Oxford: Oxford University Press, 2007), 145.

23 For instance, see the work by Christian Keysers at the Neuroimaging Center Groningen: http://www.bcn-nic.nl/index.html, accessed July 24, 2009.

24 Vittorio Gallese, "The 'Shared Manifold' Hypothesis: From Mirror Neurons to Empathy," *Journal of Consciousness Studies* 5–7 (2001): 42.

25 Brigitte Peucker has pointed out the striking similarity in appearance between the Grady twins and Diane Arbus's photograph "Identical Twins, Roselle, N.J. 1967." Brigitte Peucker, *The Material Image: Art and the Real in Film* (Stanford: Stanford University Press, 2007), 109.

26 Julia Kristeva, *Powers of Horror: An Essay on Abjection*, trans. Leon S. Roudiez (New York: Columbia University Press, 1982).

27 Peucker, *The Material Image*, 111.

28 Frampton, *Filmosophy*, 101.

29 I borrow the term from Haruki Murakami's description in his book *After Dark*: "We let ourselves become a pure single point [. . .] Our point of view draws back through the vacuum of nothingness. The movement is beyond our control." Haruki Murakami, *After Dark*, trans. Jay Rubin (London: Vintage 2008), 108, 116. The phenomenon is similar to free indirect discourse in Pier Paolo Pasolini's cinema of poetry, where "the distinction between what the character saw subjectively and what the camera saw objectively vanished [. . .] because camera assumed a subjective presence, acquired an internal vision." Gilles Deleuze, *Cinema 2: The Time-Image*, trans. Hugh Tomlinson and Robert Galeta (London: Athlone Press, 1989), 148.

30 Michel Chion, *Audio-Vision: Sound on Screen*, ed. and trans. Claudia Gorbman (New York: Columbia University Press, 1994), 129.

31 Richard Allen, *Projecting Illusion: Film Spectatorship and the Impression of Reality* (Cambridge: Cambridge University Press, 1995), 127. Yet a further distinction needs to be made here, as there is an obvious phenomenological difference between perceptual and mental subjectivity. In cinema, the spectator can inhabit a mental state that either correlates with the mental state of the character (centered imagining) or deviates from the mental state of the character

(acentered imagining). The spectator can also inhabit a perceptual point of view that is either external (perceptual objectivity) or correlates with the point of view of the protagonist (perceptual subjectivity). These types of visualization are not interdependent, since the spectators may inhabit the mental point of view of characters on events centrally, but without adopting their perceptual point of view as their "own."

32   J. P. Telotte, "Through a Pumpkin's Eye: The Reflexive Nature of Horror," in *American Horrors: Essays on the Modern American Horror Film*, ed. Gregory Waller (Urbana: University of Illinois Press, 1992), 117.

33   Deleuze, *Cinema*, 2, 7.

34   Daniel Shaw, *Film and Philosophy: Taking Movies Seriously* (London: Wallflower Press, 2008), 41.

35   Lucy Fischer, "Beauty and the Beast: Desire and its Double in *Repulsion*," in *The Cinema of Roman Polanski: Dark Spaces of the World*, ed. John Orr and Elzbieta Ostrowska (London: Wallflower Press, 2006), 84.

36   Goscilo, Helena, "Polanski's Existential Body—As Somebody, Nobody and Anybody," in *The Cinema of Roman Polanski: Dark Spaces of the World*, ed. John Orr and Elzbieta Ostrowska (London: Wallflower Press, 2006), 30.

37   Barker, *The Tactile Eye*, 48.

38   Aurel Kolnai, *On Disgust*, ed. Carolyn Korsmeyer and Barry Smith, trans. Elizabeth Kolnai (Chicago: Open Court, 2004), 47.

39   Murray Smith, "Imagining from the Inside," in *Film Theory and Philosophy*, ed. Richard Allen and Murray Smith (Oxford: Oxford University Press, 1999), 417.

40   For a definition of affective appraisal as a component of emotion, see Jenefer Robinson: "[E]motions are *processes*, in which a rough-and-ready affective appraisal causes physiological responses, motor changes, action tendencies, changes in facial and vocal expression, and so on, succeeded by cognitive monitoring. The function of non-cognitive affective appraisals is to draw attention automatically and insistently by bodily means to whatever in the environment is of vital importance to me and mine. These affective appraisals can be automatically evoked not only by simple perceptions such as a sudden loud sound, but also by complex thoughts and beliefs. The reason why we experience emotions as passive phenomena is that we are never fully in control of our emotions: once an affective appraisal occurs, the response occurs too. We can influence our emotions only indirectly through subsequent cognitive monitoring." Robinson, *Deeper than Reason*, 97.

Chapter 2

1   Irving Singer, *Three Philosophical Filmmakers: Hitchcock, Welles, Renoir* (Cambridge: The MIT Press, 2004), 30–1.

2   On the notion of clairvoyance in the cinematic experience, see Martha Blassnigg, "Clairvoyance, Cinema, and Consciousness," in *Screen Consciousness: Cinema, Mind and World*, ed. Robert Pepperell and Michael Punt (Amsterdam: Rodopi 2006), 105–22.

³ The theoretical threesome suspense, surprise, and curiosity can be discussed in terms of the range of story information: who knows what when? Restricted narration tends to build curiosity and surprise, while unrestricted narration helps to create suspense. See David Bordwell and Kristin Thompson, *Film Art: An Introduction* (New York: McGraw-Hill, 2001), 72. In the famous words of Alfred Hitchcock, "As far as I'm concerned, you have suspense when you let the audience play God." Alfred Hitchcock, *Hitchcock on Hitchcock: Selected Writings and Interviews*, ed. Sidney Gottlieb (Berkeley: University of California Press, 1995), 113. Needless to say, these narrative categories are not static. Rather, they could be seen as the angles of a narrative triangle that is never fixed but always more or less dynamic. Thus, the range of story information in cinema often oscillates between surprise and suspense, while suspense and curiosity very often go hand in hand.

⁴ This scene is cited by Quentin Tarantino in his 2004 film *Kill Bill Vol. 2*, and Rodrigo Cortés's *Buried* (2010) clearly draws from *The Vanishing* as well. In this film the only onscreen character, Paul Conroy (Ryan Reynolds), finds himself buried alive with a cigarette lighter inside a wooden coffin.

⁵ Noël Carroll, "Film, Emotion and Genre," in *Passionate Views: Film, Cognition, and Emotion*, ed. Carl Plantinga and Greg M. Smith (Baltimore: Johns Hopkins University Press, 1999), 43–4.

⁶ Murray Smith, *Engaging Characters: Fiction, Emotion, and the Cinema* (Oxford: Clarendon Press, 1995), 188.

⁷ De Sousa, *The Rationality of Emotions*, 192.

⁸ Noël Carroll, *A Philosophy of Mass Art* (Oxford: Oxford University Press, 1998), 264.

⁹ Mladen Dolar, "Hitchcock's Objects," in *Everything You Always Wanted to Know about Lacan, but Were Afraid to Ask Hitchcock*, ed. Slavoj Zizek (London: Verso, 1992), 34.

¹⁰ Tan, *Emotion and the Structure of Narrative Film*, 48.

¹¹ Carroll, "Film, Emotion, and Genre," 43.

¹² Damasio, *The Feeling of What Happens*, 16. To further expand the distinction, what Damasio calls core consciousness is roughly equivalent to pre-reflective consciousness, for example awareness of a glass on the table. Extended consciousness is similar to reflective consciousness, though. This equals "positional" awareness of the glass on the table, which is the awareness of being aware.

¹³ Carroll, "Film, Emotion, and Genre," 45.

¹⁴ The question is frequently asked, why we sometimes take pleasure in evil and/or immoral characters in cinema such as Raymond, but also in Henry Hill (Ray Liotta) in Martin Scorsese's *Goodfellas* (1990) or Tony Montana (Al Pacino) in Brian De Palma's *Scarface* (1983). From a Kantian point of view, this pleasure might reflect the private wish of the spectators to return to the "ethical state of nature" in which an open conflict between the principles of good and evil are found in each and every one of us. Catherine Wheatley, *Michael Haneke's Cinema: The Ethic of the Image* (New York: Berghahn Books, 2009), 42. On occasion it has also been suggested that this phenomenon enables us to give expression to our morally perverse desires in a manner akin to catharsis. But with his notion of "perverse allegiance" Murray Smith shows

that our fascination for immoral characters has more to do with intellectual curiosity about extreme demeanors that for most of us are inconceivable in reality, and also with "perverse delight" in provocation "that takes as its object not only depicted actions but also what we take to be accepted and responsible moral response to these actions [. . .] of a strict moralist." Murray Smith, "Gangsters, Cannibals, Aesthetes, or Apparently Perverse Allegiances," in *Passionate Views: Film, Cognition, and Emotion*, ed. Carl Plantinga and Greg M. Smith (Baltimore: Johns Hopkins University Press, 1999), 232. Furthermore, an interesting argument has been put forward by Keith Lehrer, who proposes that it is relatively easy for us to "ally with" characters who love authentically even when they live immorally. Keith Lehrer, "Love and Autonomy," in *Love Analyzed*, ed. Roger E. Lamb (Boulder: Westview Press, 1991), 116. Mickey and Mallory (Woody Harrelson and Juliette Lewis) in Oliver Stone's *Natural Born Killers* (1994) are examples of this. Yet it seems to me that we may also experience perverse allegiance to characters that are immoral not by some weakness of the will or pure ignorance, but by their own conscious (pure?) choice, such as Hannibal Lecter (Anthony Hopkins) in Jonathan Demme's *The Silence of the Lambs* (1991), The Joker (Heath Ledger) in Christopher Nolan's *The Dark Knight* (2008), or Omar Little (Michael K. Williams) in the television drama series *The Wire* (David Simon, 2002–8). Raymond Lemorne is such an immoral character "with a backbone," and this observation actually lends the phenomenon of perverse allegiance a moral dimension, so that it becomes "perverse morality" perhaps. I will return to this argument in Chapter 7, where I will discuss Stephen Frears's *Dangerous Liaisons* (1988).

[15] Elias Baumgarten, "Curiosity as a Moral Virtue," *International Journal of Applied Philosophy* 22 (2001): 169–84.

[16] Berys Gaut, "Identification and Emotion in Narrative Film," in *Passionate Views: Film, Cognition, and Emotion*, ed. Carl Plantinga and Greg M. Smith (Baltimore: Johns Hopkins University Press, 1999), 209–10.

[17] Milan Kundera, *The Unbearable Lightness of Being*, trans. Michael Henry Heim (New York: Harper and Row, 1984), 20.

[18] Smith, *Engaging Characters*, 92.

[19] Solomon, *True to Our Feelings*, 67. Sympathy is often defined as an "other-directed" emotion in its intentionality. It is a "feel for" emotion, where our attention is directed toward the other as an emotional response to the emotion of the other. By contrast, empathy requires replication of the emotion of the other, and it is both self- and other-directed, in that it consists of sharing the other's emotion in a manner of "feel with." Many film scholars, such as Carroll, have denied that there can be empathy in the cinematic experience in the first place. According to him, empathy is impossible, because the spectator's emotions cannot correspond to or replicate the emotions or any particular character, and because there is always asymmetry between the emotional state of the character and that of the spectator. Carroll, *The Philosophy of Horror*, 90. For objections to this point, see for instance Gaut, "Identification and Emotion in Narrative Film" and Tarja Laine, "Empathy, Sympathy, and the Philosophy of Horror in Kubrick's *The Shining*," *Film and Philosophy* (2001): 72–88.

[20] Rick Altman, *Film/Genre* (London: British Film Institute, 1999), 145–52.

[21] In contrast to *The Silence of the Lambs* which might be considered a film in which the spectator can "have the cake" (as an ethical agent) and "eat it too" (as an aesthetic agent), since its ending offers both morally sanctioned pleasure (Clarice Starling catches Buffalo Bill) and morally unapproved pleasure (Hannibal Lecter "will have an old friend for dinner").

[22] The church is San Nicolo dei Mendicoli, located in the Dorsoduro district.

[23] Thomas Elsaesser and Malte Hagener, *Film Theory: An Introduction through the Senses* (New York: Routledge, 2010), 42.

[24] The scene has been paid homage to by John Irvin in his film *Ghost Story* (1981) and by Steven Soderbergh in his Elmore Leonard adaptation *Out of Sight* (1998).

[25] Charles Forceville has used a similar argument concerning another film adaptation situated in Venice, Paul Schrader's *The Comfort of Strangers* (1990) based on the same-title novel by Ian McEwan (1981). Charles Forceville, "The Conspiracy in *The Comfort of Strangers*: Narration in the Novel and the Film," *Language and Literature* 2 (2002): 119–35.

[26] According to Ed Tan, the spectators' invisibility combined with their inability to act tends to enhance the diegetic effect of the film as such: "The witnesses' situation is completely analogous to that of the observer in the real world, who is neither called upon to intervene nor physically able to react." Ed S. Tan, "Film-induced Affect as a Witness Emotion," *Poetics* 1–2 (1995): 17.

Chapter 3

[1] Hugo Münsterberg, *Hugo Münsterberg on Film: The Photoplay: A Psychological Study and Other Writings*, ed. Allan Langdale (New York: Routledge, 2001), 104.

[2] Douglas Chismar, "Empathy and Sympathy: The Important Difference," *Journal of Value Inquiry* 22 (1988): 260–1.

[3] See, for instance, E. Ann Kaplan, *Trauma Culture: The Politics of Terror and Loss in Media and Literature* (New Brunswick: Rutgers University Press, 2005).

[4] See especially Linda Williams, "Film Bodies: Gender, Genre and Excess," *Film Quarterly* 4 (1991): 2–13.

[5] Williams, "Film Bodies," 11.

[6] Steve Neale, "Melodrama and Tears," *Screen* 6 (1986): 12.

[7] Jill Bennett, *Empathic Vision: Affect, Trauma, and Contemporary Art* (Stanford: Stanford University Press, 2005), 23.

[8] Ernst van Alphen, "Symptoms of Discursivity: Experience, Memory and Trauma," in *Acts of Memory: Cultural Recall in the Present*, ed. Mieke Bal et al. (Hanover: University Press of New England, 1999), 25–6.

[9] Roberta Culbertson, "Embodied Memory, Transcendence, and Telling: Recounting Trauma, Re-establishing the Self," *New Literary History* 1 (1995): 169.

[10] Theresa Brennan argues after Freud, that traumatic symptoms can progress, either through the life drive that seeks release from that what constrains it, or through the death drive that keeps the individual locked up in the paralyzing repetition of trauma: "The life drive is evident in the body's attempt to release

the trauma by repeating it in the right way. It is the death drive that diverts the repetition away from its true purpose, which is to seek release [. . .] the body knows that the freedom from trauma only comes when it is repeated in such a way that its affective direction is reversed (by love for instance), by which energy the direction or disposition the trauma establishes is cancelled out." Teresa Brennan, *The Transmission of Affect* (Ithaca: Cornell University Press, 2004), 200, fn 17.

[11] The *awe-inspiration* theme is one of three Tan and Frijda identify as variations of the "virtue in distress" motive in melodrama. This theme comes about in a larger-than-life situation, in which one feels desire to lose oneself in a sensation of "eternity" —a sensation that Freud defined as the "oceanic feeling," The other two themes are *justice in jeopardy* and *separation-reunion*. Ed S. H. Tan and Nico H. Frijda, "Sentiment in Film Viewing," in *Passionate Views: Film, Cognition, and Emotion*, ed. Carl Plantinga and Greg M. Smith (Baltimore: Johns Hopkins University Press, 1999), 48–64.

[12] Roland Barthes, *A Lover's Discourse: Fragments*, trans. Richard Howard (New York: Hill and Wand, 2001), 30.

[13] Niklas Luhmann, *Love as Passion: The Codification of Intimacy*, trans. Jeremy Gaines and Doris Jones (Stanford: Stanford University Press, 1988), 60.

[14] Pugmire, *Rediscovering Emotion*, 49.

[15] Julia Kristeva, *Black Sun: Depression and Melancholia*, trans. Leon S. Roudiez (New York: Columbia University Press, 1992), 5.

[16] Thomas Elsaesser, "Tales of Sound and Fury: Observations on the Family Melodrama," in *Home Is Where the Heart Is: Studies in Melodrama and the Woman's Film*, ed. Christine Gledhill (London: British Film Institute, 1987), 66.

[17] Ruth Leys, *From Guilt to Shame: Auschwitz and After* (Princeton: Princeton University Press, 2007), 93–122.

[18] Gilberto Perez, *The Material Ghost: Films and Their Medium* (Baltimore: Johns Hopkins University Press, 1998), 50.

[19] Kaja Silverman, *The Threshold of the Visible World* (New York: Routledge, 1996), 23.

[20] Elsaesser defines this deadlock of identity as "the failure of the protagonist to act in the way that could shape the events and influence the emotional environment [in which] the characters are acted upon." Elsaesser, "Tales of Sound and Fury," 55. Thomas Schatz, too, argues that melodrama is connected to identity crisis, since the genre often centers on the theme of the individual's sense of self in "the strictures of social and familial tradition." Thomas Schatz, *Hollywood Genres: Formulas, Filmmaking and the Studio System* (Philadelphia: Temple University Press, 1981), 222.

[21] Nussbaum, *Upheavals of Thought*, 302. Nussbaum also makes a distinction between compassion and pity. Not surprisingly, since pity has come to have an association of superiority, it is often considered an emotion that always involves looking down upon the pitied, even when feeling genuinely sad about the other's misfortune. Compassion is an emotion of equality, while pity is that of inequality that in addition can be self-serving and hypocritical. Friedrich W. Nietzsche, *The Antichrist*, trans. Anthony M. Ludovici (New York: Prometheus, 2000); Solomon, *True to Our Feelings*, 66.

[22] Nussbaum, *Upheavals of Thought*, p. 309, italics mine.

[23] Richard Wollheim's term for simultaneous awareness of the represented object and of the fact of representation. Richard Wollheim, *Art and Its Objects* (Cambridge: Cambridge University Press, 1980), 224.

[24] Lisa Cartwright, too, proposes a model of "empathy" in which one does not feel what the other feels, but feels that one knows how the other feels. This "knowledge comes from the force of the object ('you,' the image, the representation), and my reciprocal sense that *I recognize the feeling I perceive in your expression.* 'You' move me to have feelings, but the feelings may not match your own." Cartwright, *Moral Spectatorship*, 24.

[25] Mardi J. Horowitz quoted in Leys, *From Guilt to Shame*, 97.

[26] Bennett, *Empathic Vision*, 7.

[27] Isabella Winkler, "Love, Death, and Parasites," in *Mapping Michel Serres*, ed. Niran Abbas (Ann Arbor: The University of Michigan Press, 2005), 231.

[28] According to Neale, melodrama contains a built-in impossibility of happy ending, since any narrative satisfaction in melodrama results either in loss of fantasy, or the postponement of the fulfillment of fantasy: "if there is fulfillment, a happy ending, it is at the cost of the loss of the story [. . .] It can indeed last only as long as the fiction lasts. [. . .] [An] 'unhappy' ending can function as a means of *postponing* rather than destroying the possibility of fulfilment of a wish. An 'unhappy' ending may function as a means of satisfying a wish to have the wish unfulfilled—in order that it can be preserved and re-stated rather than abandoned altogether." Neale, "Melodrama and Tears," 21. This kind of pleasure is related to the so-called paradox of tragedy: the question as to why we derive pleasure from apparently unpleasant emotions, as we often do when we witness suffering in fiction. The most famous solution to this paradox is perhaps the one formulated by David Hume, which highlights pleasure in artistic representation and expression. Such pleasure outstrips the negative emotions aroused, but it is important to notice that this pleasure does not simply cancel out these negative emotions. It overwhelms and absorbs them. David Hume, "Of Tragedy," in *The Philosophical Works of David Hume. Vol. 3* (Boston: Elibron, 2007), 237–47. In the context of horror, Noël Carroll proposes a similar argument by stating that the negative emotions (fear, disgust) in horror films can be overcome by delight in the aesthetic form of the film where "the locus of our gratification is not the monster as such but the whole narrative structure in which the presentation of the monster is staged." Carroll, *The Philosophy of Horror*, 181. Kendall Walton asserts that our pleasure in tragedy as such is genuine, while the negative emotions are merely generated by make-believe, and thus there is no particular contradiction in these emotional responses. Walton, "Fearing Fictions," 25. For Neale pleasure in melodrama echoes an atavistic pleasure that resides in the articulation of a nostalgic fantasy of total love rather than in the satisfaction of that fantasy. Neale, "Melodrama and Tears," 20. Ed Tan makes a comparable distinction between F-enjoyment and A-enjoyment. The latter is the response to the film as a work of art, say, the admiration for its sublime quality, whereas the F-enjoyment is a fiction-based response that results from concern about preferred outcomes in the film. Tan, "Film-induced Affect as a Witness Emotion," 16.

29 Yet this does not mean that aesthetic appreciation of cinema should be considered as categorically pleasurable. As Lisa Cartwright argues with her notion of compulsory compassion, a film can make a demand for the spectators' compassion so that they feel compelled to act upon it (keep on watching) even against their pleasure. Cartwright, *Moral Spectatorship*, 46–50.

Chapter 4

1 Siegfried Kracauer, *The Theory of Film: The Redemption of Physical Reality* (Princeton: Princeton University Press, 1997), 158.

2 Kracauer, *The Theory of Film*, 165, 175.

3 Sergey M. Eisenstein, *Film Form: Essays in Film Theory*, trans. Jay Leyda (New York: Meridian Books, 1957), 71. In addition to Kracauer and Eisenstein, Jean Epstein also wrote about the rhythmic energy of cinema in general that affects us through the "velocities, movements [and] vibrations" of filmic symbols." Jean Epstein, "The Senses," trans. Tom Milne, in *French Film Theory and Criticism 1907–1939*," ed. Richard Abel (Princeton: Princeton University Press, 1993), 244. In the context of contemporary film theory, Janet Harbord, who follows Brian Massumi, also writes about the copresence of cinema and the spectator that produces resonance or vibration. Janet Harbord, *The Evolution of Film: Rethinking Film Studies* (Cambridge: Polity, 2007), 121.

4 T. S. Eliot, "The Dry Salvages," in *Collected Poems 1909–1962* (London: Faber and Faber, 1963), 213.

5 Bettina von Arnim quoted in Philippe Lacoue-Labarthe, "The Echo of the Subject," in *Typography: Mimesis, Philosophy, Politics*, ed. Christopher Fynsk (Stanford: Stanford University Press, 1998), 139.

6 "Anguish in fact is the recognition of a possibility as my possibility; that is, it is constituted when consciousness sees itself [. . .] separated from the future by its very freedom. This [. . .] removes from me all excuse." Jean-Paul Sartre, *Being and Nothingness: A Phenomenological Essay on Ontology*, trans. Hazel E. Barnes (New York: Washington Square Press, 1992), 73.

7 The previous two being *Breaking the Waves* (1996) and *The Idiots* (1998).

8 A. O. Scott, "Universe Without Happy Endings," *New York Times*, September 22, 2000, accessed February 19, 2010, http://movies.nytimes.com/movie/rev iew?res=9B04E3D6103BF931A1575AC0A9669C8B63.

9 On this characteristic property of music, see Robinson, *Deeper than Reason*, 376.

10 Richard Cytowic, "Synaesthesia Encyclopedia," in *Encyclopedia of Neuroscience* CD-ROM, ed. George Adelman and Barry H. Smith (Amsterdam: Elsevier, 2004).

11 Valence is a notion that is used in physics to indicate the power of combination of atoms, but that also plays a role in affective exchanges between the film and the spectator, since every sound and every image has its positive or negative valence too.

12 See Steven Connor: "Why should it be that a phrase of music, a cadence, or a figure, should be registered so immediately in this lifting, this shifting, this sizzling of the skin, as though they had not needed to be taken in and

made intelligible by the ear at all? [. . .] Is it because sound invades or comes upon us in a way that what we see does not, or not unless we apprehend it as something heard?" Steven Connor, *The Book of Skin* (London: Reaktion Books, 2004), 246–7.

13 On this phenomenon see Joshua Yumibe, "On the Education of the Senses: Synaesthetic Perception from the 'Democratic Art' of Chromolithography to Modernism," in *New Review of Film and Television Studies* 3 (2009): 257–74.

14 Bill Thompson, "Evoking Terror in Film Scores," *M/C: A Journal of Media and Culture* 1 (2002), accessed October 17, 2010, http://journal.media-culture. org.au/index.php/mcjournal. See also Alf Gabrielsson and Patrick N. Juslin's study into the ways in which musical parameters, such as tempo, volume, and articulation (legato versus staccato) convey emotions. In their outline, harsh timbre, fast tempo, and nonlegato articulation correspond to anger, and bright timbre, fast tempo, and airy articulation correspond to joy. Alf Gabrielsson and Patrik N. Juslin, "Emotional Expression in Music Performance: Between the Performer's Intention and the Listener's Experience," *Psychology of Music* 1 (1996): 68–91. Using the concept of "bipolar affective space," Emery Schubert also evaluates emotional content of music across parameters of valence and arousal. Emery Schubert, "Measuring Emotion Continuously: Validity and Reliability of the Two-dimensional Emotion Space," *Australian Journal of Psychology* 3 (1999): 154–65.

15 Peter Kivy, *Sound Sentiment: An Essay on the Musical Emotions* (Philadelphia: Temple University Press, 1989), 77. This is the reason why, despite the cultural associations that clearly contribute to the emotional qualities in music, many listeners can recognize the intended emotion in music even from an unfamiliar culture. Slow tempo, quiet sound, and complexity are associated with sadness, fast tempo, loud sound, and simplicity with happiness, and fast tempo, loud sound, and complexity with anger in both Western and non-Western cultures. This means that, even though emotional qualities of music are often governed by culturally learned associations, there actually may be some universal rules that relate certain emotions to certain acoustic cues that transcend cultural boundaries. In both cases, emotion is a matter of quality of music that is affectively appraised in similar ways across different cultures, and that is analogous to a particular human emotional state. See, for instance Laura-Lee Balkwill, William Forde Thompson and Rie Matsunaga, "Recognition of Emotion in Japanese, Western, and Hindustani Music by Japanese Listeners," *Japanese Psychological Research* 4 (2004), 337–49.

16 Unlike in more "regular" musicals, this first musical sequence in von Trier's film does not take place until the 38-minute mark of the film. The function of this delay is self-reflective, but instead of inviting the spectator to maintain a critical distance toward the film, the delay actually seems to contribute to the promise of completion of the "musical utopia." See Brian McMillan, "Complicitous Critique: *Dancer in the Dark* as Postmodern Musical," *Discourses in Music* 2 (2004), accessed October 17, 2010, http://www.discourses.ca.

17 Gabriela Ilie and William Forde Thompson, "A Comparison of Acoustic Cues in Music and Speech for Three Dimensions of Affect," *Music Perception* 4 (2006), 319–30.

[18] See Jenefer Robinson: "One emotion process can thus transform into another as grief gives way to rage or fear to amusement. Moreover, many of these emotion processes are not easily nameable in terms of folk psychology: they are blends of different named emotions or they are conflicts between one named emotion and another, or they are ambiguous between one emotion label and another. [. . .] [O]ur emotional life occurs in streams, which change all the time in response to ever-changing affective appraisals, ever-evolving thoughts, ever-changing actions and action tendencies, bodily states, and feelings." Robinson, *Deeper than Reason*, 311.

[19] Glen A. Mazis, *Earthbodies: Rediscovering Our Planetary Senses* (Albany: State University of New York Press, 2002), 25.

[20] Jeff Smith would say that the interaction of cinematic and musical elements in "Cvalda" intensifies the emotion through "affective congruence," which makes the spectators feel the emotion more strongly than they would with either image of music alone. Another strategy of musical affectivity in cinema is called "polarization," in which music moves, or even alters the affective meaning of a scene toward its own affective character. Jeff Smith, "Movie Music as Moving Music: Emotion, Cognition, and the Film Score," in *Passionate Views: Film, Cognition, Emotion*, ed. Carl Plantinga and Greg M. Smith (Baltimore: Johns Hopkins University Press, 1999), 146–67.

[21] This operative analogy also explains why music can transmit its emotional qualities to us so that we can realize them imaginatively without necessarily feeling them "concretely." As Colin Radford points out, listeners of sad music may experience the feeling of sadness without necessarily being "truly" sad. Radford, "Emotions and Music."

[22] Recitative is a style of musical delivery in which the singer adopts the intonations and rhythms of ordinary speech.

[23] Serres, *The Five Senses*, 141,

[24] See Francis Sparshott: "[The] world [of music] is experienced as in itself affectful [. . .] more directly and intensely than any other sort of object. [. . .] [I]t is the very fact that music as such has no reference, no descriptive content, and no subjectivity, that makes it directly affectful. [. . .] The music [. . .] is not located or identified as itself other or elsewhere than the listener—'You are the music while the music lasts.' The music is, perhaps, a sounding structure or a structured sound, indwelling in the [listener]." Francis Sparshott, "Music and Feeling, *The Journal of Aesthetics and Art Criticism* 1 (1994): 4.

[25] David Sonnenschein, *Sound Design: The Expressive Power of Music, Voice and Sound Effects in Cinema* (Studio City: Michael Wiese, 2002), 121. Teresa Brennan also writes that rhythms have a unifying, regulating role in affective exchanges, whereas nonrhythmic or dissonant sounds function to separate and disrupt. Furthermore, even those affective exchanges that lack an auditory dimension work in a similar way, albeit perhaps in a more subtle fashion, since every image also has a rhythm. Brennan, *The Transmission of Affect*, 70–1.

[26] Eduard Hanslick, *The Beautiful in Music*, trans. Gustav Cohen (Indianapolis: Bobbs-Merrill, 1957).

[27] Susanne Langer, *Philosophy in a New Key: A Study in the Symbolism of Reason, Rite, and Art* (Cambridge: Harvard University Press, 1957).

28 Kivy, *Sound Sentiment.*

29 Stig Björkman, Torsten Manns, and Jonas Sima, *Bergman on Bergman: Interviews with Ingmar Bergman,* trans. Paul Britten Austin (New York: Da Capo Press, 1993), 181.

30 Although a sound can never be really "off" screen, only the source of sound can, as Christian Metz points out. Christian Metz, "Aural Objects," trans. Georgia Gurrieri. *Yale French Studies* 60 (1980): 28–9.

31 Perhaps similarities with *The Shining* are also worth mentioning here.

32 If the Grady twins in *The Shining* are comparable to Diane Arbus's identical twins, then Johan in *The Silence* is a spitting image of another Arbus photograph, namely "Child with a toy hand grenade in Central Park, N.Y.C. 1962" with the difference that Johan is holding a toy hand gun.

33 Rick Altman, "The Material Heterogeneity of Recorded Sound," in *Sound Theory, Sound Practice,* ed. Rick Altman (London: Routledge, 1992), 20–1.

34 Jean-Luc Nancy, *Listening,* trans. Charlotte Mandell (New York: Fordham University Press, 2007), 7.

35 Nancy, *Listening,* 6.

36 Nancy, *Listening,* 67.

37 Nancy, *Listening,* 6–7.

38 Nancy, *Listening,* 21.

39 Nancy, *Listening,* 7.

40 Philip Brophy, *100 Modern Soundtracks* (London: British Film Institute, 2004), 6.

41 Guy Rosolato, "The Voice: Between Body and Language," in *Voices,* ed. Christopher Phillips (Rotterdam: Witte de With, 1998), 75–94; Didier Anzieu, *The Skin Ego,* trans. Chris Turner (New Haven: Yale University Press, 1989); Kaja Silverman, *The Acoustic Mirror: The Female Voice in Psychoanalysis and Cinema* (Bloomington: Indiana University Press, 1988).

42 Chion, *Audio-Vision,* 114.

43 Nancy, *Listening,* 14. Martha Nussbaum makes a similar point about (Mahler's) music: "Music is especially well-suited to express parts of the personality that lie beneath its conscious self-understanding. Music can bypass habit, use, and intellectualizing, in such a way that its symbolic structures seem to pierce like a painful ray of light directly into the most vulnerable parts of the personality. [. . .] music seems to elude our self-protective devices, our techniques of manipulation and control, in such a way that it seems to write directly into our blood." Nussbaum, *Upheavals of Thought,* 269.

Chapter 5

1 Tarja Laine, *Shame and Desire: Emotion, Intersubjectivity, Cinema* (Brussels: Peter Lang, 2007), 34.

2 See, for instance, Gabrielle Taylor, *Pride, Shame and Guilt: Emotions of Self-Assessment* (New York: Oxford University Press, 1985); Bernard Williams, *Shame and Necessity* (Berkeley: University of California Press, 1993); Michael Lewis, *Shame: The Exposed Self* (New York: Free Press, 1995); Jack Katz, *How Emotions Work* (Chicago: The University of Chicago Press, 1999).

3   Sartre, *Being and Nothingness*, 303.

4   Leys, *From Guilt to Shame*, 126.

5   Douglas Crimp, "Mario Montez, for Shame," in *Regarding Sedgwick: Essays on Queer Culture and Critical Theory*, ed. Stephen M. Barber and David L. Clark (New York: Routledge, 2002), 65.

6   Jean-Paul Sartre, *Critique of Dialectical Reason Volume I: The Theory of Practical Ensembles*, trans. Alan Sheridan-Smith (London: Verso, 1982), 536.

7   Leo Bersani and Ulysse Dutoit, *Forms of Being: Cinema, Aesthetics, Subjectivity* (London: British Film Institute, 2004), 42.

8   "For shame involves a realization that one is weak and inadequate in some way in which one expects oneself to be adequate. Its reflex is to hide from the eyes of those who will be one's deficiency, to cover it." Nussbaum, *The Upheavals of Thought*, 196.

9   On transformational shame, see Eve Kosofsky Sedgwick, *Touching Feeling: Affect, Pedagogy, Performativity* (Durham: Duke University Press, 2003), 63–4. On traumatic shame, see Kathleen Woodward, "Traumatic Shame: Toni Morrison, Televisual Culture, and the Cultural Politics of Emotion," *Cultural Critique* 46 (2000): 210–40.

10 For me the tragedy between Lester and Fitts bears similarities to a real-life situation that occurred in the United States in 1995, after taping an episode of *The Jenny Jones Show* on secret admirers. A 32-year-old man Scott Amedure revealed that he was attracted to an acquaintance. This acquaintance, Jonathan Schmitz, agreed to participate in the show, believing that the person who was secretly attracted to him was a woman. On the show Schmitz was "humiliated and angered" (in his own words) to learn that the admirer was a man, and before the show was scheduled to air Schmitz fired two shotgun blasts at Amedure, killing him instantly. Kathleen Woodward wrote about Schmitz's shame as follows, and she might just as well have described what came over to Fitts: "In such a case, we can surmise that shame, turning to rage, is the precipitate of trauma. In such a case, affect blocks thought. In such a case, what is called an 'affect storm' leads to violence. In such a case, there was not a context for a self-reflexive sequencing of the emotions." Woodward, "Traumatic Shame," 233.

11 Susan Faludi, *Stiffed: The Betrayal of the American Man* (New York: Perennial, 2000).

12 Walter Susman, "Did Success Spoil the United States? Dual Representations in Postwar America," in *Recasting America: Culture and Politics in the Age of Cold War*, ed. Larry May (Chicago: University of Chicago Press, 1989), 31.

13 Although perhaps they should be discussed as comedies of humiliation rather than embarrassment, given William Ian Miller's claim that in contemporary middle-class America humiliation has entered the center stage. According to him shame is concerned with larger, moral issues, that is not living up to what we ought to, while humiliation is grounded more trivially. It occurs when we try to live up to what we have no right to. William Ian Miller, *Humiliation; And Other Essays on Honor, Social Discomfort, and Violence* (Ithaca: Cornell University Press, 1993), 138–45. Yet *Borat*, as well as *American Beauty*, could also be about something more profound, at least

below the surface. They may cover the moral high ground of welcoming the other into one's world regardless of whatever cultural beliefs and values he or she might hold.

14 Tomkins, *Exploring Affect*, 399.

15 David Benin and Lisa Cartwright, "Shame, Empathy and Looking Practices: Lessons from a Disability Studies Classroom," *Journal of Visual Culture* 2 (2006): 156.

16 Sedgwick, *Touching Feeling*, 37.

17 Leys, *From Guilt to Shame*, 3.

18 Katz, *How Emotions Work*, 110.

19 Jack Katz makes this distinction between "doing laughter," which is a strategic weapon that communicates to the others that one "gets the joke," and 'being done by humor,' which is the 'spirit' of humor that takes over the laughing person. Katz, *How Emotions Work*, 121–30. I think that often laughing at Borat initially starts as "doing laughter" only to be transformed into "being done by humor" in a less controllable fashion.

20 Ann Homaday, "Kazakh Zingers," *Washington Post*, November 3, 2006, accessed May 27, 2009, http://www.washingtonpost.com/wp-dyn/content/ article/2006/11/02/AR2006110201876.html.

21 Slavoj Zizek, *The Fright of Real Tears: Krzysztof Kieslowski between Theory and Post-Theory* (London: British Film Institute, 2001), 73.

22 Eric Anderson, "Inclusive Masculinity in a Fraternal Setting," *Men and Masculinities* 5 (2008): 604–20.

23 Sedgwick, *Touching Feeling*, 62.

24 The dialogic mode of interpretation corresponds to the way one forms a relationship with the other in a manner that "does not result in merging or mixing. Each retains its own unity and open totality, but they are mutually enriched." M. M. Bakhtin, *Speech Genres and Other Late Essays*, trans. Vern W. McGee, ed. Caryl Emerson and Michael Holquist (Austin: University of Texas Press, 1986), 6–7. The other two modes of interpretation are projective appropriation and ventriloquist identification. Paul Willemen, "The National," in *Fields of Vision: Essays in Film Studies, Visual Anthropology and Photography*, ed. Leslie Delereaux and Roger Hillman (Berkeley: University of California Press, 1995), 28–9.

Chapter 6

1 See, for instance, Philip Hallie, *Tales of Good and Evil, Help and Harm* (New York: HarperCollins, 1998), 90.

2 Susan Sontag, *Regarding the Pain of Others* (New York: Farrar, Straus and Giroux, 2003), 106.

3 On the ways in which emotions are generated as part of power relationships between individuals, see for instance Theodore D. Kemper's "Social Relations and Emotions: A Structural Approach," in *Research Agendas in the Sociology of Emotions*, ed. Theodore D. Kemper (New York: SUNY Press, 1990), 207–37. In

his account emotions, and especially anger, are set free due to an individual's realization of either loss or gain of power.

4 Solomon, *True to Our Feelings*, 211–12.

5 This is Jean-Luc Nancy's phrase for our common responsibility for everything that could possibly be said concerning morality. Jean-Luc Nancy, "Responding to Existence," trans. Sara Guyer, in *A Finite Thinking*, ed. Simon Sparks (Stanford: Stanford University Press, 2003), 296.

6 This is Aristotle's view on the function of aesthetic emotions as found in his *Poetics*, a "cleansing away" of excessive negative emotions in order to reduce them to a healthy balance. Cf. chapter 1, endnote 7.

7 Perhaps it could also be said that *Elephant* prevents any identification with the victims, because the crime it depicts is so brutal and shocking that we "no longer think primarily of the victim but of the crime itself, of nature or of whatever it is in human nature in general that makes such acts possible." Fisher, *Vehement Passions*, 135.

8 There is an obvious comparison to be made with Michael Moore's *Bowling for Columbine* (2002). This documentary film not only attributes responsibility for both the Columbine tragedy and the general nature of violence in the United States to the American school system that does not respond to the real needs of the students, but also to the widespread availability of weapons, to the American love affair with guns, to the culture of fear created by the media, to poverty, to K-Mart, and to Charlton Heston, among other things. Therefore, although provocative, Moore's documentary seems eager to externalize the blame and to evoke self-righteous anger. In contrast to such self-righteous anger, justified anger always involves responsibility of the self, a responsibility that needs the double focalization of *Elephant*, which is predominantly lacking in *Bowling for Columbine*.

9 David Hume, *A Treatise of Human Nature*, ed. David Fate Norton and Mary J. Norton (Oxford: Oxford University Press, 2001), 250–2.

10 Nussbaum, *Upheavals of Thought*, 334.

11 Fisher, *Vehement Passions*, 15.

12 Jon Elster, *Alchemies of the Mind: Rationality and the Emotions* (Cambridge: Cambridge University Press, 1999), 143.

13 Axel Honneth, "Personal Identity and Disrespect," in *The New Social Theory Reader*, ed. Steven Seidman and Jeffrey C. Alexander (London: Routledge, 2001), 39.

14 See Murray Smith's discussion on the relation between character alignment and focalization in *Engaging Characters*, 145–6.

15 Incidentally, *Elephant* derives its title from another short film about the Troubles, a short film directed by Alan Clarke and released in 1989, by which Gus Van Sant was stylistically inspired.

16 Carl Plantinga, "Disgusted at the Movies," *Film Studies* 8 (2006): 86.

17 Julian Hanich, "Dis/liking Disgust: The Revulsion Experience at the Movies," *New Review of Film and Television Studies* 3 (2009): 306.

18 Chion, *Audio-Vision*, 129. This is a function that is not normally attributed to a female voice. As Kaja Silverman points out, especially in classical Hollywood

cinema there are hardly any female voices in the form of *acousmêtre*, with the exception of the voice of "monstrous feminine" (such as the voice of the mother in Hitchcock's *Psycho* (1960). Silverman, *The Acoustic Mirror*, 50.

19 Isaiah Berlin, *Liberty*, ed. Henry Hardy (Oxford: Oxford University Press, 2002), 36–8.

20 Marco Abel, *Violent Affect: Literature, Cinema, and Critique after Representation* (Lincoln: University of Nebraska Press, 2007), 11.

21 Abel, *Violent Affect*, 10.

22 Sara Ahmed, *The Cultural Politics of Emotion* (New York: Routledge 2004), 50.

23 See, for instance, Kaja Silverman, "Fragments of a Fashionable Discourse," in *Studies in Entertainment: Critical Approaches to Mass Culture*, ed. Tania Modleski (Bloomington: Indiana University Press, 1986), 139–54.

24 Gerard A. Hauser, "Body Rhetoric: Conflicted Reporting of Bodies in Pain," in *Deliberation, Democracy and the Media*, ed. Simone Chambers and Anne N. Costain (Lanham: Rowman & Littlefield, 2000), 138.

25 Chris Yuill, "The Body as Weapon: Bobby Sands and the Republican Hunger Strikes," *Sociological Research Online* 2 (2007), accessed June 11, 2009, http://www.socresonline.org.uk/.

26 See also Laine, *Shame and Desire*, 77.

27 See also the discussion in Chapter 2 on morality and character alignment.

28 Michel Foucault, *Discipline and Punish: The Birth of a Prison*, trans. Alan Sheridan (New York: Random House, 1995), 300.

29 Friedrich Nietzsche, *On the Geneaology of Morality*, trans. Maudemarie Clark and Alan J. Swensen (Indianapolis: Hackett, 1998).

30 Constantin Parvulescu, "The Cold World behind the Window: *4 Months, 3 Weeks & 2 Days* and Romanian Cinema's Return to Real-existing Communism," *Jump Cut: A Review of Contemporary Media* 51 (2009), accessed August 1, 2009, http://www.ejumpcut.org.

31 Thomas Elsaesser, "Pohjalla: Aki Kaurismäki ja abjekti subjekti," trans. Antti Autio, *Lähikuva* 2 (2010): 7–27.

32 Parvulescu, "The Cold World behind the Window." Yet the film's opening shot of two goldfish in a tiny, bare aquarium is also a sign of entrapment. For even though the dorm is a "safe zone" for Otilia and Gabita, it simultaneously "isolates" them from all other spaces where they constantly have to monitor their own behavior.

33 Kristeva, *Powers of Horror*, 3.

34 Thomas Elsaesser, "Was wäre, wenn du schon tot bist? Vom 'postmodernen' zum 'post-mortem'-Kino am Beispiel von Christopher Nolans *Memento*," in *Zeitsprünge: Wie Filme Geschichte(n) erzählen*, ed. Christine Rüffert et al. (Berlin: Bertz, 2004), 115–25.

35 Robert Solomon, *The Passions: Emotions and the Meaning of Life* (Indianapolis: Hackett, 1993), 44–5.

36 Solomon, *Passions*, 164.

37 Fisher, *Vehement Passions*, 144.

38 Solomon, *Passions*, 129.

39 Manning, *The Politics of Touch*, 47.

40 Nussbaum, *Upheavals of Thought*, 390.

Chapter 7

1   By affective reciprocity I mean a "method" of loving the other that avoids a desire for shared identity and mutual control, which enables the individual to love exclusively without loss of self and without a desire to obliterate the freedom of the loved one. See, for instance, Deborah Brown, "The Right Method of Boy-Loving," in *Love Analyzed*, ed. Roger E. Lamb (Boulder: Westview Press, 1997), 49–63.

2   Malte Hagener and Marijke de Valck, "Cinephilia in Transition," in *Mind the Screen: Media Concepts According to Thomas Elsaesser*, ed. Jaap Kooijman, Patricia Pisters, and Wanda Strauven (Amsterdam: Amsterdam University Press, 2008), 19.

3   Christian Keathley, *Cinephilia and History, or The Wind in the Trees* (Bloomington: Indiana University Press, 2005), 8.

4   Ronald de Sousa, "Love as Theatre," in *The Philosophy of Erotic Love*, ed. Robert C. Solomon and Kathleen M. Higgins (Lawrence: University Press of Kansas, 1991), 477–91.

5   Maurice Merleau-Ponty, *Phenomenology of Perception*, trans. Colin Smith (London: Routledge, 1962), 337. This being-in-the-world, this "style" of people, is what we love when we truly fall in love, their spirit, their manner of gesturing, their use of language, and their relationship with the world in general. It is not, say, their "properties" as is often suggested. Martha Nussbaum, too, defines false love as love in which someone takes an excessive interest in properties that are not worthy objects of true love—money, status, physical pleasure. This harms true love for people, who are worthy of love for what they are, instead of what properties they have. Nussbaum, *Upheavals of Thought*, 573–4.

6   Mazis, *Earthbodies*, 97.

7   Luhmann, *Love as Passion*, 119.

8   Robert Nozick, "Love's Bond," in *The Philosophy of Erotic Love*, ed. Robert C. Solomon and Kathleen M. Higgins (Lawrence: University Press of Kansas, 1991), 64.

9   For Jesse Prinz emotions contain valence markers, functioning as positive or negative "inner reinforcers" which "underwrite our implicit beliefs about the organization of emotion space." Jesse J. Prinz, *Gut Reactions: A Perceptual Theory of Emotion* (Oxford: Oxford University Press, 2004), 161.

10 Tomkins, *Exploring Affect*, 75–80.

11 Simone de Beauvoir, *The Second Sex*, trans. H. M. Parshley (New York: Vintage, 1989), 402.

12 Nancy, "Responding to Existence," 298.

13 Jean-Luc Nancy, "Shattered Love," trans. Lisa Garbus and Simona Sawhney, in *A Finite Thinking*, ed. Simon Sparks (Stanford: Stanford University Press, 2003), 265.

14 Torben Kragh Grodal, "Art Film, the Transient Body, and the Permanent Soul," *Aura* 3 (2000): 44. Transient meanings, according to Grodal, are the result of our concrete, basic, and embodied interaction with the world, and they evoke "tense" emotions that are based on action tendencies, such as sadness. Permanent meanings are the result of a higher and more abstract,

transcendent, and disembodied experience of the world. They evoke "saturated" emotions that are experienced simultaneously as subjective and as an
expression of some eternal and spiritual meaning, such as nostalgia. Thus,
transient meanings are considered embodied, because they evoke emotions
that have an outlet through action, such as crying. By contrast, permanent
meanings are transcendent because there is no conventional release for them.
According to Grodal art cinema can activate "higher" meanings that prefigure
some "eternal truth of human existence." Grodal, "Art Film," 44–6.

[15] This is a central argument in Laura Mulvey's polemical essay. She notes that,
since a woman connotes a lack of penis, she implies "a threat of castration and
hence unpleasure." Laura Mulvey, "Visual Pleasure and Narrative Cinema,"
Screen 3 (1975), 13. In her view traditional Hollywood cinema deals with this
problem through strategies of fetishization and voyeuristic male scopophilia,
of which the latter is by necessity sadistic, since it implies exercising dominance
over the female without consent. By contrast, if the representational structure of pornography is not based on identification, but on a more detached
form of viewing (Allen, *Projecting Illusion*, 130–1), this poses the question as to
what extent both female *and* male characters in porn function as "objects-to-
be-looked-at" for both male and female spectators. Furthermore, as Gertrud
Koch and many others have noted, the "carnal pleasure of looking" at erotic
action is not only a common pleasure among men, but also for many women,
not necessarily identifying with being a masochistic object for the male gaze.
Gertrud Koch, "The Body's Shadow Realm," in *Dirty Looks: Women, Pornography,
Power*, ed. Pamela Church Gibson and Roma Gibson (London: British Film
Institute, 1993), 22–45. Moreover, in many porn films women appear as desir-
ing subjects, instead of submissive objects, and this female demand for sexual
pleasure could be considered one of the positive potentials of pornography.
As Linda Williams points out: "pornography is perhaps one of the few popular
genres in which women are not punished for knowing, pursuing, and finding
their pleasure." Linda Williams, *Hard Core: Power, Pleasure and the Frenzy of the
Visible* (London: Pandora Press, 1990), 260.

[16] Williams, *Hard Core*, 116–18. In Freudian thinking the process of disavowal is
a male defense mechanism against castration anxiety provoked by the female
lack of penis. Given that the male implicitly believes that both sexes possess
penises, Freud argues that the male creates a fetish as a replacement for the
missing female penis, which allows him to deny the threat of castration. In
film studies Christian Metz suggested that perception of the cinematic image
is equivalent to the spectacle of a phallic lack that confronts the male child.
Christian Metz, *The Imaginary Signifier: Psychoanalysis and the Cinema*, trans.
Celia Britton et al. (Bloomington: Indiana University Press, 1982). Laura
Mulvey, too, recognizes fetishism by means of close-ups and other filmic techniques as a problem-solving strategy of classical cinema to deny castration
anxiety of which the female appearance on screen reminds the male viewers.
Mulvey, "Visual Pleasure and Narrative Cinema."

[17] Anne Gillain, "Profile of a Filmmaker: Catherine Breillat," in *Beyond French
Feminisms: Debates on Women, Politics and Culture in France, 1981–2001*, ed. Roger
Célestin, Eliane DalMolin, and Isabelle de Courtivron (New York: Macmillan,
2003), 202.

18 Sartre, *Being and Nothingness*, 770–84.

19 Kristeva, *Powers of Horror*, 1.

20 Creed, *The Monstrous-Feminine*, 17.

21 Søren Kierkegaard, *The Concept of Irony*, ed. and trans. Howard V. Hong and Edna H. Hong (New Jersey: Princeton University Press, 1989), 26.

22 Toni Morrison, *The Bluest Eye* (London: Vintage, 2007), 122.

23 Robert Nozick, *The Examined Life: Philosophical Meditations* (New York: Touchstone, 1989), 62.

24 Richard Rorty, *Contingency, Irony, and Solidarity* (Cambridge: Cambridge University Press, 1989), xv.

25 Nozick, "Love's Bond," 424.

26 Ronald de Sousa, *The Rationality of Emotion* (Cambridge: The MIT Press, 1987), 97–100.

27 Steven Shaviro, "Emotion Capture: Affect in Digital Film," *Projections: The Journal for Movies and Mind* 2 (2007): 78.

28 As quoted in Lawrence Langer, *Holocaust Testimonies: The Ruins of Memory* (New Haven: Yale University Press, 1991), 7.

29 Perhaps it could even be said that it is often, though not always, easier to fall in love, than it is to fall out of love. Ronald de Sousa writes for instance: "So we may expect great difficulty in trying to get rid of an unwanted emotion, but more success in working ourselves *into* one. [. . .] It does me no good to tell myself how foolish I am to miss her: for the thought is an enemy agent, as it were, calculated to fix my thoughts on just what I should forget. I should forget her smile, her eyes, her perfect breasts . . . The best course is to fall in love with someone else: 'it'll take my mind off her.' Or failing that, to hate her: directing my attention onto her betrayal, her levity, her heartlessness . . ." De Sousa, "The Rationality of Emotions," 141.

30 Shaviro, "Emotion Capture," 81.

31 De Beauvoir, *The Second Sex*, 654.

32 This phrase is from Luce Irigaray's *i love to you*. She considers recognition a condition for (authentic) love: "I recognize you goes hand in hand with: you are irreducible to me, just as I am to you. We may not be substituted for one another." This is why Irigaray insists on saying "I love *to* you" rather than "I love you", as the "to" adds the agential intentionality between "I" and "you" that is missing in the traditional formula, which sounds as if one's love can assimilate the other. Luce Irigaray, *i love to you* (New York: Routledge, 1996), 103.

33 Lehrer, "Love and Autonomy," 114.

34 Joyce J. Schuld, *Foucault and Augustine: Reconsidering Power and Love* (Notre Dame: University of Notre Dame Press, 2003), 33.

35 Kathryn Pauly Morgan, "Romantic Love, Altruism, and Self-respect," in *The Philosophy of (Erotic) Love*, ed. Robert C. Solomon and Kathleen M. Higgins (Lawrence: University of Kansas Press, 1991), 393.

36 Irving Singer, *The Nature of Love Vol. 1: Plato to Luther* (Chicago: University of Chicago Press, 1966).

37 Silverman, *The Threshold of the Visible World*, 78.

38 Janice A. Radway, *Reading the Romance: Women, Patriarchy and Popular Literature* (Chapel Hill: University of North Carolina Press, 1991).

Bibliography

Abel, Marco. *Violent Affect: Literature, Cinema, and Critique after Representation.* Lincoln: University of Nebraska Press, 2007.

Ahmed, Sara. *The Cultural Politics of Emotion.* New York: Routledge, 2004.

Allen, R. T. "The Reality of Responses to Fiction." *British Journal of Aesthetics* 1 (1968): 64–8.

Allen, Richard. *Projecting Illusion: Film Spectatorship and the Impression of Reality.* Cambridge: Cambridge University Press, 1995.

Alphen, Ernst van. "Symptoms of Discursivity: Experience, Memory and Trauma." In *Acts of Memory: Cultural Recall in the Present,* edited by Mieke Bal, Jonathan Crewe, and Leo Spitzer, 24–38. Hanover: University Press of New England, 1999.

Altman, Rick. "Cinema as Event." In *Sound Theory, Sound Practice,* edited by Rick Altman, 1–14. London: Routledge, 1992.

—. "The Material Heterogeneity of Recorded Sound." In *Sound Theory, Sound Practice,* edited by Rick Altman, 15–34. London: Routledge, 1992.

—. *Film/Genre.* London: British Film Institute, 1999.

Anderson, Eric. "Inclusive Masculinity in a Fraternal Setting." *Men and Masculinities* 5 (2008): 604–20.

Anzieu, Didier. *The Skin Ego.* Translated by Chris Turner. New Haven: Yale University Press, 1989.

Bakhtin, M. M. *Speech Genres and Other Late Essays.* Translated by Vern W. McGee, edited by Caryl Emerson and Michael Holquist. Austin: University of Texas Press, 1986.

Balkwill, Laura-Lee, William Forde Thompson, and Rie Matsunaga. "Recognition of Emotion in Japanese, Western, and Hindustani Music by Japanese Listeners." *Japanese Psychological Research* 4 (2004): 337–49.

Barad, Karen. *Meeting the Universe Halfway: Quantum Physics and the Entanglement of Matter and Meaning.* Durham: Duke University Press, 2007.

Barker, Jennifer M. *The Tactile Eye: Touch and the Cinematic Experience.* Berkeley: University of California Press, 2009.

Barthes, Roland. *A Lover's Discourse: Fragments.* Translated by Richard Howard. New York: Hill and Wand, 2001.

Baumgarten, Elias. "Curiosity as a Moral Virtue." *International Journal of Applied Philosophy* 22 (2001): 169–84.

Beauvoir, Simone de. *The Second Sex.* Translated by H. M. Parshley. New York: Vintage, 1989.

Benin, David and Lisa Cartwright. "Shame, Empathy and Looking Practices: Lessons from a Disability Studies Classroom." *Journal of Visual Culture* 2 (2006): 155–71.

Bennett, Jill. *Empathic Vision: Affect, Trauma, and Contemporary Art.* Stanford: Stanford University Press.

Berlin, Isaiah. *Liberty,* edited by Henry Hardy. Oxford: Oxford University Press, 2002.

Bersani, Leo and Ulysse Dutoit. *Forms of Being: Cinema, Aesthetics, Subjectivity.* London: British Film Institute, 2004.

Björkman, Stig, Torsten Manns, and Jonas Sima. *Bergman on Bergman: Interviews with Ingmar Bergman.* Translated by Paul Britten Austin. New York: Da Capo Press, 1993.

Blassnigg, Martha. "Clairvoyance, Cinema, and Consciousness." In *Screen Consciousness: Cinema, Mind and World,* edited by Robert Pepperell and Michael Punt, 105–22. Amsterdam: Rodopi, 2006.

Bordwell, David and Kristin Thompson. *Film Art: An Introduction.* New York: McGraw-Hill, 2001.

Brennan, Teresa. *The Transmission of Affect.* Ithaca: Cornell University Press, 2004.

Brophy, Philip. *100 Modern Soundtracks.* London: British Film Institute, 2004.

Brown, Deborah. "The Right Method of Boy-Loving." In *Love Analyzed,* edited by Roger E. Lamb, 49–63. Boulder: Westview Press, 1997.

Buber, Martin. *The Knowledge of Man.* Translated by Ronald Gregor Smith and Maurice Friedman. New York: Harper & Row, 1965.

Budd, Malcolm. *Music and the Emotions.* London: Routledge, 1985.

Carroll, Noël. *The Philosophy of Horror; or, Paradoxes of the Heart.* New York: Routledge, 1990.

—. *A Philosophy of Mass Art.* Oxford: Oxford University Press, 1998.

—. "Film, Emotion and Genre." In *Passionate Views: Film, Cognition, and Emotion,* edited by Carl Plantinga and Greg M. Smith, 21–47. Baltimore: Johns Hopkins University Press, 1999.

Cartwright, Lisa. *Moral Spectatorship: Technologies of Voice and Affect in Postwar Representations of the Child.* Durham: Duke University Press, 2008.

Casetti, Francesco. *Eye of the Century: Film, Experience, Modernity.* Translated by Erin Larkin with Jennifer Pranolo. New York: Columbia University Press, 2005.

Chion, Michel. *Audio-Vision: Sound on Screen.* Edited and translated by Claudia Gorbman. New York: Columbia University Press, 1994.

Chismar, Douglas. "Empathy and Sympathy: The Important Difference." *Journal of Value Inquiry* 22 (1988): 257–66.

Connor, Steven. *The Book of Skin.* London: Reaktion Books, 2004.

Cope, Wendy. *Serious Concerns.* London: Faber and Faber, 1992.

Creed, Barbara. *The Monstrous-Feminine: Film, Feminism, Psychoanalysis.* New York: Routledge, 1993.

Crimp, Douglas. "Mario Montez, for Shame." In *Regarding Sedgwick: Essays on Queer Culture and Critical Theory,* edited by Stephen M. Barber and David L. Clark, 57–70. New York: Routledge, 2002.

Culbertson, Roberta. "Embodied Memory, Transcendence, and Telling: Recounting Trauma, Re-establishing the Self." *New Literary History* 1 (1995): 169–95.

Cytowic, Richard. "Synesthesia Encyclopaedia." In *Encyclopaedia of Neuroscience* CD-ROM, edited by George Adelman and Barry H. Smith. Amsterdam: Elsevier, 2004.

Bibliography

Dadlez, E. M. *What's Hecuba to Him: Fictional Events and Actual Emotions.* University Park: Penn State University Press, 1997.

Damasio, Antonio. *The Feeling of What Happens: Body and Emotion in the Making of Consciousness.* San Diego: Harcourt, 1999.

Deleuze, Gilles. *Cinema 2: The Time-Image.* Translated by Hugh Tomlinson and Robert Galeta. London: Athlone Press, 1989.

Dolar, Mladen. "Hitchcock's Objects." In *Everything You Always Wanted to Know about Lacan, but Were Afraid to Ask Hitchcock,* edited by Slavoj Zizek, 31–46. London: Verso 1992.

Dufrenne, Mikel. *Phenomenology of Aesthetic Experience.* Translated by Edward S. Casey. Chicago: Northwestern University Press, 1989.

Eisenstein, Sergey M. *Film Form: Essays in Film Theory.* Translated by Jay Leyda. New York: Meridian Books, 1957.

Eliot, T. S. *Collected Poems 1909–1962.* London: Faber and Faber, 1963.

Elsaesser, Thomas. "Tales of Sound and Fury: Observations on the Family Melodrama." In *Home Is Where the Heart Is: Studies in Melodrama and the Woman's Film,* edited by Christine Gledhill, 43–69. London: British Film Institute, 1987.

—. "Was wäre, wenn du schon tot bist? Vom 'postmodernen' zum 'post-mortem'-Kino am Beispiel von Christopher Nolans *Memento.*" In *Zeitsprünge: Wie Filme Geschichte(n) erzählen,* edited by Christine Rüffert, Irmbert Schenk, Karl-Heinz Schmid, and Alfred Twes, 115–25. Berlin: Bertz, 2004.

—. "Pohjalla: Aki Kaurismäki ja abjekti subjecti." Translated by Antti Autio. *Lähikuva* 2 (2010): 7–27.

Elsaesser, Thomas and Malte Hagener. *Film Theory: An Introduction through the Senses.* New York: Routledge, 2010.

Elster, Jon. *Alchemies of the Mind: Rationality and the Emotions.* Cambridge: Cambridge University Press, 1999.

Epstein, Jean. "The Senses." Translated by Tom Milne. In *French Film Theory and Criticism 1907–1939,* edited by Richard Abel, 241–6. Princeton: Princeton University Press, 1993.

Faludi, Susan. *Stiffed: The Betrayal of the American Man.* New York: Perennial, 2000.

Fischer, Lucy. "Beauty and the Beast: Desire and its Double in *Repulsion.*" In *The Cinema of Roman Polanski: Dark Spaces of the World,* edited by John Orr and Elzbieta Ostrowska, 76–91. London: Wallflower Press, 2006.

Fisher, Philip. *The Vehement Passions.* Princeton: Princeton University Press, 2002.

Forceville, Charles. "The Conspiracy in *The Comfort of Strangers:* Narration in the Novel and the Film." *Language and Literature* 2 (2002): 119–35.

Foucault, Michel. *Discipline and Punish: The Birth of a Prison.* Translated by Alan Sheridan. New York: Random House, 1995.

Frampton, Daniel. *Filmosophy: A Manifesto for a Radically New Way of Understanding Cinema.* London: Wallflower Press, 2006.

Freeman, Cynthia. "The Sublime in Cinema." In *Passionate Views: Film, Cognition, and Emotion,* edited by Carl Plantinga and Greg M. Smith, 65–83. Baltimore: Johns Hopkins University Press, 1999.

Gabrielsson, Alf and Patrik N. Juslin. "Emotional Expression in Music Performance: Between the Performer's Intention and the Listener's Experience." *Psychology of Music* 1 (1996): 68–91.

Gallese, Vittorio. "The 'Shared Manifold' Hypothesis: From Mirror Neurons to Empathy." *Journal of Consciousness Studies* 5–7 (2001): 33–50.

Gaut, Berys. "Identification and Emotion in Narrative Film." In *Passionate Views: Film, Cognition, and Emotion*, edited by Carl Plantinga and Greg M. Smith, 200–16. Baltimore: Johns Hopkins University Press, 1999.

Gillain, Anne. "Profile of a Filmmaker: Catherine Breillat." In *Beyond French Feminisms: Debates on Women, Politics and Culture in France 1981–2001*, edited by Roger Célestin, Eliane DalMolin, and Isabelle de Courtivron, 201–11. New York: Macmillan, 2003.

Goscilo, Helena. "Polanski's Existential Body—As Somebody, Nobody and Anybody." In *The Cinema of Roman Polanski: Dark Spaces of the World*, edited by John Orr and Elzbieta Ostrowska, 22–37. London: Wallflower Press, 2006.

Grodal, Torben. *Moving Pictures: A New Theory of Film Genres, Feelings and Cognitions.* Oxford: Oxford University Press, 1997.

—. "Art Film, the Transient Body, and the Permanent Soul." *Aura* 3 (2000): 33–56.

Hagener, Malte and Marijke de Valck. "Cinephilia in Transition." In *Mind the Screen: Media Concepts According to Thomas Elsaesser*, edited by Jaap Kooijman, Patricia Pisters, and Wanda Strauven, 19–31. Amsterdam: Amsterdam University Press, 2008.

Hallie, Philip. *Tales of Good and Evil, Help and Harm.* New York: HarperCollins, 1998.

Hanich, Julian. "Dis/liking Disgust: The Revulsion Experience at the Movies." *New Review of Film and Television Studies* 3 (2009): 293–310.

Hanslick, Eduard. *The Beautiful in Music.* Translated by Gustav Cohen. Indianapolis: Bobbs-Merrill, 1957.

Harbord, Janet. *The Evolution of Film: Rethinking Film Studies.* Cambridge: Polity, 2007.

Hartz, Glenn. "How We Can Be Moved by Anna Karenina, Green Slime, and a Red Pony." *Philosophy* 74 (1999): 557–78.

Hauser, Gerard A. "Body Rhetoric: Conflicted Reporting of Bodies in Pain." In *Deliberation, Democracy and the Media*, edited by Simone Chambers and Anne N. Costain, 135–54. Lanham: Rowman & Littlefield, 2000.

Hitchcock, Alfred. *Hitchcock on Hitchcock: Selected Writings and Interviews*, edited by Sidney Gottlieb. Berkeley: University of California Press, 1995.

Homaday, Ann. "Kazakh Zingers." *Washington Post*, November 3, 2006. Accessed May 27, 2009. http://www.washingtonpost.com/wp-dyn/content/article/2006/11/02/AR2006110201876.html.

Honneth, Axel. "Personal Identity and Disrespect." In *The New Social Theory Reader*, edited by Steven Seidman and Jeffrey C. Alexander, 39–45. London: Routledge, 2001.

Hume, David. *A Treatise of Human Nature*, edited by David Fate Norton and Mary J. Norton. Oxford: Oxford University Press, 2001.

—. *The Philosophical Works of David Hume. Vol. 3.* Boston: Elibron, 2007.

Ilie, Gabriela and William Forde Thompson. "A Comparison of Acoustic Cues in Music and Speech for Three Dimensions of Affect." *Music Perception* 4 (2006): 319–30.

Illouz, Eva. *Cold Intimacies: The Making of Emotional Capitalism.* Cambridge: Polity Press, 2007.

Irigaray, Luce. *i love to you.* New York: Routledge, 1996.

Kaplan, E. Ann. *Trauma Culture: The Politics of Terror and Loss in Media and Literature.* New Brunswick: Rutgers University Press, 2005.

Katz, Jack. *How Emotions Work.* Chicago: The University of Chicago Press, 1999.

Keathley, Christian. *Cinephilia and History, or The Wind in the Trees.* Bloomington: Indiana University Press, 2005.

Kemper, Theodore D. "Social Relations and Emotions: A Structural Approach." In *Research Agendas in the Sociology of Emotions,* edited by Theodore D. Kemper, 207–37. New York: SUNY Press, 1990.

Kierkegaard, Søren. *The Concept of Irony.* Edited and translated by Howard V. Hong and Edna H. Hong. New Jersey: Princeton University Press, 1989.

Kivy, Peter. *Sound Sentiment: An Essay on the Musical Emotions.* Philadelphia: Temple University Press, 1989.

Koch, Gertrud. "The Body's Shadow Realm." In *Dirty Looks: Women, Pornography, Power,* edited by Pamela Church Gibson and Roma Gibson, 22–45. London: British Film Institute, 1993.

Kolnai, Aurel. *On Disgust,* edited by Carolyn Korsmeyer and Barry Smith. Translated by Elizabeth Kolnai. Chicago: Open Court, 2004.

Kracauer, Siegfried. *The Theory of Film: The Redemption of Physical Reality.* Princeton: Princeton University Press, 1997.

Kristeva, Julia. *Powers of Horror: An Essay on Abjection.* Translated by Leon S. Roudiez. New York: Columbia University Press, 1982.

—. *Black Sun: Depression and Melancholia.* Translated by Leon S. Roudiez. New York: Columbia University Press, 1992.

Kundera, Milan. *The Unbearable Lightness of Being.* Translated by Michael Henry Heim. New York: Harper and Row, 1984.

Lacoue-Labarthe, Philippe. "The Echo of the Subject." In *Typography: Mimesis, Philosophy, Politics,* edited by Christopher Fynsk, 139–207. Stanford: Stanford University Press, 1998.

Laine, Tarja. "Empathy, Sympathy, and the Philosophy of Horror in Kubrick's *The Shining.*" *Film and Philosophy* (2001): 72–88.

—. *Shame and Desire: Emotion, Intersubjectivity, Cinema.* Brussels: Peter Lang, 2007.

Langer, Lawrence. *Holocaust Testimonies: The Ruins of Memory.* New Haven: Yale University Press, 1991.

Langer, Susanne. *Philosophy in a New Key: A Study in the Symbolism of Reason, Rite, and Art.* Cambridge: Harvard University Press, 1957.

Lehrer, Keith. "Love and Autonomy." In *Love Analyzed,* edited by Roger E. Lamb, 107–21. Boulder, Colorado: Westview Press, 1991.

Lewis, Michael. *Shame: The Exposed Self.* New York: Free Press, 1995.

Leys, Ruth. *From Guilt to Shame: Auschwitz and After.* Princeton: Princeton University Press, 2007.

Lourens, Saskia. "Writing History: National Identity in André Brink's Post-Apartheid Fiction." PhD diss., University of Amsterdam, 2009.

Luhmann, Niklas. *Love as Passion: The Codification of Intimacy.* Translated by Jeremy Gaines and Doris Jones. Stanford: Stanford University Press, 1988.

MacDougall, David. *The Corporeal Image: Film, Ethnography and the Senses.* Princeton: Princeton University Press, 2006.

Manning, Erin. *Politics of Touch: Sense, Movement, Sovereignty.* Minneapolis: University of Minnesota Press, 2007.

Massumi, Brian. *Parables for the Virtual: Movement, Affect, Sensation.* Durham: Duke University Press, 2002.

Mazis, Glen A. *Earthbodies: Rediscovering Our Planetary Senses.* Albany: State University of New York Press, 2002.

McMillan, Brian. "Complicitous Critique: *Dancer in the Dark* as Postmodern Musical." *Discourses in Music* 2 (2004). Accessed October 17, 2010. http://www.discourses.ca.

Merleau-Ponty, Maurice. *Phenomenology of Perception.* Translated by Colin Smith. London: Routledge, 1962.

Metz, Christian. "Aural Objects." Translated by Georgia Gurrieri. *Yale French Studies* 60 (1980): 24–32.

—. *The Imaginary Signifier: Psychoanalysis and the Cinema.* Translated by Celia Britton, Annwyl Williams, Ben Brewster, and Alfred Guzzetti. Bloomington: Indiana University Press, 1986.

Miller, William Ian. *Humiliation; And Other Essays on Honor, Social Discomfort, and Violence.* Ithaca: Cornell University Press, 1993.

Morgan, Kathryn Pauly. "Romantic Love, Altruism, and Self-respect." In *The Philosophy of (Erotic) Love*, edited by Robert C. Solomon and Kathleen M. Higgins, 391–409. Lawrence: University of Kansas Press, 1991.

Morin, Edgar. *The Cinema, or the Imaginary Man.* Translated by Lorraine Mortimer. Minneapolis: University of Minnesota Press, 2005.

Morrison, Toni. *The Bluest Eye.* London: Vintage, 2007.

Mulvey, Laura. "Visual Pleasure and Narrative Cinema." *Screen* 3 (1975): 6–18.

Münsterberg, Hugo. *Hugo Münsterberg on Film: The Photoplay: A Psychological Study and Other Writings*, edited by Allan Langdale. New York: Routledge, 2001.

Murakami, Haruki. *After Dark.* Translated by Jay Rubin. London: Vintage, 2008.

Nancy, Jean-Luc. *The Birth to Presence.* Translated by Brian Holmes and others. Stanford: Stanford University Press, 1994.

—. *Being Singular Plural.* Translated by Robert D. Richardson and Anne E. O'Byrne. Stanford: Stanford University Press, 2000.

—. "Responding to Existence." Translated by Sara Guyer. In *A Finite Thinking*, edited by Simon Sparks, 289–99. Stanford: Stanford University Press, 2003.

—. "Shattered Love." Translated by Lisa Garbus and Simona Sawhney. In *A Finite Thinking*, edited by Simon Sparks, 245–74. Stanford: Stanford University Press, 2003.

—. *Listening.* Translated by Charlotte Mandell. New York: Fordham University Press, 2007.

Neale, Steve. "Melodrama and Tears." *Screen* 6 (1986): 6–22.

Ngai, Sianne. *Ugly Feelings*. Cambridge: Harvard University Press, 2005.

Nietzsche, Friedrich W. *On the Geneaology of Morality*. Translated by Maudemarie Clark and Alan J. Swensen. Indianapolis: Hackett, 1998.

—. *The Antichrist*. Translated by Anthony M. Ludovici. New York: Prometheus, 2000.

Nozick, Robert. *The Examined Life: Philosophical Meditations*. New York: Touchstone, 1989.

—. "Love's Bond." In *The Philosophy of Erotic Love*, edited by Robert C. Solomon and Kathleen M. Higgins, 417–32. Lawrence: University Press of Kansas, 1991.

Nussbaum, Martha C. *The Fragility of Goodness: Luck and Ethics in Greek Tragedy and Philosophy*. Cambridge: Cambridge University Press, 1986.

—. *Upheavals of Thought: The Intelligence of Emotions*. Cambridge: Cambridge University Press, 2001.

Parvulescu, Constantin. "The Cold World behind the Window: *4 Months, 3 Weeks & 2 Days* and Romanian Cinema's Return to Real-existing Communism." *Jump Cut: A Review of Contemporary Media* 51 (2009). Accessed August 1, 2009. http://www.ejumpcut.org.

Perez, Gilberto. *The Material Ghost: Films and Their Medium*. Baltimore: Johns Hopkins University Press, 1998.

Peucker, Brigitte. *The Material Image: Art and the Real in Film*. Stanford: Stanford University Press, 2007.

Plantinga, Carl. "Disgusted at the Movies." *Film Studies* 8 (2006): 81–92.

Prinz, Jesse J. *Gut Reactions: A Perceptual Theory of Emotion*. Oxford: Oxford University Press, 2004.

Pugmire, David. *Rediscovering Emotion*. Edinburgh: Edinburgh University Press, 1998.

Radford, Colin. "How Can We Be Moved by the Fate of Anna Karenina?" *Proceedings of the Aristotelian Society* 49 (1975): 67–80.

—. "Emotions and Music: A Reply to the Cognitivists." *The Journal of Aesthetics and Art Criticism* 1 (1989): 69–76.

Radway, Janice. *Reading the Romance: Women, Patriarchy and Popular Literature*. Chapel Hill: University of North Carolina Press, 1991.

Ranciére, Jacques. *The Emancipated Spectator*. Translated by Gregory Elliott. London: Verso, 2009.

Robinson, Jenefer. *Deeper than Reason: Emotion and its Role in Literature, Music, and Art*. Oxford: Oxford University Press, 2007.

Rorty, Richard. *Contingency, Irony, and Solidarity*. Cambridge: Cambridge University Press, 1989.

Rosolato, Guy. "The Voice: Between Body and Language." In *Voices*, edited by Christopher Phillips, 75–94. Rotterdam: Witte de With, 1998.

Sartre, Jean-Paul. *Critique of Dialectical Reason Volume I: The Theory of Practical Ensembles*. Translated by Alan Sheridan-Smith. London: Verso, 1982.

—. *Being and Nothingness: A Phenomenological Essay on Ontology*. Translated by Hazel E. Barnes. New York: Washington Square Press, 1992.

Schaper, Eva. "Fiction and the Suspension of Disbelief." *British Journal of Aesthetics* 18 (1978): 31–44.

Schatz, Thomas. *Hollywood Genres: Formulas, Filmmaking and the Studio System.* Philadelphia: Temple University Press, 1981.

Schubert, Emery. "Measuring Emotion Continuously: Validity and Reliability of the Two-dimensional Emotion Space." *Australian Journal of Psychology* 3 (1999): 154–65.

Schuld, Joyce J. *Foucault and Augustine: Reconsidering Power and Love.* Notre Dame: University of Notre Dame Press, 2003.

Schusterman, Richard. "Aesthetic Experience: From Analysis to Eros." *The Journal of Aesthetics and Art Criticism* 2 (2006): 217–29.

Scott, A. O. "Universe Without Happy Endings." *New York Times*, September 22, 2000. Accessed February 19, 2010. http://movies.nytimes.com/movie/review?res=9B04E3D6103BF931A1575AC0A9669C8B63.

Sedgwick, Eve Kosofsky. *Touching Feeling: Affect, Pedagogy, Performativity.* Durham: Duke University Press, 2003.

Serres, Michel. *The Five Senses: A Philosophy of Mingled Bodies.* Translated by Margaret Sankey and Peter Cowley. London: Continuum, 2008.

Shaviro, Steven. "Emotion Capture: Affect in Digital Film." *Projections: The Journal for Movies and Mind* 2 (2007): 63–82.

Shaw, Daniel. *Film and Philosophy: Taking Movies Seriously.* London: Wallflower Press, 2008.

Silverman, Kaja. "Fragments of a Fashionable Discourse." In *Studies in Entertainment: Critical Approaches to Mass Culture,* edited by Tania Modleski, 139–54. Bloomington: Indiana University Press, 1986.

—. *The Acoustic Mirror: The Female Voice in Psychoanalysis and Cinema.* Bloomington: Indiana University Press, 1988.

—. *The Threshold of the Visible World.* New York: Routledge, 1996.

Singer, Irving. *The Nature of Love Vol. 1: Plato to Luther.* Chicago: University of Chicago Press, 1966.

—. *Three Philosophical Filmmakers: Hitchcock, Welles, Renoir.* Cambridge: The MIT Press, 2004.

Smith, Jeff. "Movie Music as Moving Music: Emotion, Cognition, and the Film Score." In *Passionate Views: Film, Cognition, Emotion,* edited by Carl Plantinga and Greg M. Smith, 146–67. Baltimore: Johns Hopkins University Press, 1999.

Smith, Murray. *Engaging Characters: Fiction, Emotion, and the Cinema.* Oxford: Clarendon Press, 1995.

—. "Film Spectatorship and the Institution of Fiction." *Journal of Aesthetics and Art Criticism* 2 (1995): 113–27.

—. "Imagining from the Inside." In *Film Theory and Philosophy,* edited by Richard Allen and Murray Smith. 412–30. Oxford: Oxford University Press, 1999.

—. "Gangsters, Cannibals, Aesthetes, or Apparently Perverse Allegiances." In *Passionate Views: Film, Cognition, and Emotion,* edited by Carl Plantinga and Greg M. Smith, 217–38. Baltimore: Johns Hopkins University Press, 1999.

Solomon, Robert. *The Passions: Emotions and the Meaning of Life.* Indianapolis: Hackett, 1993.

—. *True to Our Feelings: What Our Emotions Are Really Telling Us.* Oxford: Oxford University Press, 2007.

Sonnenschein, David. *Sound Design: The Expressive Power of Music, Voice and Sound Effects in Cinema.* Studio City: Michael Wiese, 2002.

Sontag, Susan. *Regarding the Pain of Others.* New York: Farrar, Straus and Giroux, 2003.

Sousa, Ronald de. "The Rationality of Emotions." In *Explaining Emotions,* edited by Amélie Oksenberg Rorty, 127–52. Berkeley: University of California Press, 1980.

—. "Self-deceptive Emotions." In *Explaining Emotions,* edited by Amélie Oksenberg Rorty, 283–98. Berkeley: University of California Press, 1980.

—. *The Rationality of Emotion.* Cambridge: The MIT Press, 1987.

—. "Love as Theatre." In *The Philosophy of Erotic Love,* edited by Robert C. Solomon and Kathleen M. Higgins, 477–91. Lawrence: University Press of Kansas, 1991.

Sparshott, Francis. "Music and Feeling." *The Journal of Aesthetics and Art Criticism* 1 (1994): 23–35.

Staiger, Janet. *Perverse Spectators. The Practices of Film Reception.* New York: New York University Press, 2000.

Stocker, Michael and Elizabeth Hegeman. *Valuing Emotions.* Cambridge: Cambridge University Press, 1996.

Susman, Walter. "Did Success Spoil the United States? Dual Representations in Postwar America." In *Recasting America: Culture and Politics in the Age of Cold War,* edited by Larry May, 19–37. Chicago: University of Chicago Press, 1989.

Tan, Ed S. "Film-Induced Affect as a Witness Emotion." *Poetics* 1–2 (1995): 7–32.

—. *Emotion and the Structure of Narrative Film: Film as an Emotion Machine.* Mahwah: Lawrence Erlbaum Associates, 1996.

Tan, Ed S. and Nico H. Frijda. "Sentiment in Film Viewing." In *Passionate Views: Film, Cognition and Emotion,* edited by Carl Plantinga and Greg M. Smith, 48–64. Baltimore: Johns Hopkins University Press, 1999.

Taylor, Gabrielle. *Pride, Shame and Guilt: Emotions of Self-Assessment.* New York: Oxford University Press, 1985.

Telotte, J. P. "Through a Pumpkin's Eye: The Reflexive Nature of Horror." In *American Horrors: Essays on the Modern American Horror Film,* edited by Gregory Waller, 114–28. Urbana: University of Illinois Press, 1992.

Thompson, Bill. "Evoking Terror in Film Scores." *M/C: A Journal of Media and Culture* 1 (2002). Accessed October 17, 2010. http://journal.media-culture.org.au/index.php/mcjournal.

Tomkins, Silvan S. *Exploring Affect: The Selected Writings of Silvan S. Tomkins,* edited by E. Virginia Demos. Cambridge: Cambridge University Press, 1995.

Walton, Kendall L. "Fearing Fictions." *Journal of Philosophy* 1 (1978): 5–27.

Wheatley, Catherine. *Michael Haneke's Cinema: The Ethic of the Image.* New York: Berghahn Books, 2009.

Willemen, Paul. "The National." In *Fields of Vision: Essays in Film Studies, Visual Anthropology and Photography,* edited by Leslie Delereaux and Roger Hillman, 21–34. Berkeley: University of California Press, 1995.

Williams, Bernard. *Shame and Necessity.* Berkeley: University of California Press, 1993.

Williams, Linda. *Hard Core: Power, Pleasure and the Frenzy of the Visible.* London: Pandora Press, 1990.

—. "Film Bodies: Gender, Genre and Excess." *Film Quarterly* 4 (1991): 2–13.

Winkler, Isabella. "Love, Death, and Parasites." In *Mapping Michel Serres,* edited by Niran Abbas, 226–50. Ann Arbor: The University of Michigan Press, 2005.

Wollheim, Richard. *Art and Its Objects.* Cambridge: Cambridge University Press, 1980.

Woodward, Kathleen. "Traumatic Shame: Toni Morrison, Televisual Culture, and the Cultural Politics of Emotion." *Cultural Critique* 46 (2000): 210–40.

Yuill, Chris. "The Body as Weapon: Bobby Sands and the Republican Hunger Strikes." *Sociological Research Online* 2 (2007). Accessed June 11, 2009. http://www.socresonline.org.uk.

Yumibe, Joshua. "On the Education of the Senses: Synaesthetic Perception from the 'Democratic Art' of Chromolithography to Modernism." *New Review of Film and Television Studies* 3 (2009): 257–74.

Zizek, Slavoj. *The Fright of Real Tears: Krzysztof Kieslowski between Theory and Post-Theory.* London: British Film Institute, 2001.

Index